The Great Ones

JIM MURRAY

· · · · · · · · · · · · · · · · · · · ·

The Great Ones

Los Angeles Times
BOOKS

Los Angeles Times
BOOKS

Book Development Manager: Carla Lazzareschi

Editor: Mike James

Design and Typography: Mike Diehl

ISBN 1-883792-56-8

© 1999 Los Angeles Times

Published by the Los Angeles Times
Times Mirror Square, Los Angeles, California 90053
A Times Mirror Company

www.latimes.com/bookstore

First printing October 1999

Printed in the U.S.A.

Table of Contents

• • • • • • • • • • • • • • • • • • •

Foreword

One of the pleasures I always had when I came to Los Angeles was reading Jim Murray in The Times. Whether he was writing about baseball or boxing, football or golf, I knew I would get a few laughs from his column before I went out to the course.

Jim was very kind to me in print, but he had such a way with words, he could never resist a good line. He had a million of them, and some of them came at my expense.

One very nice column also contained such disclaimers as, "You watch Arnie and he looks like a guy you'd slicker into a double-press bet on the outgoing nine.... You'd swear he got his swing out of a Sears Roebuck catalog."

I never took offense at such comments; I knew Jim Murray was honestly writing what he saw, not so much with his eyes but with the incredible perception he possessed about people. That was what made him so special.

Jim was one of the most talented writers I've ever read, and he was as quick thinking on his feet as he was at pounding away at the keyboard. After a poor drive at Rancho Park during the L.A. Open years ago, I stood over a very difficult second shot. I turned to Jim standing nearby and said, "Well, Jim, what would your beloved Ben Hogan do in this situation?"

Jim looked at me and said, "Hogan would never be in this situation." Jim once began one of his columns by writing, "Nobody ever played golf the way Arnold Palmer did." I've often thought nobody ever wrote a column the way Jim Murray did. He could write about anything, but the best thing he did was tell stories about the people who made sports what it is. Can there be a more fitting combination than one of the best sportswriters of our time writing about some of the best of sports personalities he covered?

Jim is gone now, but the library he left behind remains. I'm proud to be a part of it.

—ARNOLD PALMER

Introduction

Jim Murray's Pulitzer Prize–winning career with the Los Angeles Times spanned nearly four decades, during which time he covered most of the big events that defined sports for millions of readers in Southern California. Super Bowls, heavyweight title bouts, World Series ... no coverage was really complete until Jim lent his singular style to it.

What Jim did better than anyone and what made him connect with athletes and fans alike was to tell the personal stories of the competitors involved in these events: their hopes, motivations, styles, dreams and foibles. In sum, their lives as human beings, not just as athletes.

This volume is a collection of columns about many of the outstanding athletes who competed during Jim's career, the men and women who dominated, indeed transcended, their sports. Our aim was to select only those personalities who made an exceptional and long-lasting impact in their fields. And although we've picked more than 100 sports personalities, this compilation admittedly represents only a fraction of those who qualify for inclusion. For that we are truly regretful.

We have tried to make this a representative sampling of the full range of athletes to whom Jim gravitated during his 1961-1998 career at The Times. Only the mercurial Muhammad Ali has two columns devoted to him here, and the reason is simply that Jim's opinion of boxing's biggest name changed dramatically during Ali's career.

In compiling these columns, we have made some minor editing

changes to impose consistency of style, reflect evolving social sensibil-
ities and correct the occasional mistakes that occur under the pressure
of a daily newspaper deadline. Some words and phrases that were once
considered acceptable, but are now offensive, have been omitted. Many
of these are changes that Jim adopted himself over the years; others, we
are confident, are in keeping with his spirit.

But even with these minor changes, these columns remain the heart
and soul of one of America's greatest sportswriters.

—MIKE JAMES
Senior Assistant Sports Editor,
Los Angeles Times

Baseball

• • • • • • • • • • • • • • • • •

October 3, 1963

Oh, Henry!

I like to watch Henry Aaron play ball for the same reason I like to watch Spencer Tracy act, or Jan Peerce sing, or Nureyev dance, or the sun set over an open body of water.

I don't get a lump in my throat but I have a feeling I'll remember it long after I've forgotten a lot of other things that happened about the same time, and that I'll bore people talking about it when I get old.

What I mean is, it's an EVENT in your life – like your first sight of Edward G. Robinson holding off the whole damn FBI in "G-Man" or "Public Enemy." It's Cagney yelling "Come in and get me, coppers!" Bing Crosby singing "Please," Victor McLaglen stumbling through the Irish rebellion. Your first walk home with the girl in the blond pigtails. Your first look at the Empire State Building or Spode china or a Botticelli. It's pure pleasure is what it is. You can forget the mortgage, the hole in your shoe, the fight with your wife, the date who turned you down for the prom, your boss, your income tax, your ulcer and you can lose yourself in admiration. He's a one-man escape for you.

It's an aura given only to a few athletes. With most of your heroes, you agonize. Henry is curious in this regard. He is to enjoy only. The way he plays it, baseball is an art, not a competition. He is grace in a gray flannel suit, a poem with a bat in its hands.

Hold on you say? What's that? Willie Mays has more "color?" Well, if "color" is your hat flying off, or "color" is the over-the-shoulder catch, or "color" is the wild 360-degree swing and the all-purpose pratfall, Willie is your man. Henry is mine.

With Willie the effort is there. You see it. You empathize with it. You strain when he strains, struggle when he struggles. Willie is a bit of a ham. With Henry Louis Aaron it's as smooth and effortless as a swan gliding along a lake. He underplays like a British actor. Willie attacks the game. Aaron just gets it to cooperate with him.

"He's a pretty hitter – about the prettiest I've ever seen," the Dodgers' Vin Scully, who must have seen 2,000, says. "Henry's no trouble on or off the field," his manager, Bobby Bragan says. "He's the perfect ballplayer, the kind, if you get one in your lifetime, you're one-up on most every other manager in the game. The beauty of Henry is you don't even know he's there."

With most ballplayers, when you don't even notice if they're there, it's usually because they're not – and when they're needed. No one ever needed to look around for Henry Aaron when the chips were down. And he kept his hat on.

When he steals a base, it's stealable – and necessary. He's stolen 24 of 27 this year. In his whole career he's been caught stealing only 3.4 times a year. And he's stolen 149 bases. Percentage-wise, he may be as hard to throw out as Maury Wills.

His skills are so deceptive that, when he first came up to the big leagues, his manager thought he had hired a somnambulist. "Why doesn't he sleep on his own time like everybody else?" he protested. The scout who signed him was not worried. "Unless you hear him snoring, don't throw him anything out over the plate or you'll run out of baseballs before spring training is over. He's the most wide-awake sleepy-looking guy you ever saw."

If Willie Mays gets $150,000 next year, Henry Aaron will be the most underpaid guy in the world this side of a rickshaw. Frankly, the only thing Willie Mays does better than Henry Aaron is hit home runs. Frankly, of course, the only thing Caruso did better than me was sing – but it is a fact that up until two years ago, (and if you weighted Mays' average with a year – 1952 – when he played only 34 games), Aaron led Mays in (average per year) every single category from hits to runs to runs-batted-in to home runs.

"You can't compare one man to another," Henry protested to me one night this week as he got in some hardly-needed bat work fungoing grounders to infielders. Of course, the hell I can't. I positively enjoy comparing Aaron to Mays. To me, it's a rock'n roll versus a symphony.

Of course, the only person you really can compare Aaron to is Joe DiMaggio. Like DiMag, he's in the right place at the right time. Like DiMag, he never throws to the wrong base. Like DiMag, he's one of the most consistent hitters in the long history of the game. Neither of them ever had what you could consider a slump. A "slump" for Henry Aaron is going one whole day without a hit or one whole week without a home run.

Unlike DiMag, he's dubbed "colorless." "Color" is also playing most of your career in New York. The camera lights are brighter, the ink is blacker, the Ed Sullivan Show is just around the corner. The guest panelists on "What's My Line?" have to wear masks when you come on because if you play in New York, everyone knows your face. In Milwaukee, the only recognizable thing comes in kegs! No one ever pays any attention to anyone from Milwaukee. You're just the second line of a vaudeville joke. You're better off in Sheboygan.

Henry Aaron is not my personal discovery. He's well acquainted with every pitcher around the league. "With Aaron," says Johnny Podres, "the thing you have to do is not let him come up with anybody on base. You throw your best pitches to guys in front of Aaron or you'll get dizzy watching the runs come around when he gets to bat."

"I have tried everything with Aaron but rolling the ball to him," confesses Don Drysdale. "You can get him out once in a while – but you better not count on it."

He does one thing wrong: He hits off his front foot. It's such a terrible fault some years he has trouble leading the league in everything. He could bat an annual .320 on his knees.

When he first came up, a spindly, silent kid from the streets of Mobile, he attracted so little notice that a coach once asked him, "Say, is your name 'Aaron Henry' or is it the other way round?"

Nowadays, around baseball, when you say "Henry," that's enough. There's only one of him in this game. And that's enough, too, for my dough. I mean, why be greedy? Beethovens don't come by the dozen. Baseball is not the philharmonic, but it is like it in that when you get someone who doesn't need the music right in front of him, people pay to see him. As for you Willie Mays fans – Liberace, baby. My man is not the sequined-suit type. No vulgar flash. Just hits the right notes. And the high curveballs.

● ● ● ● ● ● ● ● ● ● ● ● ● ● ● ● ● ●

MARCH 13, 1983

Alston Quietly Goes From Darrtown to Cooperstown

The soda fountains of south Florida are going to take an awful kicking around today. There won't be a plate of fudge uneaten from Indian River to Okeechobee county. They'll be celebrating in Darrtown, Ohio, all hours of the night. Probably clear up to 9 o'clock.

Walter Emmons Alston made the Hall of Fame! How nice! A little "Turkey in the Straw," Professor! It's a great victory for apple pie, ice cream soda, biscuits and honey and whole milk. Harvest moons, pinchback suites, church socials and calico dresses and surreys with a fringe on top. Mid-America, state fair country.

Darrtown, the place where time forgot, where the train only stopped when they hit a cow, where they didn't have a bank but they had a hollow tree, where they didn't have an airport but they had a birdbath, where the 11 o'clock news is the barber.

They don't have a golf course, but you can sign up for the horseshoe pit. Main Street is the plowed field that doesn't have any corn on it, and the peak traffic hours are milking time. Herb Shriner's kind of town.

I think of all this every time I think of Walter Alston, American Homespun, baseball's Grant Wood type.

Walt Alston came from a long line of people who made America great, who won our wars, grew our crops, cut our wilderness, built our cities, hewed our character. Jacques Barzun said that whoever wished to know America must first know baseball.

It's altogether fitting that Walter Alston and baseball should be intertwined. It's a marriage made in Valley Forge or the Declaration of Independence. They're as made for each other as cider and donuts. As American as pumpkin pie with whipped cream.

Walter Alston was one of the most unafraid men I have ever known. Almost everyone has the smell of fear, the hint of panic, the look of swallowed hysteria at some time or another. Alston's throat was always flat.

He was a man you'd most like to be next to in a lifeboat. Or a foxhole. Alston made mistakes, but they were never motivated by fear of failure. Alston never cut his losses. Or alibied his defeats. Walter Alston was so honest, it was embarrassing. No one ever caught him doing anything demeaning.

He could never understand the artificial life. One of the vivid memories early on I have of Walter Alston is sitting in the team bus while two savants sat and discussed their evening out the night before in some Manhattan watering place. Alston appeared puzzled.

"What is it you do exactly in a nightclub?" he wanted to know. When it turned out all they did was sit and drink, Alston was horrified.

The thought of grown men sitting in an upholstered cellar and burning up twenty-dollar bills in idle chatter when they could be home playing snooker or drinking milk and playing cards was incomprehensible to him.

I always thought his quiet confidence had as much to do with the Dodgers' success as Maury Wills' steals, Sandy Koufax's strikeouts, Don Drysdale's shutouts.

Walt Alston never did anything for show. If he fought with umpires it was not for the cameras, it was for his players. The balk rule made him see red. He had the fastest team in the big leagues, and when one of them got thrown out he took it as proof positive there was cheating afoot.

The team never got rattled because he never did. He treated victory and defeat with the same easy grace and country manners.

When his team blew the 1962 pennant in a playoff, the players sat in a locked dressing room passing a bottle of remorse around and cursing. Alston went on camera and over to the victors' locker room bearing congratulations. He never got angry when he lost, only surprised.

He always seemed oddly like a preacher running a wild animal act. Walt Alston used every four-letter word any ballplayer ever used, but you noticed a peculiar thing: he almost always used them only in uniform or within earshot of a home plate.

You never discussed Great Books with Walt Alston. You discussed the balk, the infield fly rule, the joys of possum hunting and the sophisticated charms of beautiful downtown cosmopolitan Darrtown after dark.

Walt Alston would rather play pool with his father or hearts with his grandson than post office with Elizabeth Taylor. The glitter of Hollywood eluded him. It's doubtful if Walt Alston spent an hour total on the Sunset Strip in his two decades in L.A.

The manager of the Dodgers is a social catch in some circles. Walt Alston's night life centered around the hotel coffee shop where he could usually be found loading up on coffee and a danish and chewing two toothpicks. The bat was as safe from him as it was from the Salvation Army girl.

He was a good manager because he was a good man, a walking advertisement for the Good Book, an Old Testament model. Players black and white knew him as a man of probity and character.

Fairness was taken for granted in Walt Alston. He figured anyone who made it to the big leagues was a big leaguer. It was not necessarily so, but players played better for Walt Alston.

He never had an agent; he never asked for more money, a longer contract. He came from an era where when you hired just a man, you

7

stuck with him. He redefined the meaning of the word "man." His teams won because he expected them to. Isn't that what big leaguers are supposed to do?

He belongs in the Hall of Fame if anyone does. So if you'll lift your glass, here's a toast to Walter Emmons Alston (in chocolate milk and a Girl Scout cookie): here's to a man who made his profession's Hall of Fame not because he could hit or throw a curveball better than anyone else, but because he excelled in the far more difficult area of human endeavor: he was a Man with a capital M, and he made all those around him the better for it.

● ● ● ● ● ● ● ● ● ● ● ● ● ● ● ● ● ●

OCTOBER 8, 1961

Yogi Berra, the Legend

CINCINNATI – If you turn on your television set this weekend to watch the World Series and suddenly come upon what appears to be a large, shaggy bear in baseball uniform trying to roller-skate up an icy hill, don't switch channels.

This will be Lawrence Peter Berra trying to match wits with the left-field incline in Crosley Field, a ballpark designed either by a man with the sense of humor of an urchin who puts banana peels on sidewalks or one who just hates outfielders as a class.

The outfield in this ballpark is so steep in places the players should have oxygen and a Sherpa guide to scale it. It has produced more pratfalls than Mack Sennett in his heyday, and the sight of Yogi Berra and this incline coming together in combat should be funnier than watching Jackie Gleason and Elsa Maxwell trying to cha-cha.

Yogi Berra, it happens, is funny just standing still. In many respects, he is the most famous baseball player the game has had since Babe Ruth.

8

He is ageless – and changeless. He came upon the scene so many years ago and looked so old even when he was young there are those who think he was Columbus' cabin boy.

The day he leaves baseball 2 million fans may leave it with him. He is as much a part of the legend of America as Paul Bunyan or John Henry. He is the patron saint of three generations of American kids with catchers' mitts in their hands, and no churchman could seriously object. Yogi Berra is a man who has remained a boy – a rich man who remembers what it was like to be poor.

The face is sad. It has been said it is ugly but it is not, lit in the center by large, sad and curiously gentle eyes. It is the color of gray paste – a city face. It is a comforting face, the kind one trusts. "Hey, Yogi," yell people with a chuckle who have never seen him before. A lineman outside the ballpark laughs delightedly when he looks over the fence and sees the familiar face and figure.

It is a silhouette baseball didn't know whether to believe or not when they first saw it. This lumpy man, a perfect 50 in measurements – 50-inch chest, middle and two 25-inch calves – with the two protruding ears, the head that seems to grow, neckless, right out of the shoulders, couldn't possibly be an athlete. Baseball didn't know whether to turn him over to the minor leagues or Clyde Beatty.

Yogi, of course, turned out to be one of the most superbly skilled athletes of his time. He came to symbolize the New York Yankees, the haughtiest team in the annals of sports.

He outlasted derision by his own simple dignity and friendliness. The bench jockeys at first hopped about the dugout on all fours, scratched themselves busily like caged primates, called out "Hey, Berra, what tree did they pull you out of?" and offered him peeled bananas. It was the kind of ridicule that made a Ty Cobb behave forever afterward on the field with insensate rage and vengeance but Yogi ignored – and forgave. His own dignity (and his bat) at first silenced and then made ashamed his ridiculers.

Yogi was unique. He is probably the only guy in history who wrote a book but never read one. The jokes were endless. But there was no cutting edge to them. Sometimes they even illustrated Yogi's innate kindness to his fellow man. Like the fellow who rousted him out of bed in the early morning. "Did I wake you up, Yog?" he chirped. "Oh no," apologized Yogi. "I had to get up to answer the phone anyway."

Then there was the balloon salesman in Washington who had a fistful of dirigible-sized balloons. "Want one, Yogi? For the kids." "Oh, no," said Yogi. "I'd never be able to get them in the suitcase."

People smile when his name is mentioned. Housewives who are not sure what city Yankee Stadium is in feel a glow of affection for Yogi Berra. Their kids know a cartoon character named "Yogi Bear" who owes his existence to Yogi Berra's, and they laugh with and love them both.

Yogi was a catcher who was as chatty as a Bronx housewife behind the plate. He's lonelier now in the outfield. So he chats with the fans.

The New York Yankees came into Cincinnati on their special train at 9 o'clock in the morning on Friday. Yogi Berra was out at the ballpark at 11:30. He was practicing catching fly balls on the left-field incline, a professional to the core even after so many World Series and so many records it takes calculation machines the size of election coverage computers to list them all.

There was a curiously sad tableau taking place in the park as Yogi arrived. High in the back of the stands as Yogi Berra, a study in perseverance, chased thrown fly balls, a lonely, frightened man stood poised, naked, on the roof's edge threatening to jump. He didn't. He was coaxed down. But you wonder, watching Yogi Berra, how a man could give in to despair.

Yogi Berra thinks he's lucky to be in baseball. I think it's the other way around.

● ● ● ● ● ● ● ● ● ● ● ● ● ● ● ● ● ●

Clemente: You Had to See Him To Disbelieve Him

For once, Roberto Clemente must have been taking. And God buzzed a high hard one right across the letters.

They didn't make a pitch Roberto Clemente couldn't hit. All he required of a baseball was that it be in the park. He hit with the savage lunge of a guy waiting on top of a gopher hole till the animal poked its head out. It's a good thing he didn't make his living hitting fastballs because he never got any.

Old Aches and Pains, we called him around the press room. Here was a guy you could drive railroad spikes with. You could scratch a match on his stomach. He wasn't born, he was mined.

He was the healthiest specimen I ever saw in my life. He didn't have a pimple on him. The eyes were clear. I never even heard of him having to blow his nose. Yet he was positive he was terminal. You'd get the idea reports of his birth were grossly exaggerated.

I never saw a man get so mad when you didn't believe him. Roberto would rip off his shirt, command you to put your ear to his back, then he would ripple his vertebrae like castanets for you. "You see!" he would shout. "I am a man with a broken back playing right field!" Then he would go 3-for-4 with a stolen base and three outfield assists.

He could get yellow fever in the Arctic. You could tell by looking at him that his temperature was 98.6 and that he never had a coated tongue or sore throat in his life. The sicker he got, the worse the pitchers felt.

He used to chew me out because I would write a tongue-in-cheek column after listening to a litany of his symptoms which would lead you to picture a toothless old man sitting, shivering, in an afghan bedspread with his feet in a tub of hot water and a thermometer in his mouth and a hot water bottle at his back. But every time the Pirates came to town I would hotfoot it down to the dugout because you never came away empty from an interview with Clemente.

He didn't answer questions so much as he delivered orations. He could lecture brilliantly on osteopathy, orthopedics or the anatomy. But he was Calamity Jane of the dugout. He was always playing the last act of "Camille." It was funny to be sitting there talking to this figure that looked as if it had just walked off a Michelangelo pedestal and hear it talking like something in a TB ward.

I once asked him to describe a .400 hitter, and it was everything Robert was not. It had to bat left-handed, had to be young, had to be batting ahead of somebody so it could get good pitches. And, of course, it had to have a good back and doctors and trainers who believed him. It had to sit out second games of doubleheaders and not waste its energy throwing out base runners at home plate on the fly.

Roberto didn't have the grace of Henry Aaron or the dash of Willie Mays, but if you put all the skills together and you had to play one of them at the same position, it would be hard to know which to bench. He was the most destructive World Series player I ever saw outside of Ruth and Gehrig.

The side of Roberto that everybody missed was that he was a kind man. For all the deadpan (he rarely smiled), bluster and complaints (he never talked, he yelled), he was always available. God is getting an earful someplace today because Roberto is sure he was quick-pitched.

The thing I like best is, you never heard of him doing a disreputable thing. The only thing Roberto slipped into his room at night was a book. You never found him having breakfast with a niece from Boston. The only thing he drank out of a bottle was patent medicine.

I can't believe he won't come walking out of a clearing, bent over and holding his back and complaining that the swim was bad for his sciatica. If you see someone answering that description, throw him a bad pitch down around the ankles outside and, if he hits it screaming

12

down the right-field line, it can only be Clemente, and you'll know reports of his condition have been grossly exaggerated once again.

● ● ● ● ● ● ● ● ● ● ● ● ● ● ● ● ● ●

July 7, 1994

In His Day, Clipper Meant a Winner

You know, in the press box sometimes, we old-timers used to have a bit of fun with the young guys on the bet.

Down on the field, some hotshot outfielder would go streaking back after a line drive and make a last-minute leaping catch of it at the wall. We would look on, unimpressed.

"DiMaggio would have been waiting for it," we'd tell the youngsters scornfully. "DiMaggio never had to leap for a ball in his life."

In the field, some eager young player would chase down a ground single and come up firing wildly. Only he would throw behind the runner, who would then help himself to an extra base. We would smirk.

"DiMaggio never threw to the wrong base in his life. Of course, that guy wouldn't have been running if he knew DiMag was out there."

Exaggerated? Not much. There was a large element of truth in the hyperbole. Joe DiMaggio played the game at least at a couple of levels higher than the rest of baseball.

A lot of guys, all you had to see to know they were great was a stat sheet. DiMaggio, you had to see.

It wasn't only numbers on a page – although they were there too – it was a question of command, style, grace. Connie Mack, no less, once said he was the ultimate team player. That the Yankees won the pennant 10 times in the 13 years DiMaggio was with them attests to that.

The Yankees of his era were the personification of graceful elegance.

Other teams were "the Gas House Gang," or "the Rollicking Redbirds," but the DiMag Yankees were all dignity. They beat you without getting their uniforms dirty.

They came to the ballpark in three-piece suits and shined shoes, cut hair and clean shaven. Their image was that of a company of Swiss bankers, not terrorists. Joe DiMaggio never got in a brawl on or off the field.

In sports – in all of entertainment – there is a principle known as empathy.

It has to do with the audience projecting itself into the performance of an athlete, dancer or singer. If what he does involves strain or effort, you experience it with him. Guys who balance plates thrive on it. You squirm, you strain, you hyperventilate.

But certain performers do what they do so effortlessly, you are unaware of struggle or strain. You are at ease. They are in control. So are you. Bing Crosby had that quality. It seemed so easy that every guy in the shower was sure he could sing like Bing. And Joe DiMaggio had that quality. He made it look easy.

Joe never got his hair mussed. His cap never fell off. He never lunged at a ball. In more than 600 plate appearances one year, he struck out only 13 times. People thought he was aloof. He was really shy. He once admitted that when he arrived in New York and a writer asked him for a quote, Joe didn't know what he was talking about. He thought maybe it was a soft drink.

I caught up with the great DiMaggio (as Hemingway's character, the ancient Cuban fisherman, keeps referring to him in "The Old Man and The Sea") the other day. He was in town to receive the Lifetime Achievement Award at the prestigious Cedars-Sinai Sports Spectacular, a fund-raiser for the Genetics-Birth Center at the hospital, and a cause close to DiMaggio's heart because he has his own Joe DiMaggio Children's hospital in Hollywood, Florida.

Everyone knows about the 56 straight games DiMaggio hit in back in 1941. Every fan knows that, when stopped for one night by spectacular fielding plays, he went on to hit safely in the next 16 games. So the record could have been 73. Everyone knows Joe hit in 61 straight games in the Pacific Coast League and that in his major league streak of 56 he had 91 hits, almost two a game; 15 home runs, almost one every three games; drove in 55 runs, scored 56 and batted .408. It is the most brilliant burst of batting in baseball history.

But what no one ever knew about the great DiMag is, he was the first major league ballplayer to have an agent.

His agent? Are you ready? A little drum roll, professor. Ty Cobb!

Right! That Ty Cobb. The Georgia Peach.

"He used to eat in our family restaurant at the wharf in San Francisco," Joe told me the other day. "So, he took an interest in me.

"When the Yankees bought me from San Francisco (for $25,000), they offered me a $5,000 contract. Ty Cobb was outraged. (With the volcanic Cobb, this was not an unusual state of affairs.) He wrote to the Yankees' Ed Barrow and blistered him terribly. So Barrow sent back a $500 raise. Then, Ty sat down and wrote another letter. Oddly enough, he liked to write letters. Barrow came up with another $500.

"This went on for seven letters. Finally, Barrow wrote, 'This is all! Tell Cobb to stop writing letters!'

"But I ended up with $8,500. And Cobb ate for free in the restaurant."

Another little-known fact of the DiMaggio legend is that, in 1939, when Joe won the American League batting title with a .381 average, he could have become one of the few hitters in baseball history to have hit .400. Should have, actually.

"I was hitting .412 with a little more than two weeks remaining in the season," he recalled. "Then, I had this terrible infection in my left eye. They injected it with Novocain. And [Manager Joe] McCarthy wouldn't take me out of the lineup. The eye was tearing up and painful. I couldn't really see the breaking ball. I lost 32 points on my batting average in two weeks. I shouldn't have been playing."

League rules used to provide that batting title eligibility was based on official at-bats in a season. It has since been changed to plate appearances, which include walks and sacrifices and times hit by pitchers.

But in '39, the batting title was based on times at bat. Would Joe's .412 have qualified in 1939 if he had sat out the last two weeks as he should have?

"Oh, yes," he says.

He ended up with 462 official at-bats and would have easily made the obligatory 400, he believes. As gaudy as DiMaggio's actual numbers were – and remember, he spent three seasons at the height of his career in the service during World War II – they would have been even more glittering if one of the line smashes he hit in Game 57 of the streak had fallen safely, or if he had been able to go home and put on an eye patch in 1939.

You shudder to think what agent Cobb could get for him today.

• • • • • • • • • • • • • • • • •

AUGUST 23, 1961

Drysdale's Double Life

ST. LOUIS – One reason I wanted to make this road trip east with the Dodgers was I wanted to see whether Don Drysdale needed a police escort in this part of the country.

Don Drysdale is a peculiar case. With the hitters in this league he could lose an election to Castro. They are sure, to a man, that he is baseball's version of a gas chamber and that batting against him is like playing catch with hand grenades – with the pins out.

Don Drysdale leads the league in hit batsmen. He always does. When he first came up to the league he used to knock the bat out of batters' hands. Now he's found it simpler just to knock the batters off of the bat.

There are some players who think Drysdale is miscast as a ballplayer, that he should have been a surgeon. Who else, they argue, could perform a prefrontal lobotomy with a fastball? He can lance an abscessed ear – or abscess one – with a slider. No Punch and Judy Show could match a Don Drysdale – Frank Robinson duel for multiple contusions, pratfalls and concussions. The fans love it, but the penal code takes a dim view of it.

Robinson is Drysdale's favorite target – but not his only one. The charm of Robinson is that he leans so far over the plate and crouches so low it is possible to hit him in the ear with a strike. Only the umpires don't call it. So Drysdale gets even by aiming at Robbie in the middle of an intentional base on balls.

This is like hitting a guy over the head while he's asleep, but the way Robinson is hitting, the pitchers think he should even take his chances against that. He may become the first guy ever to get the most-valuable-player award posthumously.

With this background – and considering he has hit 69 batters in his career while Sandy Koufax has hit only six and that he has hit 17 this year while Koufax hit only one, Robinson – you might expect Drysdale to look and act like a middle-aged delinquent, a guy who hides his switchblade knife in his geography book and who leads his homeroom in stolen hubcaps, a kind of Van Nuys replica of Raul Castro.

He doesn't and isn't. Don Drysdale looks as if he just stepped off a collar ad. He can't even play bad guys on television. No one would believe it.

He dries the dishes at home just like the rest of us and is so personable he could sell brushes door to door and drive a Cadillac. Off the mound, he could make Santa Claus look like a cantankerous old rascal.

If there's one thing a ballplayer hates worse than a slump, it's an autograph pest. Drysdale leads the club in autographs. Even catchers whose fingers get split trying to hold his fastball like him.

In the Candlestick Park dressing room the other day, Drysdale was sitting in a bridge game that he was playing with characteristic ferocity when a newsman brought in word that a deaf-mute couple were at the door to see him. Even the cop at the gate was afraid to disturb him, but Don got immediately to his feet and ambled out barechested to stand in cold draughts of Candlestick and talk to the couple.

It was a touching scene. The couple's name was Hammerlund, and they have been dropping by to see Drysdale, to whom they are distantly related, for years. When the Dodgers hit San Francisco, they pack a lunch, put on a Dodger cap and head for the ballpark with their eyes shining. The wife has learned to utter a few syllables in the years since they first began it, but they still communicate by scratch pad with Drysdale.

Frank Robinson wouldn't have believed his eyes. Drysdale stood for almost 45 minutes in the polar blast of Candlestick patiently exchanging written dialogue with the couple.

The conversation was hardly racy. "We have painted the pantry and the living room and put up new curtains in the bedroom," they would scribble on the paper. "What color are they?" Don would write back. "We made waffles for breakfast and put the cat out" would be the bulletin. "I like waffles. And cats," Don would answer kindly.

It went on like that till the visitors ran out of scoops. Most ballplayers in this league would have told the pair to get lost – in sign language. I had the feeling Drysdale would have stayed there till he had to excuse himself to go pitch.

In the dressing room, his bridge partners were looking at their watches and muttering under their breath, but Don wasn't about to let those wonderful people down. You had to pinch yourself when you realized he had been aced out of a win the night before by a wrong-field home run. And when a left-hander hits a left-field homer in Candlestick Park it's time for a fellow to call in the chaplain and see who's got it in for him upstairs.

It's when he takes the mound that Don Drysdale becomes Mr. Hyde. You can almost see the hair begin to sprout on his face, his teeth become pointed, his jaws drip and horns begin to show under his baseball cap.

His face twists into a snarl. He looks like a hungry tiger who has just seen his breakfast go by in a pith helmet.

"He throws baseballs like they were knives, and he will lose his letter if he misses," Jim Brosnan once told me. "His idea of a 'waste' pitch is a strike."

The record is on the side of his enemies. Drysdale's control is excellent. He only walked 72 men in 269 innings last year and can almost always put the ball where he wants it. That would be the batter's ear, is the unanimous opinion of the Cincinnati Reds.

The mystery of which is the real Don Drysdale – or how the Dr. Drysdale of the Dressing Room keeps the Mr. Hyde of the Pitcher's Hill out of his private life is part of the romance of baseball.

Anyway, I think I will stick close to Don when he gets to Cincinnati, and if I see any vigilantes lurking around with a rope, send for Marshal Dillon on the double. I don't think they'll believe me when I tell them he's a nice guy and good to his mother and cousins. Not if they've been listening to Frank Robinson. If Robbie loses a Drysdale fastball in the lights of Cincinnati, Drysdale's bridge partner may have to play a dummy hand the rest of the trip.

● ● ● ● ● ● ● ● ● ● ● ● ● ● ● ● ● ● ●

SEPTEMBER 28, 1988

They Won't Call Him Dr. Zero for Nothing

Norman Rockwell would have loved Orel Hershiser. The prevailing opinion is, he wasn't drafted, he just came walking off a Saturday Evening Post cover one day with a pitcher's glove, a cap two sizes too big and a big balloon of bubble gum coming out of his mouth.

You figure his name has to be Ichabod. I wouldn't say he's skinny,

19

but when he turns sideways, he disappears. If it weren't for his Adam's apple, he wouldn't cast a shadow.

He's paler than Greta Garbo. He's so white you can read through him. If you held him up to the light you could see his heart.

He says things like "Golly gee!" and "Oh, my goodness!" If he gets really upset, you might figure he would go to "Oh, fudge!"

He can't really see without glasses, and when he puts them on, people think he's either a sportswriter or a guy doing his thesis on major league baseball as a metaphor for the society we live in.

It should come as no surprise to anyone that he has a Roman numeral after his name. He is descended from the Hessian troops George Washington crossed the Delaware to defeat at Trenton. He is about as far from the public perception of a major league pitcher as it is possible to get. If you wanted to picture a big league pitcher, a guy like Burleigh Grimes would come to mind.

Some guys pitch out of a sidearm motion, others from a crouch, Grimes pitched out of a scowl. He had this big chaw of tobacco and a blue-black beard that could sand furniture, and the batter had two strikes on him stepping in.

Or you might prefer Big D, Don Drysdale. He pitched out of a towering rage.

Every batter was Hitler to Drysdale, or a guy who'd stolen his girlfriend. He threw the ball as if it were a grenade, or he hoped that it were. Big D didn't much care whether he knocked the bat off you or you off the bat. He hit 154 batsmen in his time – 155 if you count Dick Dietz in the ninth inning of a spring game in 1968.

If anyone told you Orel Hershiser is on the verge of breaking one of the most unassailable pitching records in the books, Don Drysdale's 58 scoreless innings, that this scholarly-appearing right-hander is almost certain to win this year's Cy Young Award, you might be pardoned for asking, "With what?"

Orel Leonard Hershiser IV does not intimidate the batter, although his nine hit batsmen last year indicate it's not entirely a good idea to lean over the plate looking to get at the curveball when he's on the mound.

Hershiser throws ground balls. This is not to say his curve bounces but that his "out" pitch is a roller to shortstop. He throws a sinker, or what we kids in the old neighborhood used to call the drop. This is a pitch you hit on the top, and it does exactly what a golf ball hit on the top does – it rolls along the ground till it hits something, usually an infielder's glove.

Hershiser also throws a heavy ball – as did Drysdale. That's a ball that comes up to the plate like a 16-pound shot. It can break your bat – and your wrist along with it – if you meet it squarely. Which you seldom do.

These are Hershiser's stock-in-trade pitches, and he can put them pretty much where he wants them, but he cut such a less-than-commanding figure when he first came into the game that the brain trusters thought he was a relief pitcher. He pitched in 49 games one year and worked only 109 innings. He started only four games. But he finished one.

One year, he pitched in 49 games, started only 10 but finished six. Somehow the message began to seep through that this guy had better than two-inning stuff and, when he came up to the Dodgers, he appeared in 45 games, started 20 and finished eight. Eight complete games is star billing in today's baseball, particularly for someone who spent more than half the season in the bullpen.

It's not that Orel Hershiser is your basic ragpicker or junk dealer. His fastball is a 90-m.p.h. horror that struck out 190 last year. Still, no one calls him Dr. K or the Big Train. They might begin calling him Mister O, or Dr. Zero if he puts up nine more innings of shutout ball. Dr. Zero has put up 49 in a row so far. Only two pitchers have logged more – Drysdale, 58, and Walter Johnson, 55.

The record was once widely believed as unattainable as Joe DiMaggio's 56-game hitting streak.

Five shutouts in a season is Cy Young stuff. Five shutouts in a row is

Hall of Fame stuff. Drysdale holds the record with six in a row in the National League, and you have to go all the way back to 1904 to find a pitcher with five in a row in the American League. (Walter Johnson set his scoreless-inning record with a lot of relief appearances.)

Drysdale's scoreless-inning progression was saved at Inning 45 in 1968 when, with the bases loaded, he apparently hit batter Dick Dietz. Umpire Harry Wendelstedt ruled that Dietz stepped into the pitch. Drysdale's argument was even stronger. "How can you hit a guy with a strike?" he wanted to know.

Hershiser's saver was an interference call on a baserunning assault that broke up a double play and apparently let a run score. Umpire Paul Runge ruled that the baserunner neglected baserunning and would have gotten 15 yards in football for what he did to the pivot man in the double play. Runge called the runner out, which disallowed the run.

It's important to remember that Drysdale had to get three outs with the bases loaded after his incident in 1968. And Hershiser still had to get the next nine outs in 1988.

Dr. Zero needs a 10-inning shutout to pass Drysdale. If he gets it, he may celebrate with a hot chocolate.

If he misses it, he'll say, "Oh, heck!"

• • • • • • • • • • • • • • • • • •

OCTOBER 19, 1977

Reggie Renames House Ruth Built

NEW YORK – Excuse me while I wipe up the bloodstains and carry off the wounded. The Dodgers forgot to circle the wagons.

Listen! You don't go into the woods with a bear. You don't go into a fog with Jack the Ripper. You don't get in a car with Al Capone. You don't get on a ship with Morgan the Pirate. You don't go into shark waters with a nosebleed. You don't wander into Little Big Horn with General Custer.

And you don't come into Yankee Stadium needing a win to stay alive in a World Series. Not unless you have a note pinned to you telling them where to send the remains. If any.

They told us these weren't the real Yankees. I mean, not like the genuine article of years gone past, the Murderers' Row Yankees, the Bronx Bombers. These were just a bunch of pussycats dressed up in gorilla costumes.

These were Yankees who had "take" signs in the playbook. These were Yankees who talked of "beating you with the glove." These were "hit-and-run Yankees," not the old kind who just stood there and hit balls into the stratosphere and played "hit and walk" baseball.

That's what they told us. That's what the scouting report said.

They said these Yankees weren't even speaking to each other. You wondered why they dared show up.

Years ago, old-timers remembered, on the 1927 Yankees the right fielder in World Series used to stand there and hit back-to-back home runs out of the park. Why, he hit three in one game in World Series *twice!*

Well, the 1977 Yankees' right fielder has just hit home runs on his last four consecutive official at-bats. And he became only the second player in history to hit three home runs in a game.

He became the first player in history to hit five home runs in a single Series.

You have the feeling the Dodgers pitchers are longing to see Babe Ruth step in there. He might be a welcome relief.

"If I played in New York, they'd name a candy bar after me," boasted Reggie Jackson before the season started. They may name an entire chocolate factory after him now.

Once again these were the Yanks who had your back to the wall when you were ahead only 2-0. Once again they were headhunters. If they were fighters they'd never go to the body. Once again, they're a bunch of guys who go for the railroad yards in bombing runs or shell Paris with railroad guns.

These are the Yankees who let you store up runs like a squirrel putting nuts in his cheek. When you get them all neatly piled up, the Yankees come along and pile up more with two swings of a bat.

These Yanks are store-bought. They're not homemade like a proper ballclub should be, stitched at home with tender, loving care. George Steinbrenner just went out and ordered them like a new car. Expense was no object. It didn't matter. With George, it was either a question of buying a ballclub – or buying Rhode Island.

There's an old familiar smell in the Yankee locker room – fermenting grapes. The wine of victory spreads across the floor, the waterfall of success. Where Ruth or Gehrig once dribbled champagne across their chins, Reggie Jackson does now.

The reporters are 10 deep around Jackson's locker in this the House That Ruth Built. It is Jackson's Yankees now. "Mr. October." The most dangerous World Series hitter since Ruth used to call his shots.

No one has ever seen more devastating home runs than Reggie Jackson ripped out of Yankee Stadium Tuesday night. Two were on so-so fastballs, but the third was a knuckler down and away. "He hit a helluva pitch," Da Manager Tom Lasorda confessed later, still in some shock.

The pitchers' union is not ready to strike its colors. The pitcher who threw it, Charlie Hough, recalls it as a knuckler that didn't knuckle.

One of the homers was a line drive that would have crossed state lines and gone through the side of a battleship on its way to the seats. The other two were booming Jack Nicklaus-type tee shots, high and far, the kind that pitchers wake up screaming in the middle of the night over.

Reggie was, for him, composed as the forest of microphones was thrust under his chin and the photographers called for one more shot of a tilted champagne bottle.

How often had Ruth struck this pose for the midnight tabloids? Mantle?

The home run is to the Yankees what the Raphaels are to the Vatican and the pyramids to the pharaohs – symbols of glory and tradition.

How many National League teams have been bludgeoned in this hallowed stadium by mighty multiple home runs? You see a Dizzy Dean struggling manfully to hold down the floodgates of homers in 1938, a Wee Willie Sherdel, a Carl Hubbell, a Charlie Root in 1932. And now a Hooton, Sosa and Hough.

The star-of-the-day, the new Sultan of Swat in Yankee Stadium, was managing to sound more like a one-man HEW bureau. "What am I going to do?" Reggie Jackson answered slowly. "First, I'm going to go out and have a few drinks and put some of this money back in circulation. Then I'm going to share my World Series money with the city of New York, which did so much for me, go to Phoenix where I live and to Oakland where I came from." What did he feel on becoming the first man to hit four home runs in a row in World Series? "Jubilation, relief, pride and some justification," added Reggie.

This was a team that was supposed to self-destruct before your very eyes about the seventh inning of every game. They weren't supposed to be real Yankees that they made movies about.

From what anyone could see in the wreckage of the Dodger planes, the only difference between the 1927 Yankees and the 1977 Yankees is a few million dollars in salaries.

The 1927 Yankees are the yardstick against which baseball historians measure all subsequent teams. Old-timers' eyes mist over when they say, "You should have seen that bunch!"

Today's bubble gum collectors can take the offensive, too. "Baby, you should have seen the 1977 Yankees, the Jackson Yankees. Four at-bats in a row, Reggie hit home runs – on *four swings*. Reggie hit the first pitch on all four of them. Match *that* around the Ruth Yankees."

Reggie gets unlimited champagne, a new Thunderbird, a page all his own in the record books and a free trip to Cooperstown. But the

Yankees get a new mythology. This stadium will be the House That Reggie Built. He goes to join Ruth's called shot, Mantle's tape measures. It's his Series. It will be remembered as the Year-That-Reggie-Jackson – the year that Reggie Jackson hit five home runs, the last four his last four times up. No one will remember anything else about it 20 years from now. The 1977 World Series is Reggie Jackson's fee simple. Everything that went on before he stepped to center stage was prologue. It was an opera that all led to the appearance of the star. When the scene was set and the overture over, Reggie gave 'em goose bumps.

It was one of sports' great moments, the kind of thing that will make 500,000 people who weren't say "I was there." The homers will get longer, higher, farther in the retelling. But nobody has to embellish the frequency.

We're not likely to see their like again.

But then, they said that about Ruth too, didn't they?

● ● ● ● ● ● ● ● ● ● ● ● ● ● ● ● ● ●

AUGUST 31, 1961

Sandy Rare Specimen

CHICAGO – For Sanford Koufax, left-handed pitcher, the 1961 baseball season opened on an unusual note – with the manager pounding on his door at 2 o'clock in the morning demanding to be let in at once.

This was unusual because the manager usually wasn't out after curfew. Neither, ordinarily, was Sandy Koufax, but this was a night both longshots came in. Well after curfew, as it happens.

The next high spot in Sandy Koufax's banner year came one August night in the Coliseum when he was betting against the Reds' Bob Purkey. Sandy swung at a thrown ball – and expected to miss it as usual. Instead, the ball rocketed out to right field.

Koufax stood there for a moment. Then he looked around to see who did it. By this time, his teammates were on their feet in the dugout waving their hats and pointing frantically to first base. Sandy set sail. But in the outfield, Frank Robinson casually picked up his base hit and threw him out at first.

The tragic part is that if Sandy Koufax had gotten that hit, he would be batting .077 today instead of .062.

Sandy Koufax is not exactly a character invented by Al Capp. But he is a rare specimen for baseball. In a game where the vocabulary runs to four-letter words and the vocal range registers from loud to hoarse, Sandy is articulate and soft-spoken. Where the musical tastes run to rock'n' roll or hillbilly gut-bucket, Sandy prefers Mendelssohn and Beethoven. Where plenty of players only act like bachelors, Sandy is one. And doesn't act like it.

Where teammates seek out the nearest cowboy picture, Sandy looks for the foreign art film. Where other players' raiment makes them look as though they're trying to be sure the deer hunters see them, Sandy's is subdued – but expensive. There are those who think Sandy's salary just pauses briefly in his pocket on the way to the alpaca sweater industry. On road trips, Sandy can be found either at the ballpark or in a men's store. He stands in line waiting for them to open in the morning, and some suspect he asks for autographs of the owners whose stock he most admires.

Sandy Koufax didn't even particularly want to be a ballplayer. He went to Cincinnati University on a basketball scholarship and had not even played a great deal of baseball on the streets of Brooklyn where he grew up. Sandy wanted to be an architect, and there are still days when he feels he has made a terrible mistake – almost as if Frank Lloyd Wright had decided to become a rodeo rider.

The trouble was, Sandy Koufax was such a natural pitcher that baseball couldn't afford to let him turn to mere bridge-building. Sandy's fastball was so fast some batters would start to swing as he was on his way to the mound. His curveball disappeared like a long putt going in a hole.

Koufax has never pitched an inning of minor league ball, which doesn't make him unique but makes him a member of a very small club. As a result, he has learned his craft slowly. And it's as exasperating as hay fever: one day you have it, the next day you don't. Sandy thinks it is basically a problem of rhythm. You don't know till you hear the music of the first pitch smacking in the catcher's glove – or off the center-field fence – whether you're going to dance or trip over your feet.

The Dodgers have persevered a long time with Sandy Koufax. On the other hand, he has given baseball lots of second chances, too, when you consider the building boom in this country. Players who have batted against him have been waiting confidently for him to elbow Lefty Grove to one side in the Hall of Fame.

This year, both have had their patience rewarded. Koufax has not only won 15 games, a personal high, but he was the man who caught the falling Dodgers on the way down the side of a cliff and held them by their heels till they could scramble to the second-place ledge. If Koufax hadn't defeated Cincinnati last Friday his team would now be as far out of it as the Andrea Doria.

When they dropped a doubleheader and came into Chicago like a drowning man with a rock in his lap, Koufax pitched a virtual no-hitter. A cacheable fly ball and a half-hit ground ball to right field represented the entire offensive thrust of the Chicago Cubs for the afternoon. A good thing, because the Dodgers didn't make anybody forget the 1927 Yankees either.

Koufax has struck out so many batters, he is approaching records set by pitchers in the prehistoric ages of baseball like Rube Marquard and someone named "Noodles" Hahn. He is a victim of his own stuff – he averaged 155 pitches a game last year, largely because batters get so little wood on the ball they can't even pop it up and foul it back instead. He has fanned 895 batters in 898 innings.

Sandy is now sure he wants to stay in baseball. And the batters wish he'd go build something. Success may go to his pocketbook – or to Hart, Schaffner & Marx. But it won't go to his head. Joe Frisco once said of Irving Berlin that he had a nice voice but you had to hug him to hear it. With Koufax even that wouldn't help. When Sandy is shouting, he sounds as if he is talking to himself.

When the Dodgers get to Chavez Ravine, Sandy Koufax may finally put the game of baseball on the run. He has won nine, lost two on the road, won six lost seven in the Coliseum. Even if he does rout the record book, you will never know by looking at him. He will be the nice young man with the gentle brown eyes standing in the corner looking as though he had come in for autographs.

● ● ● ● ● ● ● ● ● ● ● ● ● ● ● ● ● ● ● ●

JULY 12, 1988

No One Can Say the Guy Chose the Wrong Field

If you had a license from God to construct yourself a baseball manager, you would probably begin with one with a big belly and short legs that were slightly bowed or pebbled with lumps so that they looked like sacks of walnuts. You would want one who had his own syntax, a voice that sounded like an oncoming train in a tunnel. It'd have to be a nice part for Vincent Gardenia.

He wouldn't have been a big star in his youth. A .500 pitcher, perhaps. A .260 hitter who made a lot of noise. He'd have to know how tough this game is. He'd never have a self-doubt or a moment's anxiety. He'd come into a room as if he were leading a parade. Everybody would be his best friend. He'd talk to shoeshine boys, parking lot attendants. He'd sell baseball. He'd be sure God was a baseball fan. He'd know that America was the greatest country in the world, otherwise how could a poor boy like him grow up to be part of the greatest organization in the world?

29

He'd never be at a loss for words, he'd like to eat, he'd cry at sad movies, but he'd have a temper like a top sergeant whose shoes were too tight. He'd be sentimental, cantankerous, on speaking terms with the president of the United States but, if you asked him what his foreign policy was, he'd say, "Beat Montreal!"

He'd be part press agent, part father figure, all man. He'd have an anecdote for every occasion, always with a moral attached. He'd tell at the drop of a hat of the time when he knocked the big league batter down the first time he faced him because that batter had refused him an autograph as a knothole kid years before. His stories would be more entertaining than true, but no reporter ever would leave his office with an empty notebook or stomach.

He wouldn't be one of those tense, secretive guys like the manager in the World Series last year who looked as if he was guarding a gang hideout and you were the Feds. He'd be selling baseball. It would be his job, and he'd come from a long line of people who did their jobs.

He'd have a lot of con in him. He'd never forget he was dealing with kids, and that he could make them pick the shell without the pea under it if he had to.

When he'd have a player who didn't want to transfer from the outfield to catcher, he'd say, "Didn't you know the great Gabby Hartnett, the greatest catcher of all time, started out in the outfield?" Gabby Hartnett started out in a catcher's mask, but a good manager is resourceful.

When a team was floundering in a 10-game losing streak, this manager would reassure them that "the 1927 Yankees, the greatest team of all time, lost 11 games in a row that year!" The 1927 Yankees didn't have 11 losing innings in a row, but that would be irrelevant.

He'd know baseball wasn't nuclear physics. It was show business. It was "Entertainment Tonight." The pictures on his wall would not be Babe Ruth, Ty Cobb, Stuffy McInnis, Connie Mack, John McGraw, guys sliding into second. They'd be the heavy hitters of show business, Sinatra, Rickles, Berle, Kaye.

He'd be a star in his own right. People would have his picture on their office walls.

He'd be Tommy Lasorda. He'd be Mr. Baseball, a guy with his own show. He'd get the best tables in restaurants, he'd be part of the fabric of the glitter and glitz of a town that prides itself in it. He'd never be out of character when the spotlight was on. He'd be on the dais of every black-tie dinner there was, he'd make a speech at the tap of a glass.

Some managers are worth five games a year to their franchises. Sagacious moves can account for that much success. Tommy Lasorda is worth something more – a few hundred thousand in attendance.

His predecessor, Walter Alston, was a great manager. He had to be. But he was as quiet as snowfall. He officed out of his pocket. He dressed with his coaches. He led by example. His office had a picture of his wife and grandchildren in it. He never made a headline in his life. He was patient, kindly, courtly, a gentleman of the old school. A guy you would most want to be in a foxhole – or a lifeboat – with. Dependable, matter-of-fact, as untemperamental as a butler, he knew more about the balk rule than any man who ever lived.

It's not what baseball is about. It's no secret the late owner Walter O'Malley chafed under Alston's monkish managerial policy. He was stuck with him because Alston was so good. It was hard to fire an annual pennant. So he did the next best thing: he gave him an annual one-year contract.

It was all well and good to be low-key in the corner of the dugout when the Dodgers were new to the town and every night was New Year's Eve and they had Koufax and Drysdale and Maury Wills and The Duke and the Davis boys and you didn't have another major league baseball team, football teams (two) and pro basketball teams (two) and a hockey team and a lot of other promotions to vie for your space in the sports sheets.

You think the Dodgers are going to hire Tom Kelly, or the manager of Seattle (if it has one) or some minor leaguer who understands the infield fly rule backward and forward (which reads the same, anyway)?

Tommy Lasorda is as perfect for the Dodgers as peanut butter for white bread. Or Laurel for Hardy. A lot of people were surprised when the Dodgers broke precedent and signed him to an early extension on his contract. Why? Peter O'Malley is Walter's son, isn't he? The only way Tommy Lasorda could be let go is if Casey Stengel suddenly became available. God is not going to let that happen. Or the real Angels are going to have a drop in attendance.

Neither is Peter O'Malley going to let his manager become available. There are, conservatively, 14 big league teams who would sign Lasorda tomorrow for more money than the Dodgers pay him. But Lasordas do not change their religions, either. "Who gave me a chance to manage?" he yells. "The Yankees? The Phillies? No, it was the Dodgers." Lasordas dance with the one what brung them. "Lack of loyalty," Lasorda shouts, "is rooning this country!"

● ● ● ● ● ● ● ● ● ● ● ● ● ● ● ● ● ●

JANUARY 20, 1974

Mantle of Greatness

Mickey Charles Mantle was born with one foot in the Hall of Fame. Unfortunately, the other one was in a brace.

If Mickey Mantle had had TWO Hall of Fame legs, he probably wouldn't have had to go through the formality of 18 big league seasons and 12 World Series. He's the first guy who limped his way to the Hall of Fame.

Mantle probably should be in the Smithsonian, too. He may be the last of a breed, as extinct as the brontosaur – the last of the great New York Yankee myths. Mickey played most of his career on one leg – and in dead silence. I don't think I ever heard him speak above a whisper. He behaved as if a ballpark were a library. He was as shy as a schoolgirl, the only superstar I ever saw blush. He was as private as the pope.

He was, in the words of one reporter, the Man Who Wasn't Babe Ruth. And it infuriated the fans, the press, the league, the world, the front office, the backroom. He was as aloof as a German spy. He couldn't stand to be laughed at. When he missed a fly ball or a curveball, he went into a raging, silent sulk. But he punched things, not people.

"Mickey's got a hitting streak of 56 straight water coolers," Whitey Ford once observed.

Mantle gave the impression on the field he didn't give a damn, that he was just waiting for the 5 o'clock whistle. But Mantle was as competitive as a shark.

"He hated pitchers that wouldn't give him nothin' sound to hit," ruminated Casey Stengel, who managed Mantle on a more or less friendly basis, mostly less, for 10 years.

Mantle went from a zinc mine to Broadway, from Oklahoma to Times Square, at the age of 19. "He never seen concrete before," Stengel explained as Mantle stood in frightened silence in right field at Yankee Stadium.

The Yankee press, used to the gregarious, bellowing Babe Ruth, for whom the big city held no more terror than a base on balls, resented Mantle's taciturnity and it showed in their copy. I doubt any player that great got that booed. I doubt any player that disabled got that great.

When Mantle showed up in Arizona as a raw recruit signed for a miserly $1,100 bonus and bus fare, sportswriters retired his number before he had been issued one. "He could have embarrassed my writers if it turned out he could not hit the curveball. They had him in Cooperstown in knickers," grunted Stengel.

Mantle's career could have been traced in X-rays. He had more cartilage and bone taken out of him than most people have. He was built like something that should have horns. He had to be careful on hunts. Even the moose thought he was one of them.

He was a haunted figure. The men in the Mantle family, including his dad, Elvin (Mutt) Mantle, died of cancer as young men. A wellbruited story about Mickey concerns the time a TV newsman asked him what his goal was. "Forty," he responded. "Home runs?" asked the telecaster. "Years," said Mantle grimly.

He played in a World Series once with a hole where the back of his hip should be. He tore his leg apart settling under a Willie Mays fly ball in his first World Series. "He tripped over one of them faucets out there," recalls Stengel.

He started out his career with a history of osteomyelitis, a bone disease that kept him out of the Army. He was lucky it didn't keep him out of shoes. Playing a game where you run into things with osteomyelitis is like digging tunnels under rivers with tuberculosis.

"You'd see him, he'd go down the dugout steps and his knees would shake. But he was the greatest hitter for distance I ever managed," recalls Stengel. "The distance of those balls were outstanding. He hit one in Washington one day and they had to send a cab after it as Red Patterson – he was the club publicity man – stepped it off and he says, 'My goodness, what if it was a thousand feet?' And I says, 'What if you have to send a boat after it?' and Griffith – he was the owner of the Washingtons in those days – he put a mark up where the ball went out of the park. But he had them take it down as it was commencing to scare his pitchers."

Mantle's home runs, 536 of them, laid end to end would probably cross more state lines than Hank Aaron's 713. He struck out more times than any man. But he walked more times than any man except two.

When he came up out of Oklahoma with hair the color of cornsilk and eyes as pale as a summer sky, the guys in the checkered vests were as glad to see him as the Yankees. Mickey bought more of those tin watches and stocks that existed only in the back pocket of the guy selling them than a guy who just came to town on a tractor.

"It's a good thing Whitey Ford (a Manhattan street kid) is going to the Hall of Fame with him," cracked a newsman in New York. "Otherwise, Mick would try to buy it from a guy on a street corner up there."

His bare-bones stats may not compare spectacularly with those who preceded him to Cooperstown. Baseball was an easier game before the night games, the jet port ballparks, the slider, the basket gloves, the nine-second outfielders. Besides, those guys had all their movable parts. They didn't have legs like those zinc mines Mickey used to live over (and in) – apt to cave in on you at any time. They didn't start out life as a spavin from Spavinaw. The Hall of Fame is easier to get into if you dare to slide.

• • • • • • • • • • • • • • • • • •

MAY 23, 1962

Wonderful Willie

The first thing to establish about Willie Mays is that there really is one.

He's 5 feet 10, weighs 183, has five fingers on each hand, five toes on each foot, two eyes, all his teeth and a nice smile. He's quite mortal. He makes $90,000 a year but gets to keep only enough to pay off the alimony and the rent on time and is made up like the rest of us of about 87 cents' worth of iron, calcium, antimony and whatever baser metal a human being is composed of. Only in his case, it's put together a little better than in the rest of us.

All this is important to know in talking to baseball people because when you mention Willie Mays, several things happen: A film comes over their eyes, their cheeks flush and flecks of foam appear at the corners of their mouths. Listening to them, you half expect to see the Angel Gabriel running around with No. 24 on his back. At the very least, you think they are describing one of their own hallucinations – a combination of Babe Ruth, Ty Cobb and Elmer the Great, a comic strip character 28 feet tall pasted together out of old clippings of the Sporting News or conjured out of a pot of reheated Welsh rarebit.

Willie Mays is so good the other players don't even resent him. They have had his name in standing type in Cooperstown's Hall of Fame ever since he was a rookie. Leo Durocher started to drool the first time he saw Willie Mays, and he hasn't stopped since. "If he could cook, I'd marry him," Leo once announced.

The only thing he can't do on a baseball field is fix the plumbing. As a batter, Bill Rigney once said, his only weakness was a wild pitch. But he hit one of those in spring practice for a clean single from a semi-prone position. As long as gravity is working, he'll catch any ball hit or thrown in his vicinity. His vicinity is anywhere between the foul lines. Sometimes the left fielder is instructed to go after only foul balls to keep out of Mays' way.

The only place in the world they boo him is San Francisco. This makes strong men cover their ears because around the rest of the league they figure anyone who would boo Willie Mays would kick in a stained-glass window.

Part of the trouble is when the Giants transferred to San Francisco, the press there and in New York gave the impression that Willie Mays and the Seven Dwarfs were coming to the Coast with Horace Stoneham and two lame-armed pitchers. They didn't expect Willie Mays to land there; they expected the waters of the Golden Gate to part and let him walk ashore. Or, if he flew, they didn't think he would need an airplane. The first time he struck out, there was a gasp as if someone had just let the air out of the town.

It was said his life used to be 95% baseball and 5% cowboy movies. Then he got married, and the ratio went down. His life became only 93% baseball.

He can do one more thing than any other great slugger in the history of the game – steal bases. He is the only man in history to hit more than 30 home runs and steal more than 30 bases a season – and he does it habitually.

He has been shy most of his life. He needs constant reassurance. The product of a broken home in Alabama, raised by an aunt, he never takes anything for granted. He doesn't drink or smoke and scandal has never touched his life.

Off-field, he is a pleasant, rather lonely young man. He had his 31st birthday dinner alone in a St. Louis hotel room with a newspaper man, Harry Jupiter of the San Francisco Examiner. In spring training, he was a frequent dinner guest of a busboy on the base. So far as is known he has never done an unkind thing in his career – except hit four home runs in one day off Milwaukee pitchers. That's as many as anyone ever hit in one nine-inning stretch.

He is modest. When he was with Minneapolis in 1951 and a Giant official got on the phone to send for him after the Giants had just lost 11 games in a row, Willie demurred. "I'm not ready yet. I'm not coming," he protested. "What are you batting?" the official asked. ".477," Willie answered. There was a thud on the other end of the line as the man fainted.

The Giants won the pennant that year, but Willie went hitless his first 22 times at bat. Manager Leo Durocher came upon him in the clubhouse. Tears were streaming down Willie's cheeks. "I can't help it. I can't hit them cats, Mistah Leo," he sobbed. Leo put his arm around him. "I brought you up here to play center field. You are the greatest center fielder I have ever seen, probably that the game has ever seen. Get out there and play it!"

Willie Mays did. The first pitch the next day – off Warren Spahn – he put over the roof. He's been doing it ever since. "I think I'll steal less from now on," he told me Tuesday night, "because I hope I can play for 10 years more." I got news for him: Baseball hopes so, too.

• • • • • • • • • • • • • • • •

SEPTEMBER 22, 1996

Slugger's Statistics Becoming Ruthian

Mark David McGwire as Babe Ruth II? Well, you have to crunch the numbers a little bit, but a case could be made.

Mark has sent 50 baseballs into orbit this year. Only 12 other players in the long history of the grand old game have done that. Babe Ruth did it four times; Mickey Mantle and Willie Mays, twice.

But the stat on Mark McGwire you have to pay attention to is the fact that he got his 50 home runs this year in only 390 official times at bat. Mathematics was never my long suit, but I make that a home run every 7.8 times at bat. That stat is Ruthian.

In 1927, when he hit 60, Babe Ruth went to bat officially 540 times. Home run every nine times at bat, right? In 1962 when Roger Maris unaccountably hit 61, he struck a homer every 10 times at bat.

The stats take into account only official at-bats. A bit misleading. They discount bases on balls. The notion is, since they are unofficial and don't count on your batting average, they shouldn't count on your homer average either, since you had no chance to hit a home run off, say, Ball 4.

Well, not necessarily. The truth is, many a home run has been hit off Ball 4 – or Ball 1, 2 or 3. Lots of home runs have been hit on balls outside the strike zone.

The presumption is, if Ruth had waited for strikes to hit, his home run totals would be halved. Or, anyway, lowered. When he hit 60, you have to believe, based on old umpires' recollections, that he hit a considerable number of them off high-outside or low-inside pitches.

Ted Williams might have insisted on a strike to hit, but Ruth almost never got one. He led the world in walks – 2,056 of them lifetime. He

38

regularly led the game in bases on balls – 11 times by actual count. He walked as many as 170 times a season.

With Ruth, a walk was a victory for the pitcher. You will note in the record books, Ruth was not among the all-time leaders in intentional walks. This is preposterous. It is unthinkable pitchers did not try to walk him almost every other time at bat. You have to assume he wouldn't let them. You can only conclude that many a pitch the pitcher thought was outside the strike zone really was when Ruth got through with it. It was in the center-field seats.

You have to be careful comparing a hitter to Ruth for another reason: When Babe Ruth hit 54 home runs in 1920, that was more home runs than any other team in the league hit. There were 369 home runs hit in the American League that year. Washington hit only 22, for instance. Ruth hit 54, his Yankee teammates and the rest of the league 315.

That meant only one thing: The ball was not jacked up in those years. It was still a comparative beanbag. Knocking it out of the lot still requires the basic hand-eye coordination and strength, but in those days you got no help from the ball. It took massive strength to propel it out of the park.

In 1921, Ruth hit 59 home runs. The seven other teams in the league got 402.

Know how many home runs the American League had hit this Year of Our Lord as of Wednesday last? 2,578 is all.

So it's a tricky business, comparing a hitter today to Ruth's day – although the practice of juicing up the baseball apparently originated with him, and even Ruth had a missile to swing at in his later years.

But the Babe – even with his plethora of walks – had his 500-plus and 400-plus at-bat seasons. Mark McGwire went to bat only 84 times in 1993, only 135 times in 1994 and only 317 times last year. McGwire is troubled by bad feet. Ruth missed games but not parts of seasons, and mostly from suspensions for high living, not physical ailments.

McGwire looks the part. Beneath all that curly red hair, those alert blue eyes is the body of the born hitter. The powerful arms, the sloping shoulders. Sloping shoulders seem made for hitting something hard. Joe Louis had sloping shoulders. So did the Babe. He had a sloping everything.

You have to be around 6 feet 5, 250 pounds to keep hitting a five-ounce baseball into orbit with a 40-inch, 35-ounce bat as October rolls around. McGwire qualifies – when his feet let him.

He misses at-bats for another Ruthian similarity too: He has walked 108 times this year, fourth most often in the league. He led the league in walks in 1990.

I went down to the locker room at Anaheim the other night to see how the Ruth-chasing was coming along.

"Are you proudest of the 50 homers or the .322 batting average?" I ask him. Mark has never hit .300 over a full major league season.

"I'll take the 50," he says. "It's a first for me. I had 49 and 42, never 50."

Did he ever feel he had Babe Ruth in his sights as the season wore on? McGwire shakes his head.

"I can say I never thought about that. I just tried to get a hit. You never try to hit a home run. If you do, you won't."

What's his secret? Eyesight? See the craters on the moon on a clear night, can he? Got 20/15 vision? McGwire smiles.

"My vision without contact lenses is about 20/500."

Without contacts, he says, he not only couldn't see the ball, he couldn't even make out the pitcher. With contacts, he says, he does have 20/15.

Will he hit 60?

"Oh, someone could," he begins. "Oh, you mean this year? Naw. Got what? 10 games left? But some year? It's possible."

In a sense, he's fortunate. The man who goes into mid-September with 55 or more home runs would soon seem to be leading a parade. An army of photographers, TV cameramen, reporters, talk-show recruiters, sponsors, advertisers, fans and agents would be marching behind his every move. Roger Maris' hair fell out under the onslaught.

Still, if a man can hit a home run every 7.8 trips to the plate, he can expect to be noticed. If he ever got to bat 600 times – Pete Rose had more than 600 at-bats 17 times, Maris had 590 his year and Willie Wilson had 705 one year – that would work out to 75 home runs for the year.

Even in a year when there were 2,500 others, that would get attention. That would work out to "Babe Ruth? Who was he?"

● ● ● ● ● ● ● ● ● ● ● ● ● ● ● ● ● ● ● ·

FEBRUARY 2, 1966

New Pitch for Satch

Casey Stengel called him "Father Time." The people in the border ports where he threw his fastball called him "The Ancient Mariner."

He is not only impervious to time, he is allergic to it. Clocks, calendars, time tables, sextants, sun dials are alike meaningless to him. Greenwich Time might be all right for a lot of Swiss watch makers and ships' sailings but not for Leroy "Satchel" Page. "Leroy," a discouraged owner once observed, "operates on Eastern Sub-Standard Time." Leroy never moves the clock back. Or forward. "You cannot have any daylight savings," he once noted. "The sun uses it all up."

He has missed more trains than a cross-eyed hobo. He has frequently found himself a day late and a state behind his teammates on a road tour.

You can tell his age the way you do with tree rings: you only hope to get the right century. "When you get over 35," he said the other day, alluding to a human condition he had clearly achieved, "you sometimes get too old to do the things you shouldn't do." In such case, Leroy R. Paige should have been a model of human deportment ever since Halley's Comet. "There are them as disputes it," admits Satch however.

They came to draft him the other day, the joke goes – for the Spanish-American War. He played a Civil War soldier in a movie a few years back, and when the critics were surprised he had the role down so well,

41

a friend shrugged, "Why not? He played in the real one."

He tried to get into Mexico once but his passport negotiations reached an impasse over the matter of a birth certificate. "Shucks, everybody knows old Satch was born," he told the clerk who proved, nevertheless, to be the persevering type, and asked Satch how old he was. "Forty-nine," answered Satch, pulling an age out of the air. How long had he been playing baseball? "Forty-three years," said Satch. When he had established that he was real and natural born, Satch left the clerk with an autographed baseball and a piece of advice: "Learn control and respect the pitcher when he comes to bat."

Last summer, baseball history was made when Satch pitched a three-inning stint at Kansas City. History was in the form of a ballplayer getting the only hit ever in the big leagues off a 65-year-old pitcher. A young man whose acquaintance Satch hadn't made got the hit off him. "The young man's name was 'Yastrocki,'" Satch advised a few of us the other day. "He injured me."

The young man's name was actually "Yastrzemski" but men with better pronunciations than Satch have gone down swinging on that one. People's names are other things that do not weigh heavily on Satch, who likes to go through life traveling light. In his lexicon, Ted Williams comes out "Ted Lewis." ("Ted Lewis had the No. 1 eye," Satch explained the other afternoon.) Nicknames get all mixed up with real names with Satch. Bob Feller was "Robert Rapid" instead of vice versa. Joe DiMaggio was "Joe Clipper." Satch recognized people by batting stances, not the artificial amenities like surnames, and his biographer, Dick Donovan, once recalled the time the switch-hitting Mickey Mantle belted him for a hit, batting left-handed. As Satch left the game for a southpaw relief pitcher, Mickey came to bat right-handed. Satch lost him. He scoured the line-up for him without success. "Where is that boy that done me injury?" he finally queried in desperation.

Satch was probably the greatest thrower of a baseball in history. He is currently touring the country as an advance man for the clown basketball team, the Globetrotters. Baseball, you see is all heart.

He is a walking reproof to the game wherever he turns up. It is hard to see how anyone in the Hall of Fame can avoid wincing when they see him coming. I hope they have the decency to hide their plaques.

They kept him out on the leaky-roof and flat- wheeled-bus circuits for 25 years. When they did break the color line, they took in the highly publicized, highly educated youngster from Pasadena, Jackie Robinson. They had stocked two leagues before they called in Satch. Bill Veeck was the liberator. "They would've left me right there in Pitchburg (ed. note: It's in Pennsylvania, home of the Pitchburg Pirates) if Bill doesn't come along and say 'Leroy, can you still throw that thing?' and I say 'Mr. Bill, right where I want it.' And that's how I got Cleveland's into the World Series."

Bob Feller, Dizzy Dean, and other honest mounds men of the day acknowledged Satchel was the finest thrower of the baseball ever. Not that they had to. Leroy's faith in himself is boundless. When Dean, in a moment of ebullience, came up to Leroy once and announced "Satch, you 'n' me would've won 60 games between us every year." Satch answered frostily, "Mr. Bean, I would've won 60 by myself."

Someone asked him the other day if Maury Wills would have stolen on him. "Not bases, he wouldn't of," loftily advised Satch.

Satch's baseball career – which was served largely with the St. Louis Browns in organized ball which precludes calling it a "major league" career – was such a study in injustice that it is the notion here they ought to bend the rules of the Hall of Fame to let Satch in, not only in his own right, but as surrogate for all the nameless, luckless Negro players – the guys who would have been the Napoleon Lajoies, Tris Speakers, Ty Cobbs if they hadn't had to play the game by mule back, in banana republics, in the backwoods. And let the plaque so state.

If not, if they continue to load Cooperstown only with guys who came up the silk-sheet, $100,000-a-year route, why, as I said before, they ought to call it the "Hall of Shame."

• • • • • • • • • • • • • • • • •

AUGUST 31, 1995

Old School Is Fine, Thank You

Writing in the Sporting News of recent issue, Pat Jordan got it all wrong.

Wrote he: "Am I the only person in America who finds Cal Ripken's mind-numbingly plodding pursuit of Lou Gehrig's consecutive-game record a bore? I mean, this is supposed to be the highlight of the season, the day or night Ripken breaks Gehrig's record? Is this what the game has been reduced to? Awards for perfect attendance?"

First of all, before we go on, let me tell you where I'm coming from: To begin with, I've had it up to here with tabloid America. The glorification of the rebel, the outlaw, the guy who makes up his own rules. And makes you live by them. You know what I'm talking about: tennis players who get famous not for their own forehands but because of the one their wives plant on the jaw of officials, basketball players who make millions and don't show up for team practices and make magazine covers, scofflaws whose very criminality gives them celebrity, the whole sorry, sick panoply of sports in the '90s.

Forgive me, but I want to tell you about my grandfather. I don't think he ever got his name in the paper. Till he died. He worked 54 years as a millwright in a factory. He was due at work every morning at 7. So he was usually there at 6. He sat on the steps and smoked a "paper of tobacco" before he went in and put the smock on. When he got injured on the job, he went right back to work with cotton stuck in the hole in his head. Off work, off the payroll. There was no company-paid sick leave in those days.

He raised eight children. He went to church every Sunday. He worked 14 hours a day.

Dull? No hero? In my book, he was. No one ever writes any songs about a guy who shows up for work every day, who pays his bills, feeds his family, who makes the tools that build the country. He was not "colorful." He never robbed any stagecoaches, wrecked any cars (he never had one to wreck). He never went into rehab, never had to be forgiven or paroled. He was even taken for granted by his own family.

I don't want to finger Pat Jordan, a journalist for whom I have respect. It's just that I deplore the worship of the splashy and the trashy that has taken over in this country. It is when it is accompanied by sneering at the accomplishments of the dependable, the reliable, the guys who show up for work every day because that is the way they were brought up, that I rise to make a point of order.

Grandpa! Meet Cal Ripken. You have a lot in common.

Cal has been pursuing his record, Lou Gehrig's 2,130 consecutive games, to a claque of abuse. Critics derided him. They periodically called for him to abandon the chase. They demeaned it and him. Pat Jordan even reprises the derision heaped on Ripken. "Haven't there been times when he should have been benched for an injury or a slump, rather than play merely to sustain his bogus pursuit of a record that for all intents and purposes is meaningless?"

If you're asking me, Pat, in a word, No. I mean, it isn't as if he has been up there sitting on a flagpole all these years.

Cal Ripken is the fourth-best fielding shortstop who ever lived. Look it up. He once went an entire season (161 games) with only three errors. Some shortstops make that in an inning.

He has hit 322 home runs, driven in 1,241 runs, scored 1,252. He has 2,340 hits. If you don't think those numbers are legend-makers for a shortstop, you don't know baseball.

But for much of his career, you'd think Cal Ripken was doing something reprehensible. Like showing up for work on time. Doing a day's work when he got there.

He has never broken any barroom mirrors, gotten into a scuffle with the cops, missed the team plane. I don't think he even chews tobacco. He has batted over .300 four times, has gotten over 200 hits twice. Yet every time he'd go two or three games without a hit, out would come the detractors. He was being selfish, they would scream. Or they would recommend brightly that he stop his streak one day shy of Lou Gehrig's. Or stop it at 2,130, right on Gehrig's.

Let me ask you something: If you were running a business and someone came to you and said he could bring you an employee who would not only show up for work every day for 14 (or 20) years not only ready and in condition but would also be one of your most productive workers, would you start thinking of ways to get him out of the lineup? Put some no-talent goldbrick in his spot? Or would you do a little dance and buy some more shares of company stock?

I can understand some of the frustration of the press boxers. After all, I'm one of them. They like the guy who pitches two no-hitters in a row – even if that's just about all he did in his career in which he ended up a .496 pitcher. They like the guy who hits 61 home runs one year, even though he never hits over 40 any other year in his career and is over 30 only twice.

The 9-to-5 guy doesn't inspire the superlatives. I think, in a way, it's what happened to Henry Aaron. Aaron felt he never got his due for breaking Babe Ruth's all-time homer record. And he probably didn't. Aaron, like Ripken, simply did what he was supposed to do, quietly, efficiently, constantly. The kind of steady contribution that gets you a gold watch and a dinner. Willie Mays would have set off more dancing in the streets. Mays did things like hit four homers in a game and over 50 a season. His hat flew off as he caught 480-foot line drives. And, of course, he did a lot of it in New York.

Still, no one suggested Aaron quit one homer shy of Babe Ruth or retire when he hit 714.

Baseball lineups used to be full of guys like Ripken and Aaron – and Gehrig. There were Charley Gehringers, Tommy Henrichs, Earle Combses, Terry Moores by the dozen. What?! You never heard of any of them? Of course you didn't. But you've heard of tantrum-throwing and racket-throwing tennis brats, you've heard of guys who had to be bailed out to be suited up, substance abusers, wife abusers, no-shows, no-autograph, no play-today. You've heard of guys who didn't have the self-discipline of a hound dog.

They make good copy. But you can have them. I'll take Cal Ripken. I'll take Grandpa.

● ● ● ● ● ● ● ● ● ● ● ● ● ● ● ● ●

JULY 13, 1975

At Home at Third

The 10,542 onlookers at Anaheim Stadium couldn't have been more shocked if Frank Merriwell turned communist or the guys in the white hats lost on television.

There, before their very eyes, the player wearing No. 5 picked up a ground ball, aimed it carefully – then threw it into right field.

They were witnessing one of the rarest of nature's phenomena – Brooks Robinson making an error. It was his second of the year. For Brooks Robinson, that's almost a habit.

Robinson makes an error every other eclipse of the sun. When he does, it's headline stuff, ranking with catchers stealing home, outfielders making unassisted triple plays, pitchers throwing perfect games, Amelia Earhart landing. It's like watching Foyt crash, Caruso cracking on a note, the Mona Lisa with her eyes crossed.

Brooks Robinson with a glove has been a more devastating force in baseball for 21 years than Henry Aaron with a bat. Third base has been a graveyard of three-base hits. He has turned more triples into triple plays and doubles into double plays than any man who ever played the game. His glove has already gone to the Hall of Fame. It will be joined by its wearer as sure as there's a cow in Texas.

In Baltimore, they tell the story of the hit man hired by the rest of

47

the league to carry out a contract on Brooks Robinson. He turns up the next day in a state of shock. "Well, did you shoot him?" he asked. "I tried to," he admits. "I shot him four times. Three of them he caught, and the fourth he turned into a double play."

Bill Rigney used to swear that Brooks sold his soul to the devil. "Something whispers to him, 'Now, a little over to the left, it'll be along in a minute, a line drive right off your ear. Now, get your glove up, here it comes!'" There was no other way to explain how Robinson materialized on the end of the ball so often.

In the 1970 World Series, the Cincinnati Reds only got two outs an inning for all five games, thanks to Robinson. He's the only infielder in the game who ever one-handed home runs. He's the only third baseman in World Series history who ever won the car.

He has started more double plays than any third baseman who ever lived. He holds the league record for assists in a single season and lifetime. He has picked up more than 6,000 ground balls and thrown runners out in his career. He has made more putouts, more than 2,600, than any third baseman who ever lived. He has hit more home runs than any third baseman who ever lived.

Robinson shops around for gloves with hits in them the way sluggers do for bats. Whenever a teammate makes a spectacular catch, Brooks hounds him with offers to trade, buy, borrow or steal. In Baltimore, they say Brooks doesn't go after the balls, his glove does. He always keeps a backup glove which he breaks in on infield practice.

"Brooks is the only guy I know who has a farm system for his gloves," his manager says. "He's got gloves that are a year away. He retires the old ones when they can't go to their left for balls hit in the hole any more."

The other night, before he made his second error in 80 games, Brooks had a routine night for a 38-year-old third baseman. He had two hits, drove in the go-ahead run, threw one of the Angels' 9.6 sprinters out at home plate and let two bunts cannily roll foul.

"The umpires always call anything foul that goes over third base,"

Rigney once complained, "because they figure if it was fair Brooksie would have caught it."

He is the only third baseman ever to have three books written about him. The latest and best, "Third Base Is My Home," with Jack Tobin, went into multiple printings in hardcover and paperback.

In 18 years, the L.A. Dodgers have had 45 third basemen. The Baltimore Orioles have only had one. He has outlasted 37 Oriole shortstops. He is the most durable player in baseball history. He has missed only 59 games in 21 years, has played in 98% of his team's games. Lou Gehrig played in 2,130 games in a row but only 33 others when a terminal illness struck. Hank Aaron has played in more games than any player in history but missed more than twice as many as Brooks.

When he goes, he should take third base with him. Anyone else is sure to louse it up. For years, the standard press box refrain when a fielder butchered the position was, "Pie Traynor would have had it." When Brooks goes, expect to see a line drive home run disappear in the left field second deck and, at the rear of the press box, some old-timer will stir himself and snort, "Would Brooks Robinson have had it? Shoot, Brooks Robinson would have got TWO on it!"

● ● ● ● ● ● ● ● ● ● ● ● ● ● ● ● ● ●

MAY 10, 1974

Robinson's Regret

The throw was on the outfield side of second. So Frank Robinson saw a perfect chance to break up the double play.

The time was June 1967. The players were world champions, but Robinson thought they needed shaking up.

He shook them up, all right. He broke up the double play, all right. In fact, he was safe at second. But he didn't find out about it till a week later.

The little second baseman, Al Weis, blanched when he saw Robinson coming – and he danced out of the way. Robinson hit him on the kneecap. He loused up more than a double play. He might have loused up history.

Frank Robinson, at the time, was leading the league in batting (.337), homers (21) and runs-batted-in (59). Since he was defending Triple Crown champion, the Baltimore Orioles hardly counted on him to break up double plays. They wanted him to bust up fences, not knees or relays.

Frank wasn't safe for long. His head hit Weis' knee with resultant bad news for Blue Cross from both of them. They needed a stretcher for Weis; they needed a crane for Robinson. They needed smelling salts for the Orioles.

When they picked Frank up, they asked him what town he was in. "California," said Frank, who was in Baltimore. "Well, you're close. You've got the right country," the trainer told him.

At that time, Frank Robinson had 394 home runs. It's interesting that at that time Henry Aaron, with a two-year head start, had 457.

The difference was, when Frank Robinson returned to baseball six weeks later, he had a choice of two baseballs to hit – the one his left eye saw or the one his right eye saw.

Recalling the event the other night in the California Angels' locker room, Robinson admitted he changed his batting style irrevocably at that time.

"I never attacked the ball the way I had," he said. For one thing, he didn't know which one to attack. Al Weis' knee had done what a thousand knockdown pitches could not do – make Frank Robinson flinch at a curve. He hit only nine more home runs that year and only 15, his all-time major league low, the following year.

It's interesting to speculate what might have been if Frank Robinson had jogged into second base, standing up, that day. Ballclubs don't keep Triple Crown hitters around to take out pivot men. They want a Frank Robinson to be able to trot around bases, not slide around them.

Once, when the Milwaukee Braves were going to experiment with Henry Aaron at second base, the Dodgers' general manager, Buzzie Bavasi, rubbed his hands in glee. "Good! Our baserunners will shorten his career by five years!" he chortled.

Only three players have hit more home runs than Frank Robinson – Henry Aaron, Babe Ruth and Willie Mays. Only one active player, Harmon Killebrew, has any chance to catch him.

Al Weis' knee may have cost him more than all the major league curveballs he ever saw. On the other hand, Frank Robinson's style of play was controlled anger. Uncontrolled anger is hate. There is some suggestion this was Ty Cobb's way, but not the pennant way.

You know something about Robinson when you know he has played in more World Series than any man in the game today – five in two leagues. This may tell you more about the man than the fact that he is the only player in history to win the MVP in both leagues.

Still, Frank Robinson always went into second like a guy jumping through a skylight with a drawn Luger. I asked him the other night if he had any second thoughts, and if he had it to do again, would he have stopped running and turned for the dugout instead of for the double vision? Frank got a faraway look in his eyes. "I think so. There's no doubt it hurt my career, my home run total."

But I don't think Frank Robinson believed himself. I think if Al Weis were in front of him again, and it was June 1967 again, Frank Robinson again would have taken the concussion route. After all, it was his job to get base-runner Brooks Robinson safely to first, not Frank Robinson safely to the Hall of Fame. He'll make that anyway – even spotting history a hundred home runs.

● ● ● ● ● ● ● ● ● ● ● ● ● ● ● ● ● ●

JANUARY 30, 1962

Jack Be Nimble

It took baseball over 50 years to admit Negroes to our "national" pastime – a fact of life that should make it always hang its head in shame – but I was amused and gratified, both, to note the alacrity with which they admitted Jackie Robinson to the Hall of Fame.

They fell all over themselves because nobody wants to mess with Jackie. If they slammed the door of the Hall of Fame on HIM, he'd kick it in. He'd make it if he had to come in a spike-high slide and some of baseball's most hallowed custodians would have spike wounds from ankle to ear.

And if I were Sid Keener, director at Cooperstown, I'd be very careful where I put the Robinson mementos. Jackie is very sensitive about backseats anywhere.

I have always considered that Jackie Robinson was very probably the greatest athlete of my day. He was a great broad-jumper. He was the finest running halfback in college football. He was a great baseball player. And basketball may have been his best sport.

But what I admired Robinson most for was that he was a winner. The object in baseball – as it is in any other sport – is to win. But figure-happy baseball frequently forgets this. The player of the year is not always on the winner of the year. The rolls of the sport are barnacled with the names of athletes who quite clearly put individual achievement ahead of team achievement.

Ty Cobb led his team to a pennant when he was a rookie and near rookie. Then he became Ty Cobb – the superstar of baseball – and he fought his own teammates as enthusiastically as he did the others. Cobb got his hits, batting championships, stolen bases. But the guy playing alongside him, he didn't even speak to. That may have had more to do with the fact that his teams never again got in a World Series than what Cobb did at the plate.

There are many others of the same persuasion. But not Jack Roosevelt Robinson.

Before he came to them, the Dodgers had won only two pennants in 46 years. After he got there, they won six pennants in 10 years, lost another in a postseason playoff, and still another on the last game of the season. They never finished lower than second. Since he left, they have won one pennant in five years.

Jackie fought his enemies, not his teammates. He never held grudges – except against that persistent foe Jim Crow, who is in traction and whose throat is rattling today because of the number of times he got in Jackie Robinson's way on the basepaths of life.

Jackie has had to battle since he was old enough to cry. Six months after he was born in a Georgia sharecropper's cabin, his father shoved off for parts unknown with another woman. Jackie's mother, in one of the sagas of courage that should put her in whatever Hall of Fame they have for mothers, took her whole brood across the country to Pasadena, a strange city in a strange state where they were about as welcome as the smog.

Jackie got into the kind of scrapes every little kid gets into – swimming in the reservoir, swiping golf balls in the rough at the country club, dumping tar on the lawn of a cranky landlord. But he wasn't every little kid. He was a Negro. But he couldn't go bad because Mallie Robinson wouldn't let him. She hadn't struggled all the way west from a tarpaper cabin to see her children go to an indoor prison instead of a Georgia chain gang.

Jackie got into one famous scrape when he was already a famous football player. The driver of the car he was riding in got into one of those pointless traffic arguments that even the Casper Milquetoasts of society indulge in. Jackie was the peacemaker. But he made peace the way he made everything – aggressively. Before you could say Jack Robinson, he was the one in handcuffs, even though all parties, including the driver of the other car, protested his innocence.

It was a scarlet letter on a police blotter Jackie Robinson could never quite rub off. "Troublemaker!" was the whispered word the bigots hid behind and the well-meaning were troubled by.

But the trouble Jackie made was good for the country like the trouble Lincoln made. In the Army, he refused to play football in protest over a segregated post exchange. He got court-martialed for refusing to sit in the back of the bus. The charge was thrown out.

In baseball, he disagreed with Roy Campanella but didn't retreat into the childishness of not speaking. Jackie always spoke. There was no mistaking where he stood. And it was usually at home plate with the winning run.

He chided the Yankees for discrimination. The Yankees denied it. But went out the next year and got Elston Howard. Some people may not like Jackie Robinson. But they have to respect him. I'm proud he's in the Hall of Fame. But I wish he were also part of the rest of baseball.

● ● ● ● ● ● ● ● ● ● ● ● ● ● ● ● ●

JANUARY 13, 1991

Baseball Is Erasing History

Pete Rose never got 4,256 hits. Pete Rose never got 746 doubles. Pete Rose never played in 3,562 big league baseball games. Pete Rose never played in six World Series, seven playoffs.

Pete Rose never slid head first into home plate, scattering the catcher and the ball as he went. Pete Rose never ran out a base on balls.

There's no such person. Pete Rose never existed. He is a non-person. He is like one of those Soviet despots they expunge from the history books.

Pete Rose never paced a dugout with that funny little gap-toothed grin, waving his Popeye arms and explaining with gestures and rolling slides in the dirt exactly how the game should be played.

Pete Rose never played the game for 24 years with the little boy's zeal and wonder until, if you closed your eyes, you could picture him with his cap on sideways, knickers falling down to his ankles and dragging a taped ball and busted bat behind him, looking for all the world like something that fell off Norman Rockwell's easel.

Must have been some other guy. Because Pete Rose ceased to exist Thursday. He was erased from society by a group of judges they must have found in Salem.

What are they trying to tell us? There was no Charlie Hustle? There was no swaggering, pixieish No. 14 who for two decades filled notebooks and headlines and seemed to epitomize all that was fine and right with the grand old game?

There was no guy who spoke up for baseball and promoted it all he could, who never hid in the trainer's room or ducked out a side door in defeat, who never just took the money and ran?

There was no guy who, when the World Series in Boston was rained out four days out of five, came dutifully to a news conference to keep the scribes in print and the Series, which was to become one of the greatest ever played, alive?

There was no such guy as the Reds' third baseman in that Series who turned to a baserunner from the other team and said, "Ain't this great? Ain't this fun?"

Pete Rose was a figment of our imagination? He was a cartoon character like Yogi Bear?

We're supposed to forget he was ever real? We're supposed to expunge all his records? Banish him to a corner of the sports world inhabited only by the Black Sox of 1919 and one or two other non-persons in the game?

Get outta here! What for? Because he had a gambling addiction? Because he couldn't pass a bookie parlor or a 9-5 shot or the overs-and-unders on the Bears' games without wagering a few bob?

What about the guys who had other addictions? The crowd that got caught in the cocaine busts in Pittsburgh? Hey, Babe Ruth had an addiction, too. He liked rye whiskey. And that was as illegal as cocaine in his time.

I wish we could get some of those judges who voted to take Pete out of circulation to sit in on rape trials once in a while. I wish they could serve on some of those appellate court benches where they throw a serial killer's conviction out because the cop interrogating him forgot to call him "sir" or didn't have a warrant to take his knife away from him.

I wish I could figure out why guys who kill eight nurses in five states get people holding candle vigils outside their prison cells while Pete Rose gets the book thrown at him.

Do you want to stand there and tell me Pete Rose wasn't good for baseball? Lord, he *was* baseball. He's a menace to the game? Gimme a break!

I'm a law-and-order man myself. I've been known to deplore the fact that society has lost its capacity for indignation, has shrunk from punishing its criminals.

And I completely understand that you hold the highly successful to a different set of standards than the less privileged. You want to kick a president out for hushing up a robbery, that's OK with me.

But hey! Pete Rose didn't go to Harvard. Pete Rose never took prelaw. Stop and think about it, Pete made a living in an industry where it's not only all right to steal, it's expected of you.

Pete never discussed Stendhal. Pete never went to the opera. You don't take Pete to Buckingham Palace. Pete played baseball for a living. It was probably that or mow lawns.

A lot of people have sympathy for Shoeless Joe Jackson. He was even the hero of a movie, for cryin' out loud!

But wait a minute! Shoeless Joe Jackson was a crook. He was an accessory before the fact. He was part of a conspiracy to throw the World Series, no less. That's major league trifling with the faith of a nation. Whether he threw the Series or not is beside the point. He agreed to do it. His silence made him a co-conspirator.

If Pete threw ball games, why don't they tell us about it? Why don't they prove it? Ax murderers get a better day in court than he did.

He couldn't have thrown any World Series. His team won three of the six he appeared in.

Oh, he cheated on his income tax? He didn't declare some income he earned?

Noooo! Who could believe a person would do that? Try to pay as little as they could to the government?

I'm not saying you overlook lawbreaking. You don't excuse bank robbers because lots of other guys do it.

He didn't fill ballparks for all those years. He didn't have the dirtiest uniform in the National League. He didn't wisecrack around the batting cage each spring: "I'll tell you three things gonna happen this summer – the grass gonna get green, the sun's gonna get hot and Pete Rose is gonna get 200 hits." He'd like to tell you: "I may not be the best hitter on this club, but I'm the best white hitter!"

But he never did those things. They never happened. He never happened. Ty Cobb's the only guy in history who ever got more than 4,000 hits. They're going to take Pete Rose away.

I don't know about you, but I'm going to miss him.

● ● ● ● ● ● ● ● ● ● ● ● ● ● ● ● ●

MARCH 15, 1988

How Many Strikes Must He Throw?

KISSIMMEE, Fla. – The best pitcher never to have won a Cy Young Award shifted in his seat and looked around the Houston Astros' locker room.

"I think I finished second in the voting once. I'm not sure," drawled Lynn Nolan Ryan.

Let's see. Could that have been the year he pitched two no-hitters, won 21 games, had an earned-run average of 2.87, struck out 383 batters – the most anybody ever has – and pitched 326 innings?

Naw. Jim Palmer won it that year. He won 22 games, struck out 158 and pitched 296 innings. Nolan might not have been close.

Maybe it was the next year, 1974? Nolan pitched another no-hitter, won 22 games, struck out 367, had an ERA of 2.89, pitched 333 innings and allowed 221 hits.

Not very likely. Catfish Hunter won it that year with 25 victories. He struck out 143, pitched 318 innings and only allowed 268 hits.

What about 1972, when Ryan first struck out 300 batters – 329 to be precise – fourth all-time behind Sandy Koufax, Rube Waddell and Bob Feller; won 19 games, had an ERA of 2.28 and pitched 284 innings?

Forget it. Gaylord Perry won that year. Perry had 24 wins, 343 innings and 234 strikeouts.

How about the strike-shortened year when Ryan pitched his fifth no-hitter, had an ERA of 1.69, struck out, like, his 3,300th batter and pitched one of his two-hitters in the playoffs?

No, Fernando Valenzuela won that year. He had an ERA of 2.48, struck out 180 and won 13.

Why would they ever give Nolan Ryan the Cy Young Award? He has only struck out 1,000 more batters than Walter Johnson did. He has struck out 400 more than anyone else ever did. He has struck out 10 or more batters a game 174 times. He averages 9.4 strikeouts a game. The only other pitcher who averaged more than nine was Koufax.

Besides his five no-hitters, Ryan has had nine one-hitters, 18 two-hitters and 26 three-hitters.

Give him the Cy Young Award? Don't be absurd! Not when you have pitchers like Pete Vuckovich, Steve Stone, LaMarr Hoyt and Steve Bedrosian to give it to. You don't give the Cy Young Award to a guy just because he has set or broken 38 major league records. After all, did

Chaplin ever win the Academy Award?

The best 41-year-old sore-armed pitcher in the big leagues last year shifted in his locker-room seat.

"Do I think about it? Oh, not really. What I do think about is, I'd really like to get in one more World Series. I'd like to start a World Series game."

Nolan Ryan is more than an athletic marvel. He's a medical marvel. His glove should go to Cooperstown, but his arm should go to the Smithsonian.

It is a fact of baseball life that the fastball is the most perishable commodity in the game. It's not only supposed to go late in life, it's supposed to go late in a game.

Nolan Ryan's never has. You had to get Nolan in the early innings or not at all. The velocity increased as the game wore on. Your only hope against Ryan was that the ball moved at such speed that it tended to want to orbit like something filled with liquefied oxygen and a booster.

The first guy Nolan Ryan ever pitched to, he hit on top of the head. The second guy, he broke his arm. The third guy went down to his coach before going to bat and said, "Do I have to?"

Last year, at 40 and with a throbbing elbow, and a limit on the number of pitches he was allowed in a game, Nolan Ryan led the major leagues in strikeouts for the sixth time in his career. He led it in ERA for the second time in his career. He became the first player in history not to win the Cy Young Award after leading the league in strikeouts and ERA.

So what else is new?

On Sept. 9 last year, against San Francisco, Nolan Ryan, for the 22nd time in his career, struck out more than 15 batters in a game when he struck out 16 Giants – including Mike Aldrete for the 4,500th strikeout of his career.

Nobody else his age had ever struck out as many batters in a year, 270.

What made this more remarkable was that the Houston general manager, Dick Wagner, deferring to Nolan's sore elbow the year before, had decreed a 110-pitch limit on Ryan's turns on the mound.

For the first time in his career, Ryan had no complete games, but it didn't stop him from leading the world in strikeouts again. He was fifth in the Cy Young balloting.

Fastball pitchers are supposed to go to the artifices of pitching as they get into their late 30s and 40s. Nolan Ryan still muscles up a ball in the 97- to 98-m.p.h. hour range. He averages over 90. It has been said his changeup is 89.

He is the only guy in history whose fastball, certifiably, on sophisticated aeronautical equipment, exceeded 100 m.p.h. – and it did it seven times.

Baseball historians of the future are probably going to wonder what Nolan Ryan did in his off-hours that ruled him out of baseball's pitching award after hanging up those kinds of numbers. Did he rob banks, kill kittens, sell government secrets, set fires?

Nolan doesn't drink, smoke, chew or swear. He raises cattle, not hell, in the off-season. He's polite, approachable. He takes the position that God gave him that arm, he didn't have to work down a mine shaft for it. He's the most unimpressed guy in the world with the fact that he's Nolan Ryan.

Well, almost the most unimpressed. The Cy Young voters have managed to stay pretty *blase* about it, too. Maybe they're waiting for him to cure cancer.

● ● ● ● ● ● ● ● ● ● ● ● ● ● ● ● ●

JULY 8, 1983

Scully Handles a Mike Like Ruth Did a Bat

It took baseball in its wisdom 10 years to turn Babe Ruth, the most perfect hitting machine of all time, from a pitcher into a slugger.

It took football seasons to figure out Marcus Allen wasn't a blocking back and to hand him the football.

And it took network television forever to get the message that Vin Scully should do major league baseball and stop fooling around.

It wasn't that Scully was inept at other sports. It was just that he was miscast. It was like Errol Flynn playing a faithful old sidekick. Scully could do golf and do it well. Rembrandt could probably paint soup cans or barn doors, if it came to that. Hemingway could probably write the weather. Horowitz could probably play the ocarina. But what a waste!

Nobody understands baseball the way Vin Scully does. He knows it for the laid-back, relatively relaxed sport it is. Scully is the world's best at filling the dull times by spinning anecdotes of the 100-year lore of the game. He can make you forget you're watching a 13-3 game, as we were Wednesday night at Chicago, and take you with him to a time and place where you are suddenly watching Babe Ruth steal home. He is like a marvelous raconteur who can make you forget you're in a dungeon. He can make baseball seem like Camelot and not Jersey City.

He knows baseball fans are ancestor worshipers, like the British aristocracy, and he can invest a game with allusions to its gaudy past that give meaning to the present. We suddenly see knights in shining armor out there carrying on a glorious tradition instead of two rival factions of businessmen trying to land the order.

Football requires screaming. "They're on the five and it's second down and goal to go!" "They're on the three and it's third down and there's 29 seconds left to play!" Baseball requires humor, deft drama, a sprinkling of candor, mix well and serve over steaming hot tradition.

Scully knows the sport as few do. He learned it at the knee of Branch Rickey at the time he was most impressionable, a young, ambitious, career-oriented student out of Fordham. Scully will tell you why a batter should try to hit to right with a man on first and none out. ("The first baseman has to stay on the bag to keep the runner close. The second baseman has to cheat a step toward second in the event of a steal or a double play. There's a hole there you could dock ships.")

But finally, the pairing of Scully with Joe Garagiola was an inspired piece of casting, not quite like Burns and Allen or the Sunshine Boys but a matchup quite as important to baseball as Ruth and Gehrig or Tinker and Evers and Chance.

It was originally thought that was a lot of ego for one stage, or one microphone, but the two have locked into place like tongue in groove, or, in this case, tongue in cheek.

Garagiola is the locker-room wit, the jokester from the team bus. Scully brings out the best in him, and he brings out the best in Scully. When the ballgame starts with the pitcher throwing two baseballs out of the infield and the third baseman following suit in the bottom half of the first, Garagiola pronounced it "a real Halloween inning" and later suggested that the ritual disclaimer, "This game is the property of major league baseball," be waived since presumably nobody in the big leagues wanted to claim this game.

Later, when Scully noted that a certain pitcher had "retired 53 of 58 batters who faced him," Garagiola wondered, "Why wouldn't you try to sign those five guys?"

When a pitcher built along the general lines of King Kong took the mound, Garagiola observed, "He's an 8 on a seismograph. His birthday is Monday, Tuesday and Wednesday." Later, Joe said of a pitcher with a roundhouse, hanging curve, "He throws an American Legion curveball."

Later, when Scully said that a bearded infielder "looks as if he fell off a box of cough drops," Garagiola noted: "If he shaves, he only weighs 91 pounds." When a pitcher wearing more gold chains than a wine clerk appeared, Scully noted that "he looks as if he just came from Westminster Abbey."

It was all good clean fun. They brought out the best in each other. No one noticed the game was boring. Because it wasn't in the broadcast booth. That's one of the things that made this game great all along.

● ● ● ● ● ● ● ● ● ● ● ● ● ● ● ● ● ●

Almost Too Good to Be True

The first thing to do with a person like Tom Seaver is to establish that there is one. You have to make sure he didn't just walk in of the pages of "A Lad's Pluck" or "How Frank Merriwell Saves the Day at Yale."

You have to find out if he isn't a public relations hoax like the Hindu quarterback at Plainfield State Teachers or some other figment of the overheated imagination of a press agent.

You figure somebody read the life and times of the late Christy Mathewson and decided it was about time baseball had another one of them.

If George Thomas Seaver was real, why doesn't he get thrown out of a bar occasionally for busting a mirror with a bar stool? How come he isn't paying alimony to two or more wives?

What's a goody-goody like him doing with a 97-mile-an-hour fastball? Why is his skin so clear and kind of baby-fat, his eyes so hazel? Why doesn't he spit more? At least wear an earring?

If God gives you a 97-m.p.h. fastball, he gives you the barbed-wire beard, the busted nose and the rotten disposition to go with it, right? Seaver should look more like Burleigh Grimes than Christy Mathewson.

It was not only the fastball. Seaver could get the ball by you on sheer guile if he had to. He was always two pitches ahead of the batter. One of his early managers, Solly Hemus, announced that when he came up he had "a 35-year-old head to go with a 21-year-old arm." Here was an instant veteran.

Even New York was awed. "Tom Terrific," the writers called him. Fearless, faultless, a hero out of the dime-novel era. The guy who would rescue the orphan from a burning building, warn the train the trestle was out, capture the runaway horses with the heiress in the carriage. Thrash the bully. Tom Swift and his Electric Fastball.

The New York Mets were the Gabby Hayes of Baseball when he came along. Comedy relief. Casey Stengel's burlesque. They should have played in noses that would light up.

But G. T. Seaver was not anybody's laughingstock. He was insulted by defeat. To go along with the collar-ad good looks, the college education and the slider, he was as intense a competitor as Rocky Balboa. Clark Kent turned into Super pitcher when he put No. 41 and the orange and blue pinstripes on.

He pitched the Mets to two World Series. That was when the team had to rely on such batting "stars" as Al Weis, Rod Gaspar, J. C. Martin and Ron Swoboda. In 1973, the team got in the World Series with the worst won-lost percentage (.509) in the history of baseball.

Seaver was as motivated as a monk. Lots of pitchers in the big leagues will discuss good places to eat with you, booze, broads, hockey, football, jazz, even the stock market.

If you braced Tom Seaver in the locker room, you got an illustrated lecture on how many fingers you put on the fastball, how many seams you gripped for the slider and a detailed physiological description of the proper wrist snap for the outside curve.

Tom was as interested in the mechanics of the pitch as Edison was in the electric light.

He struck out people by the gross. He holds the major league record for the most seasons with 200 or more strikeouts (10). He tied the record for most strikeouts in a nine-inning game (19).

And he holds the record for the most strikeouts in a row. He once struck out the last 10 batters to face him in a game. Nobody hit a fair ball from the middle of the sixth inning on. Only five guys hit fair balls in the whole game.

Seaver made few mistakes on the mound. But when he finally made one off the field, it was like giving a high, inside fastball to Henry Aaron with three on.

In the fall of 1977 when he was 21-6 with a 2.59 ERA and 19 complete games and 7 shutouts, Seaver took on the front office, the lawyers and, ultimately, the New York Daily News and its sports editor, Dick Young, in a contract dispute that got so acrimonious it could only result in his trading. Tom Seaver went to Cincinnati.

It was like Frank Merriwell at Harvard. Or Ohio State. Just not right. Tom Seaver never won 20 games at Cincinnati, never threw double figures in complete games. The franchise was in the business of dismantling one of the game's all-time great aggregations. Seaver was as wrong for Cincinnati as Wall Street. It wasn't a career, it was an exile.

Tom Seaver has now found his way back to Shea Stadium and the orange and blue of the Mets. It's not the same, he admits. The fastball is down to 88 m.p.h. The curveball doesn't always curve. The slider is too slow, the changeup too fast.

Seaver still looks like the kind of guy who would save orphans or run for student body president, but now the body is as old as the head.

Tom has one important piece of unfinished business that the Cincinnati sidetrack stalled: He'd like to win 300 games. I mean, Frank Merriwell would. Christy Mathewson did.

"Think of it – only 11 pitchers in the history of baseball have won 300 games!" said Tom Seaver bravely as he dressed for a game in Dodger Stadium the other night. "Steve Carlton will make it 12. I'd be cheating myself if I didn't go for it."

He'd also be cheating all the kids who believe in eating their spinach and doing their homework, all the authors who believe in the words "clean-cut" and "forthright" and "pluck" and that the America of the Rover Boys, Tom Swift, and Dauntless Dick and True Grit – and Tom Terrific – is not dead yet.

● ● ● ● ● ● ● ● ● ● ● ● ● ● ● ● ● ●

MARCH 29, 1962

Title for a Duke

VERO BEACH – You look at Edwin Donald Snider, occupation outfielder, and you rub your eyes. There is a spring in the step, a sparkle in the eyes, a song in the heart, canary feathers drip from the mouth.

Can this, you ask yourself, be the Duke? The ex-Grouch?

It can. You conclude that one of these things has happened: Either (1) the slider has been outlawed: (2) the Russians have quit; (3) all left-handed pitchers have been ordered to report to their draft boards; (4) his mother-in-law has moved to Alaska; or (5) his brother-in-law got a job.

None of them. What has brought the sunshine to the hoary locks of the Duke is a simple commute. From the players' entrance of the L. A. Coliseum to the traffic jam of Chavez Ravine is not even a decent cab ride. For Duke Snider, it may be the difference between a glass case of one's own at Cooperstown or a life that's just a bowl of avocados.

Of all the current Dodgers, only Duke Snider seems likely to figure in the early returns of his first eligible ballot for the Hall of Fame. Some of the "phenoms" who have been supposed to replace him over the years seem more likely to figure in the first waiver lists for Spokane and points north.

Duke Snider is seventh on the list of all-time home run hitters, the only man to hit four home runs in two World Series. He has one of the most perfect batting swings the game has ever seen. There is little doubt his name would long since have been in standing type at Cooperstown except for one slight change in the geography of baseball – and a slightly more major one in the geography of right field.

When the Dodgers moved the franchise from Ebbets Field to the Coliseum in 1958, they all but shattered the glass in the Snider case, turned him for a long hitter to a long out. It was like putting the Hope Diamond in a pile of coal. Snider turned white when he first saw the dimensions he had to overcome.

His career became a four-year struggle to maintain his temper, poise, average and, above all, his sanity. If the Coliseum had been dynamited any time in the interim, Snider would have been the first man arrested.

It was an economic as well as artistic disaster. Snider today is a $38,500 ballplayer. He was that five years ago. In the normal course of things, he would be now by matching salaries with Mickey Mantle ($85,000), Willie Mays (ditto) and Roger Maris ($75,000). Home run hitters drive Cadillacs, and Snider could have had a fleet. He had hit 40 home runs or more for five consecutive years when the team came West. He has been hard put to total 15 a year since.

He became the game's all-time leader in 400-foot outs. Good pitchers just lobbed the ball up to him high and inside and then held their sides laughing as the ball sailed out to right center, where two outfielders who were waiting fought to make the catch. "All things considered," Snider grated through set teeth, "I would rather strike out."

Sometimes, of course, he did that, too. He was ready for an analyst. Where, in Brooklyn, when he came to bat, they yelled "Bed-fud Aven-ya, Dook," in the Coliseum they yawned and looked around for something to read.

He took his pique out by trying to throw the ball out of the Coliseum. A psychiatrist would understand, but the management didn't. The scoldings got loud enough to make page one. The Duke took it because the label "crybaby" is worse than a built-in pop-up. His cursing was under his breath. Occasionally a helmet splintered on a wall as another perfectly placed outfield came up with a tape-measure out.

The Snider drive to immortality seemed caught in a permanent traffic jam of banjo hitters. Born and raised in L. A., the Duke had been one of the few to throw his hat in the air when the move out of Brooklyn was announced. He should have stomped on it instead.

In Brooklyn, even when he was hitting an annual 40 homers, no one was measuring Snider for a statue in the park. In the midst of his greatest days, he allowed himself to be cajoled into a ghostwritten article in a national magazine, "I Play for Money Not Fun," a bit of honesty that earned him a shower of beer cans, beer can openers, open switchblade knives and open obscenity at home. Snider returned the fire. "Brooklyn," he observed, "doesn't deserve the Dodgers."

It was an idea that occurred simultaneously to Walter O'Malley. If there was one thing Snider would have liked to have taken with him, though, it was the right-field fence, which he didn't think Brooklyn deserved either.

In the years that followed, the Duke began to long for the good old days even with the shower of beer and utensils. The Los Angeles fans were polite, but the politicians foundered the Duke's career in a shower of referendums, land clearances, hair pulling contests and construction delays. Every time someone threw sand in O'Malley's bulldozers, he blew smoke on Snider's records. He was ready to be carried out with the Arechigas. He even began to get a faraway look in his eyes when a rumor of a trade back to New York brewed.

One night, in a ninth-inning tie, the final indignity occurred. With the winning run on base, the manager ordered Snider to bunt. He hit a winning home run – to the wrong field – instead (after fouling two bunts).

But the Snider swing was as unsuited for wrong-field home runs as it was for bunting. Choking Snider's switch was like cloaking Elizabeth Taylor in overalls. The management got used to platooning Snider. It cost the team the pennant as Snider was on the bench in the late innings and his "caddie" was batting cleanup when a home run was needed.

It won't happen this year. At the age of 35, he is no longer the Bedford Avenue bombardier he was. His power is shortened by several feet. But so is the fence.

A measurement of the reliance of the Dodgers on Snider can be seen in his appointment as captain, the first the team has had since Pee

Wee Reese. To the cynics this means chiefly that Snider gets $500 more a year and gets to carry the lineups up to home plate during the National Anthem.

To the Dodgers – and to Snider – it means he is the Duke of the Dodgers again. To the other pitchers it means the sweat can start to trickle down the backs of their necks again when Snider comes up with a fence he can reach, and if they lob one high and inside they can start for the showers before the ball gets to the plate.

It means the home folks can wave the fielders back again when Snider comes up and shout "the Pasadena Freeway, Dook." It may be Duke's last chance to play for fun and money – and fame (Hall of).

● ● ● ● ● ● ● ● ● ● ● ● ● ● ● ● ● ●

OCTOBER 1, 1975

Death of an Heirloom

Well, God is getting an earful today. I hope He understands the infield fly rule, the hit and run, how to pitch to Hornsby with men on, when to platoon, when it would do you some good to bunt, and what really happened in the 1913 World Series. He will get an illustrated lecture on the hook slide, the best place to play Babe Ruth, when to order the infield in and how to steal on left-handers.

At the end of all this, the narrator will doff his cap and a sparrow will fly out.

They finally slipped a called third strike past Casey Stengel. He can't argue the call. The game is over. Dusk is settling on the bleachers, the lights are turned on in the press box where "my writers" are putting "30" to the final bits of Stengelese they will ever type, and, if you look in the gloom, you can probably see the ghosts of John McGraw, Uncle Wilbert Robinson, Cobb, Ruth, Gehrig and Frisch, and Ring Lardner and Damon Runyon. Someplace, it's 1912 again, and there isn't a lawyer, agent, ad executive or TV camera in sight.

I hope they've got a team that needs platooning, a pitching staff that bears watching in the late innings, a pugnacious umpire or two. I hope the sun is out, the grass is cut and they have somebody who can make the double play. Above all, I hope they have a sportswriter or two to translate. Casey takes his language with him.

A lot of people are going to be surprised that Casey died. Because they didn't think he was born. Casey just came walking out of the pages of Grimm's Fairy Tales years ago. He escaped the wicked old witch's oven, or jumped the club on Snow White. Disney invented him. Part moose, part mouse, sometimes he was all seven of the dwarfs. His rubbery face, his rumbling voice that sounded like a distant artillery barrage, those gnarled old legs so full of lumps from balls bouncing off them that they looked like two socksful of plums.

Casey had a terrible hang-up. He thought baseball should be fun. World Series or spring exhibition game, either one. He used to infuriate the types that thought baseball was a Solemn High Mass. Casey treated the high priests of the game with the disrespect they deserve, whether they were 50-homers-a-year hitters or chewing gum magnates.

There was a lot of little boy in Casey, the eternal kid-at-a-circus. He was the world's oldest 9-year-old. He was always leading a parade. He was a genuine American heirloom, like a railroad watch. What Fernandel was to the eternal Frenchman, Cantinflas to the poor put-upon Mexican, Chaplin to tramps, Stengel was to Americana.

Watching this rumpled Rumpelstiltskin waddle bowleggedly to the mound and lift a pitcher with the elaborate courtesy and manners of a maid being presented at court was as much fun as a car full of clowns.

They said he was a bad manager because he never won till he got to the Yankees, but I always liked the answer Doc Green gave to some humorless types who were complaining about Stengel's inability to manage one night. "I can't," commented Doc, "imagine anything more beside the point."

A lot of laughter goes out of baseball with Casey. I know the upcoming World Series is going to have a big hole in it. One of the delights of the Series buffet and hospitality room was always old Case holding court in a corner in a monologue in which the hearer couldn't tell to the nearest decade which World Series he was talking about. There's going to be one corner of this Series with a deafening silence to it.

I hope they don't cut the whiskey where Casey's going because Casey liked a glass with his maunderings. I don't expect the keeper of the gate up there will come out too well in the translation. If I know Case, and I do, he'll come out as "Peterson." Casey dropped proper names about the time baseball put numbers on players' backs, and even 10-year veterans came out as "my switch-hitter" or "the big fella hisself."

Heaven won't need much for old Case. A lineup he can juggle, an ill-fitting uniform, a dependable relief pitcher and a hotel bar that stays open after night games.

The scouting report on his entrance to that big-clubhouse-in-the-sky must be eye-opening. "There's an applicant out here of indeterminate national origin, speaking a language we do not know, nonstop, wearing a wrinkled uniform with the logos of 10 teams on it, bright blue eyes which he winks incessantly, cereal bowl haircut and a straw suitcase carrying a bottle and bat, and says he knows Heinie Groan personally and has a lineup card in his hand."

And over the intercom will come the voice of The Owner himself. "Why, that must be Casey Stengel! Tell him to come right in. Mr. Hornsby and Mr. Ruth and the 1923 Giants and the 1912 Dodgers are all waiting. Tell him to come in and make himself right at home, platoon Ruth and Hornsby, and lift Mathewson for a pinch-hitter in the eighth inning, and after the game, I'll send over my writers, Matthew, Mark, Luke and John, so he can tell them how he won the 1953 World Series by holding Robinson on."

● ● ● ● ● ● ● ● ● ● ● ● ● ● ● ●

MARCH 28, 1985

Fernando Throws Age a Screwball

VERO BEACH, Fla. – When Fernando Valenzuela came to the big leagues, Bob Lemon, then a Yankee scout, stared in disbelief. He leaned over and asked a Dodger scout, "How old is he?"

"Twenty," was the reply.

Lemon thought about it a moment. "Twenty what?" he wanted to know.

Fernando Valenzuela was the unlikeliest character to put on a big league uniform since the day Babe Ruth hung his up.

"It's Orson Welles," Don Rickles guessed.

"It's Montezuma," someone said.

Still others thought it might be Santa Claus.

"Grover Cleveland Alexander with an accent," suggested baseball men.

The silhouette was a cross between that of a guy with a pillow tied around his middle and an Irish bartender. Jackie Gleason got the part if they made it into a movie.

Prevailing opinion was that Valenzuela's age was somewhere between 45 and infinity. A large school of thought held that he had been found frozen in the ruins of Machu Picchu and thawed out for the season. There was no way this could be the body and the arm of any recent teenager.

When he pitched, the perception was heightened. He threw the kind of canny twisters only a guy who had spent a lifetime in the bush leagues could throw.

His poor pitches were hard to see. His good pitches disappeared altogether. He never lost his cool. He left the middle part of the plate alone and dealt in corners.

Rival managers not only wanted to see the ball, they wanted to see his birth certificate. There was some notion that he might have learned to pitch against General Custer.

He never did any of the things rookies do. He never kicked the water cooler when he lost. He never threw his cap in the air when he won. He treated baseball as if it was just another day in the fields.

He not only spoke no English, he spoke not much of anything. He seemed to wonder what everybody was getting excited about. He was paid to strike those guys out, wasn't he? He came from a long line of people who gave a day's work for a day's pay and didn't expect a ticker-tape parade for it, or their names in the paper.

He didn't exactly save baseball, but he gave it a shot in the arm. Baseball is a game that must have its dreams if it is to live. The legend of this old-young man with the devastating screwball walking out of the dry-bed lands of western Mexico and standing the flower of major league baseball on its ear was the stuff of legend, part Pancho Villa, part Cisco Kid.

America went wild. Television crews were on hand every time he stepped off a team bus. Magazines wanted to do in-depth stories, reporters swarmed over his childhood home in Etchohuaquila, ballparks were jammed on the nights he would pitch, players who got hits off him were booed.

Fernando was privately astonished, even if his face never changed expression. The joke was, Fernando didn't know the meaning of the word "pressure." But then, he didn't know the meaning of the word "cat," either.

The club assigned the Spanish-speaking broadcaster Jaime Jarrin the delicate task of interpreting for Fernando. Jarrin felt the pressure more than Fernando. Fernando just seemed to think all these gringos were crazy.

"I knew that one faulty translation, one missed interpretation could do great harm, could create a false impression which, like all false impressions, could grow into false reality," Jarrin recalls.

He needn't have worried, he says today. The simple, basic honesty of Valenzuela charmed the media, won over a country. Probably no player since Ruth ever had the same unreserved affection in the hearts of his sport's fans as Valenzuela. The critical writer disparaged Fernando at his peril.

Despite his seeming diffidence, Valenzuela worried more about his role in public than his one on the mound.

"I knew I was representing more than myself," he says today. "I knew I was representing Mexico to many people. I was aware of that."

Not for him the midnight trips to the discos. Not for him the curt refusals of autographs, the temper tantrums. Even his arguments over money were conducted in the polite dignity of summit meetings.

Even his appearance had to be modified. Although it contributed to his lovability – Fernando had some of the characteristics of a well-loved cartoon character in his makeup – Fernando slimmed down.

He'll never look like something out of the Louvre, but it's no part for Wallace Beery anymore. Valenzuela would not disgrace a suit of lights.

Although his season last year was sub-legend for Fernandomania, it was hardly substandard for a pitcher who is still only 24 years old, give or take a generation or so.

He pitched the second most complete games in the league. His record of 12-17 looks less unimpressive when it is known that the team scored one run or none in 13 of those games, and fewer than two in 18 of them.

"He is probably the only pitcher in the big leagues who gets younger as he gets older," complained Sparky Anderson, who wishes he had him. He looked 40 when he was 20. Maybe he'll look 20 when he's 40.

Meanwhile, the National League has this recurring nightmare. Valenzuela might just disappear into the mountains some day, like Jane Wyatt in "Lost Horizon."

They're not worried about his getting old. He's already been that. They're worried about his getting young, fading away into youth, the only guy who came into baseball at the age of 3,000 and left it when he lost his curve at the age of 2.

Football

● ● ● ● ● ● ● ● ● ● ● ● ● ● ● ● ●

SEPTEMBER 17, 1989

He Paid Big Penalty
For Dumb Rap

He could throw long. He could throw short. He could scramble. He was probably the most effective quarterback who ever played the game.

But he had this weakness. He was too happy. He always had this silly little grin on his face. He laughed a lot. Smiled a lot. He always gave the impression he had just ridden into town on a wagon and two mules. He giggled. He was as country as grits, red-eye gravy and biscuits. He was as hyperactive as a puppy with a carpet slipper.

If Terry Bradshaw had gone around Pittsburgh in a three-piece suit, carrying a briefcase, if he had frowned a lot, wore horn-rimmed glasses, thought before he spoke, had an unlisted phone, if he had played Mozart instead of Eddy Arnold, he might have gained recognition for what he was – maybe the best quarterback in history.

Instead, he got this reputation as a guy who had a great arm – he used to throw javelins with it, so a football was a piece of cake – but it came attached to a guy who would buy the Brooklyn Bridge.

It wasn't as if being quarterback in the NFL called for a Phi Beta Kappa or a rocket scientist, it was just that society instinctively thinks that anyone who looks cheerful all the time must not understand the situation.

The sporting press latches onto an angle. And the angle on Bradshaw was Dummy. His teammates did nothing to disabuse it. After a losing game, you're supposed to sit in front of your locker and hang your head and look mopey. Bradshaw would be in the shower slapping and tickling with a towel or handing out exploding cigars.

Terry went along with the gag. If someone said, "Hey, Terry, if Farmer Jones had 10 apples and Farmer Brown bought three of them, how many would Farmer Jones have left?" Or, "Hey, Terry, can you name the state capitals – can you even name the states?" Terry would laugh.

Terry thinks the whole question arose because he deliberately flunked an ACT test for admission to Louisiana State University. He wanted to go to Louisiana Tech, closer to home. The skyscrapers of Baton Rouge frightened him, and the simplest way to get out of it all was to not pass the admission test.

A reporter found out about it and, since not making LSU is not exactly like blowing Harvard, a legend was born. Terry Bradshaw became L'il Abner and Ozark Ike rolled into one.

It was a bum rap. But it detracted from Bradshaw's monumental achievements in the game of football.

They're hard enough to decipher anyway. You examine a record book and you look in vain for Bradshaw's accomplishments. He's 130 touchdown passes behind Fran Tarkenton and 78 behind John Unitas, for instance. His 2,025 completions lag behind Tarkenton's 3,686 or Unitas' 2,830.

But when you talk of Super Bowls, Bradshaw stands alone. His nine touchdown passes lead all quarterbacks. So do his 932 passing yards.

So does his getting there. The object of the game is to get to, and win, Super Bowls. Terry Bradshaw did this better than any quarterback who ever played. It's possible nobody ever threw as many quality passes. For one thing, Terry Bradshaw disdained the little dump-off pass that looks so good on the stat sheet but never the scoreboard. "If I had a little flare pass called for, I would always try to squeeze 20 more yards out of it by finding somebody downfield," he grins. "My arm would freeze up on me if I wanted to dump it off. It didn't want to do it." Like all great passers, over 10% of his completions were for touchdowns.

But you measure a Terry Bradshaw, just as you measure a Roger Staubach, Fran Tarkenton, Otto Graham or any great quarterback, by how well the franchise has done since he left. In the case of the Pittsburgh Steelers, not very.

The symbiotic relationship of coach and quarterback in football is fascinating to study. In the days of the great Pittsburgh Steeler hegemony, and they won four championships in a decade, Coach Chuck Noll was hailed as the dominant mentor of the game. Paeans of praise were sent up over his "Steel Curtain" defense, his masterful organization of the game.

But he never won before Bradshaw – and he has never won since Bradshaw.

It's really a Quarterback Syndrome. Vince Lombardi, to my mind, was the best coach in the history of the pro game. If he wasn't, then Paul Brown was. If he wasn't, then Tom Landry was. If not him, Bill Walsh.

But Vince Lombardi had Bart Starr at the keyboard his glory years at Green Bay. We never got to see how well he would have done without his guiding Starr because he died shortly after leaving Green Bay for Washington. Paul Brown was great, but he was greatest when he had Otto Graham. When Otto left, the Browns went from super to so-so. Tom Landry had Roger Staubach his title years. The Cowboys were never the same when it was Roger and out. Bill Walsh is a great coach. But he had Joe Montana in the irons for his great Super Bowl runs.

And Noll had Bradshaw. So it was a great relief to a lot of people when Terry Bradshaw went in the Hall of Fame on the first bounce this year. Because there was a tendency to conclude that the unprecedented four Super Bowl championships by the Steelers were ascribable not to the guy in the dunce cap but that solemn, unsmiling head guy on the sidelines and the presence of so many other outstanding talents on the field. Well, how dumb could Terry have been? He's the last quarterback anyone knows to call his own signals in this league. He has not only read books, he has written one. "Looking Deep," with Buddy Martin as coauthor, is largely a chronicle of how difficult it was for the quarterback to overcome his relationship with his coach. It was hardly Damon and Pythias. More like Punch and Judy. "When I was a rookie, Chuck jerked me around on the sidelines during the games. Against the Giants my second year, he grabbed me by my face mask in front of my teammates, dragged me around like an animal and screamed at me. It was humiliating."

Terry Bradshaw blew it. He should have shown up aloof, cantankerous, silent and menacing his first year. He should have worn purple glasses and carried books of Russian poetry and had a doormat that said "Go away!"

If he did all those things he wouldn't be bothered today with his new four-year deal as expert analyst on CBS football telecasts or be delivering four to five motivational speeches a week all over the country at a take close to seven figures annually.

He does that because people like him. Some dunce! With a football in his hands, he was Einstein.

● ● ● ● ● ● ● ● ● ● ● ● ● ● ● ● ●

OCTOBER 5, 1971

Butkus Speaks: 'Bleepandblurkandgetthe-freakouttahere!'

Dick Butkus is one of the leading pass receivers of the National Football League. He led the entire Chicago Bears' wide receivers in passes caught Sunday against the Rams at the Coliseum. He caught two footballs on the fly and one on the ground.

What makes Butkus so valuable is, he often catches a football before it is thrown. This is because, in addition to catching footballs, he also catches people who have them. He shakes them upside-down till they let go.

Butkus has 19 lifetime receptions, which is remarkable since he wasn't the primary receiver – or even the secondary – on any of them.

Roman Gabriel completed 15 passes against the Bears Sunday – four to Josephson, three to Snow, two each to Rentzel and Ellison, one to Smith, one to Masslowski and two to Butkus.

Butkus recovered his 18th career fumble in the second quarter, and four plays later, the Bears had scored their only points of the day, 3. He is the nearest thing to an offense the Chicago Bears have. Only the quarterback gets his hands on the football more than Dick Butkus.

I thought I would go down to the locker room Sunday to interview this All-Pro wide receiver of the Bears, find out how he ran his patterns, what moves he put on the defenders (anyone moving into Butkus' zone hoping to catch a football has to be classified as a defender).

I expected, of course, the conversation to be in sign language, and I brought a stalk of bananas, my bush hat, an elephant gun, and scribbled my will on the back of an envelope. It is inadvisable to approach Dick Butkus on the heels of a 17-3 loss in anything less than a reinforced Land Rover with a white hunter, armed, aboard.

They say Fay Wray locks herself in her room when Butkus comes to town. And when he hits New York, the Army surrounds the Empire State Building while the Air Force buzzes it. Other players play in a face mask, with Butkus, it's a muzzle.

First of all, I'm happy to report it can talk. The rumor going around that Dick Butkus went through college on a vine, or that he was discovered by a scout for a Tarzan picture is not true. Neither is the report that he dresses by himself because his fur makes his roommate sneeze.

I know it can talk because when I knocked on its dressing room it said clearly, "fuzzandblurkandgetthefreakouttahere!"

I went over to safety man Ron Smith's cubicle. "If I come flying out of there," I said, pointing to Butkus' locker, where shoulder pads, helmets, socks and cleated shoes came flying through the air accompanied by screams of rage, "will you call for a fair catch?"

Smith grinned. "He'll be all right as soon as he has his couple cups of blood," he soothed. "You see, he hasn't had his quarterback today yet."

"Does he shower or just lick himself clean?" I asked.

"Listen," said Smith, "I knew Butkus when I was a sophomore at Wisconsin and he was at Illinois and he was mean then and he was still mean as of a few minutes ago. He chews cement and spits out sidewalk."

I tapped on his cage again. "Bleepandfreakandblurpandcrockand-chickandcreep!" it roared. "Cantcha wait till I get dressed?!"

He came out of the shower a few minutes later. Mighty Joe Young would have run screaming up a tree. I gave a nervous laugh.

"I didn't recognize you without a quarterback under your arm," I joked feebly. Butkus glared. He never smiles.

"Listen, did you see what they've done out there with their little fairy plays? Those little end-around tippy toes, that chicken-trip stuff and then those twerps sneak back on you, those little elves give you a clip, and those bleep-censored officials say 'one more word out of any of you and it's 15.' You call that football?! If I came out here for a dance, I'd have worn pumps. Lemme comb my hair, fer cryin' out loud!"

A moment later, the defensive genius of the Chicago Bears, the last Monster of the Midway, stalked out with that rolling gait of his like a charging rhino. "Hey, Butkus!" yelled the crowd. "You got quarterback sticking to your whiskers." "Hey Butkus, yourself at home! Eat somebody!" "Hey, Butkus, do they let your cage on the airplane with the rest of the people?" "Hey, Butkus, do they bring your food on a plate or on a rope?"

Butkus just glared. "Bleepandfleepandtwerpandfagandbagand," he growled. "Girls' football!"

Someone nudged me in the ribs. "You're lucky he's in a good mood today," he said.

● ● ● ● ● ● ● ● ● ● ● ● ● ● ● ● ●

SEPTEMBER 29, 1985

Howard Has Much To Be Vain About

"Who the hell made 'Monday Night Football' unlike any other sports program on the air? "If you want the plain truth, I did."
– Howard Cosell in "I Never Played the Game."

"As for Monday Night Football, an additional factor came into play: me! I am sure my absence had a negative effect on the ratings. Without me, the nature of the telecasts was entirely altered. I had commanded attention. I had palpable impact on the show, giving it a sense of moment, and now it seemed no different from an ordinary Sunday afternoon telecast. If that sounds like ego, what can I say? I'm telling it like it is."
– Ibid.

Normally, when an employee leaves a longtime job in industry, there is a protocol to be observed. He can say:

♦ "It has been fun working with you guys."

♦ "I'll miss each and every one of you."

♦ "The (choose one) boss/company has been a brick about the whole thing."

When Howard Cosell left "Monday Night Football" a year or so back, he must have felt as if he were leaving Devil's Island or Stalag 17 or getting thrown into the sea in a shroud off a dungeon wall.

Howard, you will remember, was a member of a rollicking trio of entertainers – the others were Frank Gifford and Don Meredith – who brought you the thrills and excitement of Monday night NFL football games – sort of. When they weren't too busy bickering among themselves, introducing Burt Reynolds or Angie Dickinson, exchanging inside jokes or getting sick on the floor, that is. One of them just sang.

It was all supposed to be great good fun. Turns out it was World War III. Armageddon in a glass booth. Two ex-jocks and an ex-lawyer. An invisible bloodbath.

Cosell is not going gently into that good night. Howard is going down like the Sundance Kid or the Merrimac. With all guns out and firing.

"To begin, Gifford's greatest talent is not broadcasting. He is what he is, a physically attractive man with a matchless ability to charm almost everybody he meets. After so many years of playing the role of hero, he has grown so accustomed to the part that he often seems more concerned with preserving the image than expressing feelings.

"He is a Teflon man. No matter how many mistakes he makes in a telecast, no matter how glaring his weaknesses as a performer, nothing sticks to him.

"For my money, Gifford is far from your classic play-by-play man. He is not in the same league with NBC's Dick Enberg or CBS' Pat Summerall. Gifford's voice is thin and monotonic and he is incapable of using it with rhythm and pace for dramatic effect. In addition, he stumbles over words, and it's not uncommon for him to lose his train of thought. His propensity for error was embarrassing. He's not a natural performer, never was, never will be."

Well, so much for the old Giff.

How about the old Danderoo, the other guy in the booth, the free spirit, the comic relief, the good ol' boy?

"I do not understand Don Meredith, and I never will. In the beginning I loved the guy. He was terribly insecure about his performance and I'd often counsel him. Eventually, he ended up winning an Emmy. I was genuinely pleased for him, in spite of the fact that I realized he had won a popularity contest.

"Meredith rarely prepared for a telecast in the manner of a professional. He often showed no interest at all. He'd try to compensate for his lack of knowledgeability by singing a song or talking to his imaginary alter ego, Harley Smydlapp. And everybody would write about how funny and irrepressible he was. Meredith's lackadaisical attitude never bothered me as much as it did Gifford. His disinterest in what he's doing must surely be apparent to anyone over the age of 2. (Without me) Meredith was lost. He had nobody to react to. I didn't know whether he was a singer, a cowboy, a philosopher, a clown, or what.

"He thought he had the kind of talent he didn't remotely possess. There's a mean streak within him. He groused and grumbled, snapped at people, and he could be contrary to the extreme. He was hardly the lovable ol' cowboy with the homespun view that was so ingratiating.

"It really didn't matter, though. When push came to shove, Gifford and Meredith were as thick as thieves. They would never take sides against each other. I could never really trust either one of them."

You can see from the foregoing that ABC had the cameras trained on the wrong action during the years the threesome was together. The action down on the field was inconsequential. Who cares if Miami beats New England? Give us Cosell against the world, the network, his own colleagues. I mean, that was the Super Bowl!

Is Howard like that Peter Finch character in "Network," railing against TV corruption: "I'm mad as hell and I'm not going to take it anymore!"? Or is he just a grumpy old party who has been dismissed with a shrug and a gold watch after putting the company on the map?

Probably both. First of all, you have to understand that Howard is a man who can hear an insult drop two continents away. Sensitive doesn't begin to describe his reaction to even the mildest criticism. In his book, he tells of the time he picked up a New York Times and read a review of his debut on the Monday night game. "Maybe his sport is boxing," it read. "It's certainly not football."

Now, most of us in this business would be glad to get off with so light a chest tap as that. But Howard, as he admits in his book, almost quit the business on the spot. "I'm not going to take anymore! I want out!"

It could be, of course, that much of his bile is justifiable. Did Howard really make "Monday Night Football"? Or is he like the vainglorious old actor who thinks Shakespeare would be nothing without him?

Just maybe he has a case. He probably should have taken the gold watch and the handshake and just gone off into the sunset like the rest of the world.

But Howard is not the rest of the world. Howard is not your grateful old retainer. Howard is a star, and he doesn't want you to forget it.

The book is Howard. Even without the warts. I'm glad he didn't go out any other way. It would have been out of character.

You know, somebody once said to Winston Churchill that his successor, Clement Attlee, was a very modest man.

"Yes," Churchill agreed. "With much to be modest about."

Howard Cosell is a very vain man. With much to be vain about.

• • • • • • • • • • • • • • • • • •

JANUARY 22, 1987

Seems This Guy Is Your Regular One-Man Gang

It's real easy to recognize the Denver Broncos.

The Denver Broncos wear No. 7. The Denver Broncos are about 6 feet 4 inches tall, weigh, oh, 215, have these dimples, an easy smile and are a 9½-point underdog to the New York Giants.

Most teams have 45 guys in the game plan. The Denver Broncos are going to try to get by with one.

Fortunately, the rules permit you 11 men on the field at one time. But they don't say you have to have them. If you think you can do it with one, I guess that's your business.

You get the impression down at the Super Bowl training camps here this week that the New York Giants are going to play John Elway in Super Bowl XXI Sunday. And they're only favored by 9½.

You wonder what would happen if Denver showed up with a whole team.

You show up at picture day in Costa Mesa and all of a sudden someone says, "Oh-oh, here comes the Denver Broncos." You look over, expecting a stampede, and here comes this one blond guy, smiling and walking this kind of pigeon-toed walk to the center of the field, and it's the team.

You talk to the Giants individually or in groups and all they talk about is Elway. The Giants seem to have as much trouble as the rest of the world remembering who the other guys on the team are – or if there are any.

You hear people talk and you get the impression Denver must have gotten the rest of the team out of the Yellow Pages. Or maybe they're just migratory workers.

You get the confused notion that John Elway cranks up and throws this long pass – and then runs out and catches it.

He must not need blockers because nobody ever mentions them.

You know, at a Super Bowl, it's a media crush and the league sets up an hour and a half a day for the thousand or so print and electronic types to crowd around the players who are seated at marked tables in the interview area.

The room opens – and about 988 guys rush to John Elway. One or two wander up to other players and say airily, "How's it going, Studs? Now, you're – a, ah, er, wait a minute, don't tell me – oh, Keith Bishop, right? Oh, no? You're who? Oh, you're Rulon Jones? Er, exactly what is it you do on the Broncos, Rulon? And what do you think of John Elway?"

Now the Giants open their room and groups stand indecisively. Do they want the quarterback, Phil Simms? Nah, how about the superlative running back, Joe Morris? Big crowd around him? OK, how about the ferocious linebacker, L.T.? Jim Burt, the mauling tackler? Maybe Harry Carson, the all-everything linebacker? Carl Banks, the unsung?

Then, there's Mark Anthony Bavaro, the strong, silent type. Or Phil McConkey, the helicopter pilot, officer and a gentleman.

There are 8 million stories in the naked city. This is an all-star cast.

A repertory company.

There is only one story in the Mile High City. Elway is like Caruso in the opera, Paderewski at the piano, Nijinsky at the Bolshoi.

If he wins, it'll be "Elway Slays Giants."

If he loses? Well, how about "Elway Can't Do It All Alone." The whozits let him down.

Is this pressure? How does it feel to be the key to the game? Horatius at the bridge? The boy with his finger in the dike. The only hope.

Elway grins this little crooked grin. "It's fun," he says.

Fun being chased around by 280-pound defensive ends, strangleheld by homicidal linebackers, having your knees cut from underneath you by a blitzing safety, a cutting cornerback?

"It's fun till you get caught," he says, grinning.

Is he that good? Is anyone that good?

Well, John Elway inspires the kind of legends Ben Hogan did in golf and Satchel Paige did in baseball, or the myths that followed Lincoln into history.

They'll tell you of his high school days in Granada Hills when he would stand on the 50-yard line and a teammate in the end zone would throw a ball up in the air and Elway would hit it dead center, like shooting a duck from midfield. They told him to hit his receiver in the numbers once and Elway asked, "Which one?"

At Stanford, they liked to say Elway was protected by 10 guys who learned to play football having catches with their butlers or who came to practice with their governesses, but he threw 77 touchdown passes – 25 more than Jim Plunkett – and most of them, to hear Stanfordites tell it, went through two time zones.

He could write his name with a football, make it sing "Dixie" or open a bottle with one at 20 paces. He completed more passes than the Fifth Fleet on leave.

Defensive ends, to a man, hated to play him. "He stands there and laughs at you," Lyle Alzado once growled. "It's like a Tom and Jerry cartoon."

Other linemen thought he was more like the league's Bugs Bunny. He kept them bumping into one another.

It isn't laughter, exactly, Elway thinks. It's just a preoccupied look he gets trying to read a defense.

Elway watchers say he just starts to smile as he gets this little mental picture of a completion over an all-out blitz and he gets this look on his face of a guy who just won a lottery.

And then, of course, there's The Drive. This is one of the historic events of football history. It goes direct to the Hall of Fame, whatever else John Elway does in his career.

Trailing by seven with the ball on your own 1½-yard line with only minutes to play in the biggest game of your career and engineering a textbook drive in the face of a hostile crowd is the stuff they write songs about. Elway put on the kind of downfield march and the kind of plays coaches only draw on blackboards but seldom see played out on the field in front of them.

It was the nearest thing to a one-man show since John Wayne cleaned up the Burma Road or Errol Flynn won the West. It was movie stuff – Elway picking apart a loose Cleveland defense like a master locksmith opening a vault.

It's no wonder the public gets the impression this week that little John with his slingshot is the thin orange line going out by his lonesome to take on the big bad fe-fi-fo-fums from the badlands of New Jersey.

It's no wonder that, when someone asked who the rest of the Broncos were this week, someone else answered, "Oh, let's see. Dopey, Grumpy, Doc, Sleepy, Sneezy – and Sammy Winder."

Reading the papers, you would get the idea Elway has the lifetime contract but the rest of the Broncos get paid by the hour. If their bus hits an abutment, the headline is going to read "John Elway, 44 Friends Hurt in Crash."

The rest of the team might as well take the field in masks. Or under assumed names. John Elway and the Mighty Elway Art Players.

Do they resent it? Any institution is the lengthened shadow of one man, but is this ridiculous?

Winder, the running back who is the nearest thing to a second banana the Broncos have, is one who thinks not. Sammy doesn't mind playing the star's best friend.

Says Sammy: "John is like a lightning rod, he takes the media blitz off us. Personally, it'd be OK with me if I never got in front of a camera or a microphone. I like not being in the spotlight."

If so, he has come to the right place. The Denver Broncos this week are the perfect hideout for a guy on the lam or a guy craving anonymity. The only trouble is, he may have trouble cashing a check.

If he ain't John Elway, the public will have a hard time believing he's a Denver Bronco. Everybody knows the Denver Broncos consist of John Elway and some barefoot kicker. And that's enough.

● ● ● ● ● ● ● ● ● ● ● ● ● ● ● ● ●

NOVEMBER 31, 1974

Woody's Own War

A lot of people were surprised to hear that Woody Hayes suffered a heart attack last spring, because they didn't think he had one.

When a stranger wanted to know if the incident had mellowed the old coach, the answer was, "Well, he called off practice for the day."

A visitor once wanted to know why a reporter didn't stand up to Woody Hayes, and the answer was, "I can't. I've got relatives in Germany."

When a Woody Hayes squad was circled around him at the start of a game once, a youngster in the press box asked an old-timer what he thought Woody was telling them. "Not to take prisoners," was the cynical response.

Woody Hayes' Ohio State squad is not a team, it's a horde. It is going through the Big Ten like Attila the Hun through the gates of Rome. When someone wanted to know which way the team got back from the Rose Bowl practice session each day, an observer said, "The usual way – by goose step."

Lots of guys lock the press out when their team loses 42-17, as Woody Hayes' did in the Rose Bowl once. But Woody locked the TEAM out.

Coach Hayes, whose idol is Gen. Patton, also slaps his troops in the heat of battle. He throws projectors at assistants, stomps on his wristwatch and once crumpled a pair of eyeglasses in his bare hand. George C. Scott gets the role if they make a movie.

There are new books about him in the stalls this fall, "Woody Hayes and the 100-Yard War," by Jerry Brondfield, and "Buckeye, a Study of Coach Woody Hayes and the Ohio State Football Machine," by Robert Vare.

Brondfield's is a little more on the advocacy side, but he points out that to understand Woody you have to understand Columbus, Ohio, a place where, if you buy a piano at a certain music store, they throw in a free shotgun.

Hayes' success is no secret. He leaves no coal mine unturned in his search for players. He goes after great players like a playboy after chorus girls. Millionaires like John Galbreath and Jack Nicklaus help the program. You couldn't throw a handful of birdseed in any direction in Ohio without hitting a crack football player. The state even raises them for export. Millionaires are not supposed to lure kids with new convertibles anymore, but there is no rule preventing them from hiring kids in the summer to count paper clips at $10 an hour or to guard the portrait of the company's founder for $15.

But Ohio State has always had great football players. It was good coaches that were in short supply. "You would think," once complained a sportswriter, "that a state that could produce seven presidents could produce ONE football coach." But in its long history, Ohio State produced only one coach before Woody Hayes who could be said to be successful. And Paul Brown didn't stay around long enough to produce what is usually referred to in football as "an era."

Vare points out that football grosses $3.5 million at Ohio State, but coach Hayes makes only $29,000 a year. He used to hand out part of that to his players till they caught him at it. Three times he has turned down raises because he thinks he is stopping inflation that way. He once turned back a car because he didn't want to contribute to pollution. He has lived in the same modest house for 20 years and drives a pickup.

There is less of an air of sanctimonious hypocrisy about Woody than some coaches. "Some coaches play on the emotions of the kid," a longtime friend confides. "But Woody really believes it." The most famous story about him is that he once pushed an out-of-gas car across the Ohio state line because he couldn't bring himself to buy anything in Michigan.

His attack is about as subtle as a brick through a plate-glass window. He regards the forward pass as subversive. He didn't throw a pass until there were only 61 seconds to play in the Michigan game last year. Just as he suspected, it was intercepted.

Still, his team, or rather teams, have averaged 47 points a game this season. On Nov. 23 his team meets Michigan in what may be the most thunderous collision since the Titanic. Woody intends to be the iceberg. Since the game is in Columbus, which becomes Convulsion, Ohio, for the day, Michigan can be expected to be down by 14-0 by the kickoff. And no team can spot Woody Hayes' 14 points and hope to escape alive, not even the Miami Dolphins – and maybe not even the Red Army.

• • • • • • • • • • • • • • • • •

NOVEMBER 17, 1968

The Deacon Is Double Trouble For Ram Rivals

The first thing to establish with David (Deacon) Jones, who eats quarterbacks for a living, is not that there is one but that there's only one.

Asked to describe him, an offensive tackle said: "Well, first of all, there's all those arms – at least six, I think."

Another said, "David puts his pants on one leg at a time same as the rest of us. Only trouble is, he's got three."

When someone asked what color his eyes were, the answer was, "Red." The answerer thought a minute, then added, "At least the three I saw were."

Still another player came back to the locker room after a four-nosebleed game and explained, "They double-teamed me. They put David Jones on me."

Quarterbacks he has scrambled are convinced there are at least two of him. "He's twins," they explain. "You stop one and the other one comes out the back of the uniform. He's like that vaudeville horse."

Since it is well-established that David Jones comes in duplicate or triplicate, rival coaches have no qualms about assigning two and three men to block him. Anyone who played him one-on-one would get investigated by the league president for consorting with gamblers. Deacon Jones is, quite simply, 20% of the Ram defense. Just to equalize him requires 2.2 players.

The Rams score goals by setting goals. The gaudiest goals posted in the locker room are for the defense. With space set aside for games in which they achieve them, the goals include things such as, "Not letting the enemy get outside its 15-yard-line." Incredibly, this happened once this year. The others include things such as, "Not letting the enemy gain more than 26 yards on any one play," "Not letting the enemy past midfield," "Intercepting at least two passes a game." Every game is a climb up the Matterhorn for the Ram defense.

The Rams have a defense manual that comes in more volumes than Churchill's Memoirs. You have to be 240 pounds just to lift it. It has more plane geometry than Euclid. A defensive lineman has more "keys" to learn than a night watchman.

The crowd thinks all you do with a defensive end is cut the tusks off it and teach it not to bite. This annoys Deacon Jones. People think what he does is about as athletic as pushing people off high cliffs.

"Listen," he hisses, "I am not an animal. I don't go around scaring women and children. They don't have to lock me up after a game. What I do is as athletic as rushing the net in tennis, stealing a base in baseball, faking a guy out of the pivot in basketball. Sometimes it's even like a poker game. I gamble a lot out there. You have to have STYLE out there or you get eaten alive. Look at me! I weigh 239 pounds now. I have weighed up to 270. But you have to be FAST when you're double and triple teamed. You have to dance your man a little. It's not brute strength."

It's not Swan Lake either, but the mystique of Deacon Jones is he's probably the first lineman since Pudge Heffelfinger to make headlines, to get linemen out of the agate type and into the big money of testimonials and recognition.

The "Seven Blocks of Granite" achieved a measure of notoriety for Fordham in the days when they played so many scoreless ties and 2-0 games that they had to rummage through the book to find out how much a touchdown counted when somebody finally made one. But individually they were as anonymous as headstones.

Sam Huff achieved a breakthrough for linebackers but it was not until an end zone crowd unfielded a "David Jones For Secretary of Defense" banner at a game last year that a tackler became a bona-fide drawing card in the league.

You might say the fame went to Deacon's head. Because that's where tight ends began to clobber him till his ears rang. Clubs began to appoint "policemen" whose sole job was to unfrock the Deacon. "That's all right with me," says Deacon. "That leaves us with seven men to cover three."

He still got to the quarterback 26 times last year and piled up 100 unassisted tackles. He has what John Brodie calls "deafening speed." He bats down almost as many passes as a safety man. He played one game this year with a bone sticking out of his thumb and Jack Pardee had to push it back into place.

Come to think of it, he does so many things it's surprising there's only the two of him.

• • • • • • • • • • • • • • • • • •

DECEMBER 2, 1963

Veni, Vidi, Vincie

If you saw Vince Lombardi in a crowd of truck drivers and were asked to guess his occupation, the next to last thing you'd pick would be football coach. But that's all right, because you'd NEVER guess he was a Latin teacher.

Vince Lombardi looks as if he should be climbing down from behind the wheel of a six-wheeled semi and saying "Okay, lady, where do you want the piano?" Or he should be down on the waterfront with a longshoreman's gaff unloading olive oil.

The face is swart and strong. The eyes are friendly but wary. This is a city boy who has been offered the Brooklyn Bridge before. It is not the face of a pedagogue. It is hard to imagine it in front of a blackboard teaching "hic, haec, hoc," the fact that "to, of, with, by, from, since" and "toward" always take the dative and the fact that all Gaul is divided into three parts.

But Vince Lombardi also taught physics. And the last guy who dug both physics and Latin was Leonardo Da Vinci and he wouldn't know an inside-right counter play from a zone defense or a button-hook pattern.

Vince Lombardi was a career assistant coach when he came to the Packers in 1959. This job is as anonymous as the signature in a motel registry, and after years of working for Red Blaik at Army and Jim Lee Howell at Yankee Stadium, Vince still had to show his pass to the gate-man and stand in line for tables at Toots Shor's.

He had played football at Fordham in a line so tough bullets would bounce off it. The so-called "Seven Blocks of Granite" could have dammed a river without losing a drop and played in so many scoreless ties the scoreboard looked as if it had developed a stutter. The only way they could win was by a safety. The line was equal parts Italian and Polish, with names that ran right off the page in the better tabloids and had so many "i's" and "e's" and u's" an "z's" that linotypers had to send out for reserves in a Fordham-Pitt game.

Lombardi was a recognized genius at football many years before the public found out about it, since it was a trade secret. But by 1959, the Green Bay franchise had fallen into such despair that it needed either a genius or divine intervention. The team had won one game the year before. It was run by a committee consisting of 13 members, which is the same thing as saying it wasn't run by anybody. It was parked by the side of the road.

Lombardi was out of place in that setting, where you could see cows instead of subways and hear crickets instead of cab horns. Green Bay was as secret as a naval code in war, and draft choices were found wandering all over the hills of Wisconsin with bloodhounds when they were asked to report.

Vince first demanded a five-year contract and the general manager-ship. He told the committee he would send for them when he needed them but not to wait around the phone. He went over the list of his personnel and briefly considered trading it off to the Mayo Clinic for their outpatient list. This was the only team he had ever seen that had more whirlpool baths than it had players.

You can always tell a losing team. It has more aches and pains than a bus wreck, and Lombardi first walked through and announced he didn't want to see anybody in a whirlpool bath unless he had already had the last rites. As a result, he has players playing 60 minutes today in such bad shape vultures are circling over them.

His first action reporting to camp was to pick up one of the biggest stars, a player who reported to practice only when the taverns were closed, by the scruff of the neck and slam him against a dormitory wall. He called for the dossier on Paul Hornung and, when they handed him a copy of "Playboy" magazine and said "Open to any page," he set his kickers to pointing the ball at Hornung until he had Hornung too tired even to read "Playboy," never mind to act it out.

It took him two whole years to build a championship team and it took the FBI to wreck it.

Ironically, Vince Lombardi, the New York boy, the city kid who knew all the angles, was way ahead of his league in warning his superstars. In his fine book "Run to Daylight," put together by my friend Red Smith and ghosted by Bill Heinz, Lombardi tells how he laid it on the line to his club. "I had a visit the other day," he said, "from two FBI men. They told me they're keeping a closer watch on professional sports than ever. The Attorney General reads every report...."

"Any one of you, you meet a man, and he says if it's you, Jim, he's an old friend of Ben Schwartzwalder of Syracuse. He talks about his friend, Ben, and what a great coach Ben is. He's a nice-looking guy and very friendly and he buys you dinner.... He isn't a friend of Ben Schwartzwalder. He's never met him, and he's a hoodlum."

The lesson was lost. The man who could teach Latin, physics or football tripped over simple American morality. Or his team did. Vince comes to the Coliseum this weekend, and he thinks he sees a bare thin crack of daylight still showing for his team to run for this year. When asked if he will make it, he smiles a wistful smile. But if I were George

Halas and the Bears, I think I'd remember what Confucius said: "When a crocodile smiles, count your limbs."

● ● ● ● ● ● ● ● ● ● ● ● ● ● ● ● ● ●

JANUARY 18, 1985

And at QB ... Warren Beatty

SAN FRANCISCO – Dan Marino is the best-looking young quarterback I have ever seen. No contest.

Now, I am not talking about his quick release, quick drop, fast read or eerie aim. I don't care whether he wins or loses.

I'm talking dimples. I have never seen such dimples on a quarterback in my life. I'm talking peaches-and-cream complexion. Bright blue eyes. Curly, honey-blond hair. I mean, we're talking matinee idol looks. Cupid's bow mouth. Just for one night, you'd like to look like that.

To look like that and be the best football player on the planet is overkill. It's unfair. It's like a Rockefeller finding gold, Liz Taylor having brains.

Great quarterbacks should be these kind of hunchbacked, pigeon-toed guys in high-top shoes like Unitas. Scarecrow-skinny pieces of rawhide like Sammy Baugh. They should kind of look like an unwrapped mummy like Kenny Stabler. Have a face like an exploded tomato like Billy Kilmer.

This guy doesn't have a wart on him. These nice, even white teeth, movie-star smile.

Nobody should get all that and the Super Bowl, too. When does God even up?

Look at him – 6 feet 4 inches, 220 pounds, all these gorgeous muscles. Then he goes out and obliterates all these records. I mean, 48 touchdowns passing, 362 completions, 5,804 yards. It's obscene. And to look like something Hollywood would cast for the part is depressing.

A rival coach points out that Marino throws for a touchdown every eighth pass he completes. Or, for that matter, every 12th pass he throws. Match that around New York. He scores every 16 plays, Dick Vermeil points out.

You know something? He's 23 years old. You heard me. He's still got his baby teeth almost. He's broken the league regular-season records for passes completed, yardage, touchdowns, 300-yard games with nine, and 400-yard games with four. No telling what he'll do when he grows up. Probably walk across Biscayne Bay.

It's enough to make every quarterback who ever lived want to go home and trash the trophy room.

You're surprised he doesn't show up at the Super Bowl press conferences in a sedan chair, blessing the sick. As it is, he sits on a raised dais in the interview room. Reporters are perforce clustered around his feet. They do not have to kiss his ring, however, but the other mere players are more humbly arrayed at eye level with their interviewers.

A little waitress came in at breakfast the other morning and surveyed this gift of God to womankind. "My God, he's cute!" she said, overawed.

If you have to wonder why the Miami Dolphins waited till the 27th player (and six quarterbacks) to draft him, the clue may be found in the profile. The scouts took one look at that and decided nobody who looked that good could concentrate on football. You wonder how he gets out of bed. Away from a mirror.

Rookie quarterbacks, even ugly ones, aren't supposed to make it in the NFL. Not for three years. Marino made it in three games. They're supposed to throw a football like a guy loading pumpkins. Marino gets rid of his like it was an olive.

You're supposed to grasp the ball with two hands, hoist it behind your ear, wind up, plant your feet, close your eyes and heave. Marino just kind of flicks it 55 yards like a guy flicking lint off his tie. His father, he says, taught him that little trick.

No one had to teach him how to hit a receiver with it. He got that gift along with his dimples. He may be the deadliest end zone passer in the history of the game. He may not be able to hit a squirrel in the eye with a spiral but he can hit either one of two 5-9 receivers with it. Miami mythology has it he could complete a pass through two key-holes if he had to.

The Miami Dolphins are kind of an ordinary team without him. With him, they are a juggernaut. He can run just faster than junk mail but, at 23, he may be more dangerous than he'll be five years from now. Like all 23-year-olds, he's doesn't always know what he's going to do next but what he often does next is throw a 50-yard touchdown. He hasn't yet learned how tough that is, to the despair of defenses. And he's never mastered the art of eating the football. He could get rid of it from an iron lung.

Still, you're pretty sure no one consulted the homecoming queens when they put this hunk in a football suit instead of something he can tango in. In fact, it's a good thing he wears that mask. If the belles in the seats got a load of those dimples and curls, they might sack him before San Francisco could.

But one thing is for sure: When they say Marino throws the prettiest passes in the NFL, you can be sure they're right. Even if they get intercepted.

● ● ● ● ● ● ● ● ● ● ● ● ● ● ● ● ●

JANUARY 15, 1990

Even for 49ers' Montana, This Was a Real Beaut

SAN FRANCISCO – I thought they'd miss Bill Walsh.

I thought Joe Montana was human.

I thought Roger Craig could be tackled, John Taylor contained. Forget it.

The 49ers wouldn't miss the Archangel Gabriel. You and I could coach them into the Super Bowl.

Joe Montana glows in the dark. I don't think he can see himself in the mirror. Check and see if anyone's ever seen him after midnight. His name should be Joe World. A state isn't enough for him.

The score was 30-3, if you're into trivia. It wasn't that close. The 49ers just got bored. So did everyone else.

It was supposed to be Dempsey-Tunney. It was more like Tyson-Spinks. The last time anyone saw anything this one-sided, they got the lifeboats out. And radioed for help.

The Rams' game plan, if they had one, appeared to be a complicated suicide pact.

Look, you don't get in a slugging match with Dempsey, a shootout with Wyatt Earp.

You don't give Nick the Greek the deal and his own deck. You don't give Minnesota Fats a table to run. You don't give a guy named Slick the dice and then bet against him. You don't give Ruth a fastball. You don't send Magic Johnson to the line in a tie game. You don't come to the net on Boris Becker. You don't hit a ball to center field with Mays there. You don't walk Rickey Henderson.

And you don't give Joe Montana the ball any more than you have to.

Giving Joe Montana the ball is like giving Rembrandt a brush or Hemingway a pen.

He doesn't need it much – the ball, that is. For Joe Montana, "good field position" is his own three-yard line. If he can be guaranteed the ball a maximum of 10 minutes a game, that may be enough.

Joe World gave a clinic in quarterbacking at Candlestick Sunday. The Rams were just the blackboard.

You had a mental picture of Joe Montana standing in front of the class and turning to the Ram corners and safeties and linebackers and saying "Now, Jerry Gray, you stand over here. Yeah, that's good! Now,

LeRoy Irvin, you're in a zone, Michael Stewart, you guard the middle. Now, try to knock this pass down as I throw it through you."

It was like watching a guy with a snake in a basket. He had the Rams hypnotized. He was taking quarters out of their ears all day, producing their wristwatches in knotted handkerchiefs. He was pulling Rams out of a hat all game.

It was a dazzling performance. If you never saw Tracy act, Heifetz fiddle, Cobb bat or Nijinsky dance, watch Montana quarterback. It's the same thing. Art.

So what the Rams have to do is make sure this artist doesn't get his easel, his stage. Take the ball and hide it, if you can.

The Rams were as careless with the ball as a sailor on leave with his pay.

In the first quarter, they were leading, 3-0. They had stopped Montana on his first series and they were driving toward another score. They had the ball on the 49er 40-yard line, second down and three to go.

They got greedy. Twice, Ram quarterback Jim Everett disdained the first down and launched buzz bombs at the horizon. They missed. Now the Rams – on the 49er 40 – punted.

The 49ers got the ball on their own 11. And marched 89 yards for their first score.

The Rams didn't learn much. In the second quarter, trailing 14-3 now, with only three minutes to play in the half, they had the ball on San Francisco's 40 again, fourth down and two. Again they punted. To the San Francisco 13. Again the 49ers marched the length of the field to a touchdown, scoring just as the half ended.

Now the moral of the story is, you don't give Montana the ball when you have only a yard or two to gain for a first down in his territory. Because Joe Montana only needs the ball – it doesn't matter where he gets it. He marches 40 yards or 90 with the same degree of skill and enthusiasm.

Now, blaming the ultimate deluge on these lapses is, as the late sports editor Stanley Woodward once said of a similar cataclysm, "like blaming the Johnstown Flood on a leaky toilet in Altoona."

But it was symptomatic of the Rams' cavalier approach generally. Not even Joe Montana can win from the bench. If you can find a way not to blow up the football, he can be had. Once the ball is inflated, your next ploy should be to see to it that Montana doesn't have it long enough to read the commissioner's signature. Giving Montana the ball is like giving a German general an army. You'll be sorry.

It wasn't a game, it was an exhibition. A recital. Joe Montana at the console.

Joe's next concert will be the Super Bowl in the Superdome in New Orleans. But it doesn't matter where Joe makes an appearance. Wherever he goes, it becomes Carnegie Hall. And it doesn't matter who the other guys are. They're just the chorus. Twenty years from now, no one will remember whom he beat, just that they saw Joe Montana beat whoever it was. Anybody remember whom Babe Ruth hit his home runs off?

The way Montana plays football, every note is high C. When you complete 26 of 30 passes – and throw two of them deliberately out of bounds – you belong to another dimension of your craft. He makes coaches geniuses, receivers millionaires and teams dynasties. It was a good thing it was cloudy and damp in Candlestick Sunday. He probably doesn't cast a shadow.

As far as the Rams are concerned, they couldn't be sure he's flesh and blood. They never got close enough all day to know whether he's animal, vegetable or mineral. As long as they keep giving him the football, he's the creature that ate (and is eating) the NFL.

• • • • • • • • • • • • • • • • • •

A Little Guarantee Makes A League of Difference

In baseball, "Joe" meant DiMaggio. In boxing, it was Louis.

Tennis never had any "Joes." Guys with "Baron" in front of their names or Roman numerals after it or guys named Ivan or Boris.

But when you allude to the Joe in football, whom do you mean?

Joe Montana, of course, you dummy, you immediately reply.

But wait a minute! Before you retire the name and the position as the property of Joseph Montana, ask yourself if you've ever heard of Joe Willie Namath.

Not your average Joe, Mr. Namath.

You know, some guys can boast they made their team what it is. Gave it respectability, credibility, so to speak. Namath made a whole league. The AFL (now the AFC) is his monument.

When Namath came along in 1965, the American Football League was widely held to be a collection of castoffs, rejects who couldn't make the senior circuit NFL – backups, wanna-bes, placekick holders, second-stringers. They played a kind of no-contact air-ball version of the sport that made the critics sniff "Volleyball!" They played a zone defense to make up for their deficiencies in the more manly (or more man-to-manly) game preferred by the NFL.

All that was pre-Namath. What Joe did is summed up in a book that followed his emergence, "The League That Came In From the Cold." It credited him with bringing the AFL into the warmth of public acceptance.

In the little world of sports, there are words and incidents that come ringing down the corridors of time. There is Ruth calling his shot, Louis summing up an opponent with "he can run but he can't hide," Bill Terry saying, "Is Brooklyn still in the league?"

And there is Joe Namath on the eve of the 1969 Super Bowl saying "I guarantee it!" right after predicting a victory over the Baltimore Colts, who were only three-touchdown favorites over Namath's New York Jets.

Joe Willie guaranteed it, all right, with a flawless, no-interception, call-his-own-plays performance against the Colts the next Sunday in Super Bowl III.

It was one of the great upsets of sports history. In a real way, it made the Super Bowl the instant equal of the World Series, the Final Four and the Triple Crown, a permanent fixture in the American sports firmament.

Joe brought a lot of firsts with him. He was, in a very real sense, the first athlete to bring an agent to the negotiating table with him. A college quarterback at Alabama, he had such impressive credentials, he had three franchises bidding for his services. Show-biz-wise Sonny Werblin, who had run MCA and had Johnny Carson as a client, knew the value of promotion, publicity and hype generally, and Joe Namath was the first athlete to have big money flying around the table. He got a package totaling $427,000 to sign.

Werblin also paid the agent's fee, $30,000, and hired members of Namath's family to work for the Jets.

Namath revolutionized the business of sports. Every guy with a multimillion-dollar contract should put a candle in front of his picture.

Joe knew what to do with his fame. He became "Broadway Joe," a Great White Way character who kept the headlines big and black and bold and the 11 o'clock news hopping. Werblin didn't hire him to hide in a locker room or say "No comment." It wasn't Joe's style anyway. Joe knew how to be a star and, in case anybody missed the point, the first thing he did was buy a fur coat.

Joe had an ongoing relationship with Johnnie Walker Scotch and most of the chorus girls of his day. I once wrote that Joe didn't know any women named Mary or Alice or Margaret or Jane, they were all named Candy, or Cherry, or Mitzi or, maybe, the Va-Va-Va-Voom Girl!

Joe never had any trouble with zone defenses, but he was intercepted regularly by curfew. But no one ever threw a football or ran an offense with more authority than Joe Willie Namath. Vince Lombardi, no less, once called him the "perfect passer."

So Joe Montana may not be the greatest Joe who ever took a deep drop. Joe Willie might provide an argument.

They're honoring Joe Willie at the 10th Annual Cedars-Sinai Sports Spectacular at the Century Plaza on Sunday night, along with other sports spectaculars like George Foreman, Junior Seau and Raul Mondesi. Joe is getting a lifetime achievement award.

I caught up with Joe Willie the other day (something safety blitzes never could seem to do) and asked him if the "guarantee" quote he made all those years ago was sincere or just something made tongue-in-cheek.

"It was made in anger," he said. "I was mad. We were not given our due. We had beat a very good Raider football team to get there, but you'd think we snuck in through a hole in the fence. I went to the Miami Touchdown Club banquet and some guy in the back of the room stood up and began with that 'We're gonna kick your butt!' stuff and I got mad. 'Let me tell you something,' I told him. 'We're gonna win that game. I guarantee it!' Weeb [Jet Coach Weeb Ewbank] was very upset. 'Don't be giving them something to pin up on the locker-room wall!' he yells. 'I like them overconfident!' I thought to myself, 'If they need locker-room-wall quotes to get up for a game, they're worse than I thought!'"

Joe never needed any wall quotes. He played 13 years in the NFL, most of them on knees so sore they had to be drained before every game. He's the only guy who ever limped into the Hall of Fame.

He's not Broadway Joe anymore. He's proud papa Joe with two lovely daughters in Tequesta, Fla. "I get up at 5:30 every morning with them," he laughs. "I can remember when I was just getting in at that time of the morning."

He ranks right there in popularity and numbers with any Joe who ever played any game. He was not only a good Joe, he was a great Joe. I guarantee it.

• • • • • • • • • • • • • • • • • •

MAY 8, 1997

He Thinks, Therefore He Wins

Only a few football coaches achieve the status of legend in their lifetimes. Knute Rockne, Howard Jones, Fielding Yost, Amos Alonzo Stagg, Bear Bryant, Vince Lombardi. And, of course, Joe Paterno.

In another era, all of them would doubtless be generals. If they had one thing in common, it was their ability to motivate and inspire the troops, to get them to sublimate their welfare to the good of the cause.

They were all different. Though Norwegian-born, Rockne had the wisecracking presence of the Irish. Yost was cerebral, Bear Bryant a grizzly of a man who rumbled when he talked and convinced his forces it was us-against-the-world. Jones was aloof, seigneurial and made it clear he expected nothing less than your best.

Paterno may be the best of them. He came along in an era when you could no longer simply suit up the graduating class or get your line out of the chem lab and play some other coach similarly circumspect. After all, the "Four Horsemen" produced three coaches and a federal judge. Today's backfields sometimes seem to produce more defendants than judges.

On the other hand, Rockne's Old Gipper was ahead of his time, was more what used to be called a "tramp athlete" available to the highest bidder or the school where he could make the most out of the pool hall. George Gipp was a great football player, but a greater poker player.

Still, Paterno is a throwback. His football players do not star in court cases a decade from their prime. His teams graduate – 87% one year (compared to a national average of 54%). In the Big Ten, only Northwestern matches Paterno's Penn State record of 80% graduation rate.

He looks more like a nuclear spy than a football coach. Paterno gazes at the world through these thick-lensed glasses and the perpetually perplexed look of a guy who's trying to remember what he did with his keys. He looks lost. He doesn't look threatening at all. Lombardi could terrify you with a growl, Bryant could make you reach to check your wallet, Rockne could make you cry. Paterno looks like a guy waiting for a bus.

The looks are deceiving. Nobody ever was more sure of where he was going and what he was doing than Joe Paterno. There are few secrets in coaching, but what there are, he has.

He speaks in a laryngitic rasp that makes you pay close attention to get what he's saying. But it's worth it. They call him "Joe Pa" back at University Park, Pa., which if you're looking for it, first get a dog. And turn right at Altoona.

The only reason football players go there is because Joe Paterno is there. The only reason the Big Ten let a non-Midwestern school in its conference is Joe Paterno.

I tell you all you have to know about Paterno when I tell you the building named after him on campus is a library. Most coaches when they achieve fame get a field house, a stadium, practice field or arena named after them.

He was a literature major, not P.E., at his alma mater, Brown University. He wasn't going to be a coach but a lawyer. But law schools cost money, and he took a job on the coaching staff at Penn State to raise tuition. That was 48 years ago.

A Paterno team is, like its coach, a conservative bunch, calm, unhurried, unstoppable and everything you try they've been briefed on. Paterno just stands on the sideline blinking and clapping his hands. He takes the field with his pants legs rolled up so high, writer Rick Reilly once snickered he looked as if he were expecting a recurrence of the

Johnstown Flood any moment. If you didn't know, you'd think he was the trainer.

His team's uniforms, like him, are not flashy. Just dark blue with white helmets. It's like getting beat by the 1908 Frank Merriwell Yales.

Joe Pa was in our midst early this week. Looking for 9.3 sprinters, 300-pound pancake linemen, rubber-armed passers, safeties who can jump seven feet straight up? Naw. Paterno was here to participate in the 1997 GTE Academic All-America Teams program. This honors athletes who led their classes not only on the field but in the classroom.

Paterno presented the award to his former quarterback, Todd Blackledge, who not only led his school to its first national championship in 1982 but made Phi Beta Kappa (as well as the Kansas City Chiefs) along the way.

In his 32 years as head coach (with 298 victories and 28 bowl games), Paterno has had many chances to go pro, but didn't, largely because he preferred remaining a pedagogue to being a CEO.

"College coaching today is difficult enough. Before you get down to game plans, you have to call the squad together to meet with agents and lawyers. You have to discuss drugs and alcohol, date rape, sexual harassment, things that have nothing to do with football. Or maybe everything to do.

"Girls are more aggressive today. So are agents. They all see that pot of gold, the professional contract, in the distance.

"It's hard to keep your feet. You have all these things to get out of the way before you can teach a line about football. I make more money than I should, but it's the future of the game I worry about."

Would he ever join what I call the "Yeah but" coaches, as in "But, coach, he raped four nurses!" "Yeah but he runs the 40 in 4.3!"

Would Joe Pa sign up a known rogue because his skills could lead the team to the Rose Bowl?

Joe Pa shakes his head. "You know it's going to be trouble down the line. You don't need that."

Trouble runs a 4.3 40 too, Joe knows.

• • • • • • • • • • • • • • • • •

NOVEMBER 29, 1994

You Can't Burn Rice, But He Can Easily Burn You

Jerry Rice, like secondhand smoke, germ warfare and insider trading, should be banned. At least, that is the view of NFL defensive backs. He should carry a surgeon general's warning on his helmet.

He's not really a player, is their view. He's a terrorist. He works undercover, so to speak. He's the NFL's Jackal.

He's so invisible, you'd think he came on the field in disguise. Claude Rains gets the part. He just vanishes like a wraith, only to materialize under the ball. He's 6 feet 2, 200 pounds, but he's as difficult to find as Jimmy Hoffa.

Is he even real? Defensive backs are not so sure. They think he just might be another E.T. They try to remember if they ever heard him, or it, talk.

They can't prove anything because, first, they have to find him. They panic. You can almost hear them when the ball is snapped. "Anybody here see No. 80?" they'll call out in rising panic. "I thought I saw him over there a moment ago," someone will answer. "What's he look like? Anybody know what he looks like?"

Hardly anybody does. He's the phantom of this opera. If you took three NFL defensive backs and had them make a police composite drawing, you would have three different pictures. No one gets close enough to tell what color his eyes are.

Even the public is vague about how he looks. Rice goes through life the way he goes through zone defenses. Everybody in San Francisco could describe Joe Montana, right down to the dimple in his chin. They all know what Barry Bonds looks like. Ask them to describe Jerry Rice, you might get a blank look. He would make a world-class spy.

Defenses track other wide receivers in the game. With Rice, they need radar. The only way to play Rice is to track the ball. Where it comes down, Rice will be. He's a size 46 long, but the 11-inch ball is easier to keep track of than the grain of Rice.

He's Public Enemy No. 1 in pro football. He has a rap sheet longer than the Gambino family. He has caught 788 passes. He's as indefensible as a flood. Teams have tried zones, man-to-man, prayer, intimidation, fouls, trash talk, sobs, pleas – everything short of armed intervention. Rice merely races through it. He's got a rendezvous with the football.

Candlestick Park is Rice's paddy. But he could catch balls on an ice floe if he had to, get open in a swamp.

He's fast. But, then, so is almost everybody else in the league. There's hardly a secondary that doesn't have Olympic speed, or isn't capable of pressing a world-record relay team.

Bill Cosby used to say of Gale Sayers that he split himself in two at the tackler and the part with the ball went on its way. Jerry Rice is somewhat this way. Except that when he catches the ball there are rarely tacklers. His uniform never gets dirty.

He begs the question as to which is the most important position.

It used to be the running back. The game belonged to the left halfback in the old days. Star players were known as Galloping Ghosts, Four Horsemen, Choo-Choos, Six-Yard Sitkos. Teams were built around George Gipp, Jim Thorpe, Red Grange, Ernie Nevers. The quarterbacks just blocked. The T-formation changed all that. With its man-in-motion formations, its pass-oriented attack, it reduced the running backs' role to that of quasi-decoys. They were used to draw the defense in, not to win games. You won games up top. In the early days, a team that threw the ball 10 times a game was known as an "aerial circus." With the T, you threw the ball 10 times before the anthem died down.

Instead of Galloping Something-Or-Others, the game was given over to Slinging Something-Or-Others or Springfield Rifles.

The most famous pass receiver in history was Knute Rockne. He and quarterback Gus Dorais brought the little-used long pass into the game at West Point in 1913, defeating the heavily favored Cadets, 30-13, with this new ploy. They completed an unheard-of 13 passes.

That wouldn't be a good drive today but outstanding receivers always manifested themselves. Don Hutson was probably the most famous of these. Like many who came after him – Raymond Berry, Steve Largent, Tom Fears, Jim Phillips – he was known less for his speed than for his sure-handed elusiveness. "Possession receivers," the game called them.

These were augmented by the "bomb squad" receivers – Cliff Branch, Crazylegs Hirsch, Lance Alworth, Bob Boyd and Cloyce Box – who regularly ran 90-yard routes. They didn't get the ball much. They didn't need it much.

Jerry Rice has it both ways. He can outrun you. Or he can outsmart you. Since his specialty is disappearing at the line of scrimmage, the defense doesn't know whether he's going long or doubling back.

Wherever he goes, he inspires the dread of an epidemic. You can almost see the defensive backs trying to look over both shoulders at once, silently screaming, "Where'd he go? Anybody here see a guy with brown eyes and gold helmet, wearing No. 80? He's probably carrying a football." They're almost ready to call 911.

He's an uncontrolled substance. He should be illegal anyway. He's probably responsible for more nervous breakdowns in the NFL than any receiver in the game. He has the most touchdowns of any receiver in the history of the game – 130 – and is third in yards gained with 12,885. It's easy to see why defenders in this league think he's from another planet. Probably arrives by saucer. From outer space.

• • • • • • • • • • • • • • • • •

MARCH 24, 1989

Pete Rozelle Sold Entire Nation on His Sport

Paul O'Neil, the late, great Life magazine writer, once approached me with a problem. He was doing a piece on the commissioner of football, Pete Rozelle. He knew I knew him.

"Underneath that poached-egg-on-toast exterior, what's the interior?" he wanted to know.

"Well," I told him, "you will find some iron filings in the yolk if you try to take a bite. But he will give you to believe the interior is poached egg, too. This is the supreme Organization Man. Madison Avenue times two. As a PR man, he's without an equal. He could make Castro president of the U.S."

Rozelle's great strength was in appearing to compromise without really doing so. He made everybody feel he was their best friend. He understood public relations as few people have in our generation.

The Super Bowl is his monument. It exists because of Pete Rozelle. He built it from scratch. Michelangelo has his David, Da Vinci his Mona Lisa – and Rozelle has the Super Bowl.

Few people remember that the first Super Bowl was almost a disaster. It fell 30,000 short of selling out as it was, but it might have been much worse if Rozelle hadn't come to town, rolled up his sleeves and put it on Page 1 and the 11 o'clock news.

At last year's Super Bowl, $100 seats were going for $1,000. Rozelle made the Super Bowl an American tribal rite. He made it easy for scribes to get their stories. He courted publicity. He would call the competing teams together and explain to them the importance of media cooperation. He encouraged media wives to attend by arranging tours and Super Bowl week activities for them. No other sport did that.

When Coach Vince Lombardi wanted to keep his team in Green Bay before the first Super Bowl game, Rozelle needed smelling salts. He ordered Lombardi west – to Santa Barbara – on the double. The game needed the ink. He was almost the only guy who could tell Lombardi what to do. Lombardi loved him.

The World Series was the great American hype when Rozelle came along. A heavyweight championship fight. A bowl game was the Rose, the Orange. Basketball was hopeful but rudderless and unfocused. It used to have to play doubleheaders with the Globetrotters to attract crowds. Pete made Super Sunday into the single biggest sports event of the year. Not since Dempsey-Tunney had the whole nation come to a halt around a sports event.

He was not a flamboyant character but he had a grasp of show biz and hype P. T. Barnum would have envied. He had network television eating out of his hand.

Pete knew the last spontaneous entertainment on the tube was sports. And he believed pro football was the ultimate in television entertainment. If you sat up for a decade, you couldn't design a sport that would fit the rectangular dimensions of the TV screen any better.

Pete didn't give the game away. He was in his element with all those button-down collars in the TV executive suites. He was equally smooth in the corridors of power in Washington, where he wrung concessions from the solons with a suavity and an air of sweet reasonableness and eagerness to please that was disarming. He always had a tan and a smile. He didn't manipulate, he bargained. He could have been a great lobbyist. Congress loved him.

He never took it for granted that you just had to throw a football out on the field, blow a whistle, and the public would break down the doors. He promoted football as energetically as Barnum had his circus.

When Pete came up, the game was run by a lot of crusty old football types, secretive, suspicious, in some cases superannuated. Pete's greatest coup was getting them to share the wealth. He got them to split the television pot equally. The last time anyone looked, that was $17 million per team.

Pete also got Congress – and the White House – to overlook the fact that this violated several provisions of the antitrust act while some other industries looked on in envy. He learned how to handle stubborn rich men the hard way.

The first time I met Pete Rozelle, he was handling the tour of the great Australian miler John Landy for an Aussie airline. Landy was the world's second four-minute miler, but he wasn't Babe Ruth. I was coaxed into a magazine piece and, later, the whole world was teased into watching the Commonwealth Games in Vancouver, featuring Landy and Roger Bannister. Pete was master of the soft sell.

But later, when he was hired back by the Rams to act as buffer between the warring owners, Dan Reeves and Ed Pauley, he had to learn to walk a tightrope the Wallendas might have fallen from. It was a job that called for a referee more than a general manager, but Rozelle handled it, as usual, so smoothly that both sides thought he was their best friend in the world. In a way, he was.

And that was how he brought pro football into the 20th century. The game hired him after Bert Bell died. It was kind of a cult game up till then. It flourished in the Northeast with the slow, steady retreat of the Ivy League from big-time football, but it was little known in other hotbeds of football, notably the Southeast and Texas, and only beginning to catch on in the West.

Rozelle changed all that. Bell had sort of officed out of his pocket. Pete Rozelle took the business to Park Avenue – literally.

Pete was known as the Boy Commissioner when he joined the great game. He leaves with the stature of Lombardi, Art Rooney, Well Mara or any of the great coaches or great players.

He always managed to retain a little-boy attitude toward the game. You could always say Pete was a fan. He loved the game and understood it from his days as sports information director at Compton College and, later, the University of San Francisco (Pete still thinks of Ollie Matson as the greatest running back in the history of the game).

But his legacy is the wedding of pro football and television. He was, as Tex Schramm of the Cowboys – who hired Pete when they were both with the Rams – put it the other day, "a man for his times."

Every sport, every business, has to be in awe of what Pete Rozelle has done for his sport. That he did it without making an enemy in the game is remarkable. It's hard to build an empire without killing a few people.

But for Rozelle, that poached-egg exterior – and iron filing interior – worked beyond anyone's dreams. If you don't think so, just try to get a Super Bowl ticket next time around.

● ● ● ● ● ● ● ● ● ● ● ● ● ● ● ● ● ●

JANUARY 19, 1979

As Graceful as a Swann

MIAMI – The first thing to establish about Lynn Swann is whether that's his name or a description. You wonder whether the Pittsburgh Steelers found him on a pond in Holland or in the third act of "Lohengrin" or "Siegfried." He could be a ride at Disneyland. Tchaikovsky would build a ballet around him.

He's only rarely at sea level. If Nijinsky could catch passes, you'd imagine this is what he'd look like in a football uniform. Swann caught 61 passes this season, only about five of them with one or more feet on the ground. He sort of floats up to meet a thrown ball. If he were playing in the street, some of the receptions would be at the second floor window or the bottom of a street light.

Swann beat the Dallas Cowboys the last time the teams met in the Super Bowl. Not Terry Bradshaw, not Franco Harris, Rocky Bleier nor the Steel Curtain.

Swann is miscast with the Steelers, who are basically an other-side-of-the-tracks team. They are company-town bullies who talk out of the sides of their mouths, smoke cigars and spit tobacco. They're hit men, football's version of a gang that would put a horse in your bed. In another life, they'd be piano-wire killers. Hold your hand over a hot stove.

Swann's way is as ethereal as his play. He writes poetry, he was a tap dancer, he composes music. Watching Lynn Swann catch a football is like reading Browning for the first time, or Byron. There's a purity to it that transcends the violence. Michelangelo would want to sculpt it. It's an art form, not a dock fight. It belongs in a museum, not an arena. It's not Dempsey-Firpo, it's Swann Lake.

Wide receivers are the ballerinas of football. Whatever grace and beauty there is in the game, they furnish. It's what keeps the game from being a mindless slugfest, ignorant armies battling in the dark. A Swann catch looks choreographed. Sol Hurok must cry when he thinks why someone put a football in this young man's hands instead of a "Rite of Spring" score.

His parents named him Lynn because they wanted a girl. Coaches wouldn't care if they named him Mabel. The minute coaches saw him run a pass route, they all went to church that Sunday and sang all the hymns. Legend has it, one coach at San Mateo watched him catch a 70-yard touchdown pass and asked who that kid was, and was told "He's a Swann." The coach, irritated: "I can see that. I want to know his name."

Swann claims he became a resourceful receiver not because of his speed or agility but his imagination. "My brothers and cousins were bigger and stronger than I was, so I had to outwit them. You know, in basketball they wouldn't ever let me shoot. The first shot I took at a basket was in my senior year in high school."

Swann starts out a pass pattern like an ode. It flows in lyric pattern. There's not an awkward move in it. He has caught more than 200 passes for 4,000 yards and 40 touchdowns. Only one player in football caught more passes this season, and only one scored more touchdowns.

You probably never should play cards with him, either. His imaginativeness does not end on the goal line. For a term paper at USC once, Lynn delved into the history of plantation slavery. With a perfectly straight face, he wrote that tap dancing evolved as an art form because the slaves wanted a way to communicate where the overseer could not catch on. Hence they tapped out a code with their toes and smiled and grinned the whole time till the slave master thought they were just dancing.

The professor was as fooled as any defensive secondary or cornerback. He gave Lynn Swann, boy historian, an "A." If you come across this splendid legend in some anthology some day, don't fall for Lynn's head fake. Tap dancing was probably invented the same way the gavotte was.

Dallas coach Tom Landry took note of the fact in his press conference Thursday that "Swann beat us last time. We have to find a way to cope with him."

No one ever has. In Super Bowl X, Swann caught four passes for a record 161 yards, including the crucial 64-yard touchdown pass that defeated the Cowboys.

To give you an idea how critical the catch was, the thrower, Terry Bradshaw, got knocked out on that play and was so amnesiac he didn't know until the next day that Swann had turned it into a touchdown.

For those of you who like nosebleed football, trench warfare, teeth-loosening and quarterbacks who have to be led off the field because they've forgotten their names and think they're in downtown Pittsburgh and it's raining, the Steelers can give you Franco and Rocky and Mean Joe and L. C. and a couple of homicidal linebackers.

But if you want to see the kind of football Monet would want to paint or that should hang in the Louvre, keep your eye on that graceful Swann. If it's artistry, not butchery, you want, keep your eye on the only flying Swann in the park. Never mind those thugs with the casts on their punching hands. It may be your last chance to see this graceful Swann go drifting along before someone tries to buy him for the lake at

Windsor Castle. If everybody played football this way they'd soon move the Super Bowl to the Met. Nureyev would be second string, and they would have to play Super Bowls with Swann in them to the strains of "The Nutcracker Suite."

• • • • • • • • • • • • • • • • • •

JUNE 3, 1986

Nobody Ever Had Him In His Pocket

They called him frantic Francis. They couldn't keep him in the pocket, not two generations of coaches, not relays of 250-pound defensive ends, blitzing linebackers, not life itself. He gave elusivity a new dimension.

The eyes give him away. He's not physically prepossessing at 5 feet 11 inches and 190 pounds, but the eyes are the eyes of a forest creature on the prowl for food and on the lookout for enemies. Or of a guy with his own deck looking for suckers. They are survivors' eyes, wary, inquisitive, quick.

This is the look of a guy asked to go through Indian territory at night with only a map and a canteen, which is a fair description of his life in the NFL. You can tell that every sense is alert. He looks like a guy who never sleeps and rarely stands still.

He is football's equivalent of Bugs Bunny. His whole career was a Saturday afternoon serial. He made "The Perils of Pauline" look like "Rebecca of Sunnybrook Farm."

In the NFL, the suspense is supposed to be whether anybody can catch the ball. With Francis, the suspense was whether he would ever throw it. He ran for more yards than any quarterback who ever lived. And that was only the ones beyond the line of scrimmage. If you counted the yards behind, he has more than any running back who ever lived.

He wasn't fast. He didn't have the strongest arm. He tended to dart, duck, twist and squirm. "Hit 'em where they ain't" was baseball player Wee Willie Keeler's motto. Francis threw it where they weren't.

By any yardstick you want to use, Francis Asbury Tarkenton was the best quarterback pro football ever had. He threw for more touchdowns, 342, more yards, 47,003, and more completions, 3,686, than any other quarterback. He took his team to three Super Bowls in four years. He ran for 30 touchdowns and 3,669 yards.

Which makes you wonder why Fran Tarkenton didn't get into the Pro Football Hall of Fame until this year, three years after his initial eligibility. He threw for 52 more touchdowns than any quarterback, had nearly 1,000 more completions and almost 7,000 more yards. You would think the Hall of Fame would have come to him.

The rap against Fran Tarkenton has always been that he threw short passes, that his completions were just complicated handoffs. The spuriousness of this argument can be seen in the yards rolled up, four to 20 miles more than other Hall of Fame quarterbacks like John Unitas, Sonny Jurgensen or Roger Staubach.

Tarkenton rebuts the charge. "In the first place, the long ball is the easiest to throw," he says. "The Hail Mary is a test of luck, not skill. It's like putting a note in a bottle and launching it over the side. If the arm were all there were to quarterbacking, a guy named Rudy Bukich was the greatest quarterback who ever played. He could throw the ball overseas."

Tarkenton also says that his scrambles were actually artful geometric patterns. They looked on paper like a chart of a Rube Goldberg invention: Player A takes ball to Point B where he bumps into Defensive End C and reverses his field to Point D where water is dripped into hole which makes Linebacker E slip and allows Player A to duck under arm (F) and release ball (G) into air where it skids off helmet (H) of Cornerback I into waiting arms of Tight End J, who falls over Safety K into end zone for touchdown.

"I was never out of control back there," Tarkenton says.

"You see, what the drop-back quarterbacks would do, they would peel back 20 yards or roll right 15 yards, then they would throw to a wide-out who had gone down the field 15 yards and then ran an 'out' to the left sideline. So what you're talking about is a 50- or 60-yard pass to make 10 or 15 yards.

"I would scramble to a prepared position. I would never release a ball 30 or 35 yards behind the line of scrimmage. My purpose in scrambling was two-fold: tire out the pass rushers and psych out the secondary.

"So the theory gained credence: If Tarkenton has to scramble and run, he must not be a very good passer. If you can punch, why box? One time, the Green Bay Packers decided, 'OK, we won't rush him.' They stopped their pass rush. I picked them apart. The next time, they came in with their ears laid back and growling again.

"A quarterback is a passer, not a thrower. Fernando Valenzuela doesn't need a 100 m.p.h. fastball. Putting the ball where you want it is more important than putting it in orbit."

No one was any better at putting the ball where he wanted it than not-so-frantic Francis.

The world still can't keep him in the pocket. Tarkenton was through town the other day, and he still manages to go through a hotel lobby as if it were stacked with Deacon Joneses, who used to say he trained for a game against Tarkenton by locking himself in a roomful of mosquitoes and turning out the lights. You find Tarkenton by looking for the nearest cloud of dust.

He looks at an interviewer as if he were deciding whether a down-and-out, a simple swing pass or a quarterback sneak were called for. His television career – "That's Incredible" and "Monday Night Football" – behind him, he is now concentrating on his advertising and motivational business, Tarkenton Production Group.

"We deal in telling company executives how to be executives," he said. "We tell them you cannot ignore good behavior and only attend to the bad behavior, which is the way most people seem to run their businesses – and lives."

Tarkenton should know. He spent 17 years listening to the negatives – "He can't do that. He can't run around outside the cup like that" – to the point where it took the Hall of Fame three years to realize he was their shiniest ornament.

They probably figured they couldn't keep him in one place long enough and didn't want to plan an induction where they have to chase the honoree down the street to enroll him. If he had a football, they'd never catch him.

Basketball

• • • • • • • • • • • • • • • • •

MAY 14, 1989

Kareem Is Now
Winning on Class

He dominated his sport in the way few have in the long history of games men play. God made him more than 7 feet tall. He took care of the rest.

It was said that if you sat up nights trying to design a sport that would more nearly fit his qualifications, you couldn't come up with a better one than basketball. But being a 7-footer is no longer nearly enough.

In another time, another era, he would have been considered a freak. He might have been tearing phone books or bending crowbars in a circus. The 7-footers of another time had short, unhappy lives.

But Kareem Abdul-Jabbar was no runaway glandular case. He was just a perfectly formed, perfectly proportioned big man. The legs didn't end up under the shoulders. He didn't clank when he walked. He didn't move like a prehistoric bird. He took quick sprinter's steps. He was graceful, agile, a 6-footer in a 7-foot body.

He didn't play the game of the 7-foot bully. Most men his size rough up the competition, don't so much take the ball away from them as them away from the ball.

This was not his style. He never shattered backboards, strong-armed rebounds, threw his weight – and his elbows – around. He played the full-court game. It was like watching a 7-foot Cousy on some nights. Everything but the behind-the-back dribble.

His legacy to basketball is a shot he didn't invent, just reincarnated – the hook shot. There is a story behind it. When he was in college, the powers-that-be, frightened by his proficiency at it, outlawed the dunk shot. This was like outlawing the home run because Babe Ruth came along, but Abdul-Jabbar, then Lew Alcindor, lived with it. He went to the skyhook. "It ain't sexy – but it counts two," he used to say. Even in the pros, he seemed to be saying "I'll show you – I don't need the dunk." The skyhook became his signature shot, his trademark.

He scored more points than anyone who ever played the game, 38,387 (43,900 if you count playoffs), and hardly any of them were what the trade calls "garbage points."

Wilt Chamberlain had 31,419 points in his career but only a handful of them were more than 10 inches long. Laid end to end, Wilt's baskets would probably add up to a half-dozen good three-pointers. Kareem's would stretch across Rhode Island.

He was almost a force of nature. But he was a team player. He never scored more than 50 points a game. He was never giving a solo out there. He was trying to win games, not trophies. He was not that easy to deal with. He was a man of monumental reserve. He wasn't haughty like a Bill Russell, opinionated like a Wilt Chamberlain, but neither was he a man you came up to clap him on the back and call him "Tiger." Even on court, he had this four-mile stare. He was aloof, suspicious, guarded. He was an only child and he carried this moat of privacy with him wherever he went. No man is an island, but Kareem Abdul-Jabbar gave it a good shot.

When he changed his name, it was widely perceived as just another way to slap society in the face and give it a message – he rejected its values. Actually, it proved to be a deeply held religious belief.

The world left him alone. People have always feared great size. Fairy tales are full of ogres and giants and Gullivers, and Kareem Abdul-Jabbar was widely feared to be The-Creature-That-Ate-Basketball.

He seldom smiled. He scowled a lot. He never courted the press. He was the first out of the locker room after a game. He was polite but not expansive. Television was afraid to ask him tough questions. He didn't inspire the hokey camaraderie. He was hardly everybody's pal.

The facts of the matter were, he took criticism very well. He was reserved, not egotistical. He treated you the same whether you wrote flattery or censure. He didn't hold grudges. The only time his private life made the papers was when his house burned down or when eight people were killed in a home he owned in Washington, D.C. Religious fanatics are the most dangerous of God's creatures. Kareem was as sick about it as the rest of the country.

The world tried hard to make him like them. The outpouring of gifts in every franchise city when he announced his retirement must have stunned him. It certainly did Doug Moe, a rival coach from Denver.

"Here's a guy who has been pretty much a jerk his entire life," Moe said bitterly. "He's been one of the least-liked guys in NBA history – by fans, media, players."

Yet rivals showered him with motorcycles, paintings, jazz collections, Oriental rugs, jukeboxes, sculptures, furniture, sailboats, surfboards – everything but his weight in diamonds. His teammates even gave him a new Rolls Royce.

"What're they going to give Magic when he retires – Rhode Island?" demands Moe.

Is Moe right? Or is the rest of the world?

Well, Abdul-Jabbar showed up for work for 25 years, always on time, always in shape to play, always at the top of the key, the low post, wherever he was wanted. In a world plagued by drugs, alcohol, scandal, he maintained a positive image. You don't have to like him. You have to respect him.

You're not supposed to be able to play basketball at the age of 42. Golf, maybe. Even baseball. Nolan Ryan can still throw one-hitters.

But basketball is a game where you get 24 seconds to get up and down a hardwood court all night long. While guys are sticking elbows in your ribs and fingers in your eye and kicks on your shins and shoes on your toes.

But you watch Kareem in the present playoffs and you have to shake your head. When he's on court, the game subtly changes. A kind of film seems to come over the eyes of the opposing team. Their shoulders slump; they almost start to pant. They get out of their game, lose their rhythm. Their centers get less aggressive, their guards more tentative. Kareem's team, on the other hand, reacts as if the cavalry just arrived. They go into battle singing.

Around a racetrack when an old stakes horse beats a field of younger but lesser horses, they describe it as "winning on class." This, it seems to me, is what Kareem Abdul-Jabbar is doing on his last go-round. Winning on class. Because, never mind that forbidding exterior, it's something he's always had plenty of.

• • • • • • • • • • • • • • • • • •

FEBRUARY 3, 1963

Elgin Has Elegance

DETROIT – The phone rang in the hotel room, and Elgin Baylor picked it up: "Sherwood Forest, Robin Hood speaking," he announced.

One night in New York, a cabdriver lifted Baylor's bags into the back seat, looked at him and a fellow basketball player, Tommy Hawkins, and asked: "You fellows athletes?" It was a little like asking if there were bear tracks in the woods, and Elgin was equal to it "We're fighting the main event in the Garden tonight. I'm letting him win," he said, pointing to Hawkins.

In Syracuse at a lunch counter, a bleary-eyed bottle fighter surveyed the troop of egrets in topcoats and demanded, "Are you some kind of a team?" "Midget wrestlers," Elgin told him. "You've heard of the Los Angeles Mothers?" "Oh, sure," said the befuddled drunk.

Elgin Baylor puts the world on. Five nights a week he does it with a basketball. A defense man on the court never gets a straight answer, either. It is easier to pick which shell the pea is under than to figure which hand the basketball is going to come off of. He is a con man on or off the court.

But if all this gives the impression Elgin Baylor is the latest product of that well-worn American stereotype – the happy-go-lucky, levee-singing Negro – it is the biggest con of all. Elgin Baylor is a proud, sensitive, suspicious and generally aloof man whose complexities cannot possibly be summed up in a series of road trip gags.

He is, as it happens, the best basketball player on the Lakers and probably in basketball. He became the 15th player in National Basketball Assn. history to pass the 10,000-point mark Friday night. All he has to do to make 20,000 points is live.

It is possible to sense stardom in Elgin even without a basketball in his hands. The eyes are insolent and the message is clear: "Don't mess with me." He cannot stand to be touched, and irritability even shows on the basketball court where elbows and arms are locked around shooters under the basket. Elgin impatiently jerks them off him and catches a pass in the same motion.

It's easy to get on a first-name basis with Elgin. All you have to do is know him three years and always let him speak first. He is his own man. When he refused to suit up in Charleston for a game in his rookie year because the all-white hotel refused to check him in, the NAACP didn't talk him into it – but his coach couldn't talk him out of it either. Elgin Baylor fights for the rights of man by fighting for the rights of Elgin Baylor. "They don't expect me to come and play if they're going to treat me like a circus animal that stays in a cage till the show goes on," was his simple explanation.

But even if he keeps the real world at arm's length, he is as at home in the extroverted, uninhibited traveling carnival that is the Lakers basketball team as he is on a jump shot.

The Lakers don't know that other Elgin Baylor. The one they know is the one written up in a national publication as "Motormouth," an affectionate, chatty mother hen of a man who loudly presides (and surreptitiously chats) at every card game played, the horse player addicted to longshots, the affable roomie who takes four showers a day and douses roomies like Rudy La Russo or Jim Krebs with deodorant so they won't mar the fastidiousness of their home away from home – and the negative in any debate.

He is the club champion in the in-flight, impromptu "Can you top this?" games. "No matter what outlandish story you come up with, Elg has got a better one," complains roommate La Russo. "If you saw a four-car crash, he saw a 54-car crash. If you caught a 10-pound fish, he caught a 100-pound one. He tells a story, and if it doesn't get the proper reaction, he tells it all over again, only more so. He keeps embellishing it till you finally say, 'Oh, Elg, you're kidding. It couldn't happen.' Then he swears it did and goes away happy."

He has told so many conflicting stories about his age and the number of years he dropped out of school that even the U.S. Army has two different birthdates for him, and Jimmy Krebs, his verbal spar mate, once announced: "The Elgin Baylor doll – you wind it up and it gets a year younger."

"Put him in a war and he'd cheat," allows Hot Rod Hundley, who has caught the queen of spades in a few hearts games where Elgin preferred playing to win to playing to rules and to following his instincts rather than following suit.

There is no subject too recondite for Elgin to expound on. "If you order mutton in a restaurant, Elg gives you a lecture on animal husbandry as it affects the lamb and sheep," Jerry West notes. "If you see a jetliner go by, Elg gives you its specifications – such as exact cruising speed, number of rivets in the fuselage and angle of descent over Cleveland. No one has ever heard Elg say 'I don't know.'"

Even though he was a Washington, D.C., high school phenom, Elgin received scholarship offers only from Negro colleges. He had had enough segregation and accepted a football scholarship at College of Idaho, where the enrollment was 480 and 380 of them were girls. The first time a Seattle basketball recruiter got a load of his form, he sent his own plane down in the most daring daylight kidnapping since John Dillinger got shot.

Most Negro stars hold the pro contract offerers at gunpoint by threatening to join the Harlem Globetrotters, but Elgin Baylor won't even mention the Globetrotters out loud – even for money. Baylor is a competitor, not a clown, and can't bear to have strangers laughing at him, even when he's getting paid for it.

In short, he comes from a long line of warriors, not end men, and society is lucky someone put a basketball in his hand instead of a blade.

He is as conservative as his clothes, and the $60,000 a year he grosses from all sources is as safe as blue chips.

"Elg is the only born Republican I know who campaigned for Kennedy," Hundley observed. He is disciplined and – unlike a Wilt Chamberlain who recognizes no authority shorter than he is, which restricts potential bosses to one small tribe in a corner of India – Elg is as coachable as a three-point average guard. "I obey a coach just like I obey my parents. That's what authority means," he says simply.

It is these things – drive, determination, confidence but, above all, grim pride – that make Elgin Baylor not only the greatest basketball player but one of the great athletes of his time. "A Negro, to make it, has to be just a little bit better," he explains. "If a white and a Negro have equal ability – and play up to it – they keep the white. I can at least make sure I play up to my ability."

If you don't think he does, ask the man who plays him. "His name," says Bob Cousy, "should be 'Elegant Baylor.'"

• • • • • • • • • • • • • • • • •

FEBRUARY 28, 1984

Bird Really Turns
Pale With Losing

When the Boston Celtics run out on the floor these nights, it often seems that they have forgotten something important – like a fifth man.

Oh, they have a fifth man. Only you can't see him. He's probably real enough, has a pulse, a temperature of 98.6 and he may have to open doors before he goes through them. But if you saw him in the attic of a haunted house at midnight or walking around the Tower of London with his head tucked underneath his arm, you'd faint dead away.

To say Larry Bird is "white" is like saying a desert is "sandy." If Larry Bird were any more white, he'd be invisible. You could read through Larry Bird. If you held him up to the light, you could see what he had for dinner. He's the only guy in the game who doesn't need X-rays. You just stand him next to the window and count the bones. He'd make a great Halloween decoration.

He'd make Casper the Ghost look as real as Orson Welles. He's got a mustache, but nobody knows it. Even his eyes are white. His hair looks like a halo. If you wrapped him in a sheet, 100 million people would fall down and repent. He looks like something that fell off a Sistine ceiling.

He's as conspicuous as Moby Dick out there on that floor. But there are times when he tends to disappear into thin air. Particularly when the Celts are wearing their road whites. There are nights when the only way the guy guarding him knows he's there is by the swish of the basket. He's the original White Shadow. If the guy assigned to him gets in trouble and asks for help, a teammate will say: "I'll be glad to help out. Could you point him out?"

"Well, no, but if you hear this rush of air and see this No. 33 kind of floating through space, foul it."

This great white shark goes through the league like a runaway iceberg. If there were a white quota in the league, Bird would fill up three franchises worth. He makes white-on-white look like a rainbow.

But the central fact of Larry Joe Bird is not his whiteness, his outside shot, rebounds, dribble or half-court pass, it's his conscience. Larry Bird wears fame like a hair shirt. Larry Bird makes your average front-line perfectionist look nonchalant, happy-go-lucky. Larry Bird is one of the most tormented superstars in any league or sport.

The other night, Larry Bird and the Celtics came into town sporting an eight-game lead in their conference and the best record by seven games in the NBA. They had won 22 games at home, 20 on the road. They could be pardoned if they swaggered a bit coming into the locker room.

Larry Bird doesn't swagger. Larry Bird worries. His team went out and got beat by the hometown Lakers, 116-108. Not one of your basic disgraces. Not even in the top ten.

After the game, you would have thought Bird was explaining an affiliation in the Communist Party, explaining where he was the night the Lindbergh baby disappeared or why he left the scene of an accident. You half expected you should read him his rights or recommend that he have a lawyer present before you went on with the questioning.

Bird was tormented by the defeat, even though it was only the 14th in a season in which one team (Indiana) had lost 39 already.

"We haven't beaten a good team all year," Bird moaned. "We're supposed to be a team-oriented group of players, and we get beat by a running team. We have to be disciplined, and we let them run us out of our game. And they beat us without two of their best, Jamaal (Wilkes) and (Bob) McAdoo. If they're in there, that's 20 more points."

Bird, who's averaging 23.8 points a game, was held to 14. He reacted as if he should join a monastery. "When you're getting paid the money I'm getting paid, you should go all out every game. There's no excuse for not playing your best."

Dumping ashes on his head and rending his garments is not new to Larry Bird.

During the 1983 season, the Celtics finished nine games behind Philadelphia in the conference and lost to Milwaukee in the second round of the playoffs, four games to none. Bird publicly took the blame – "I'm just sick. Sometimes I wonder where our hearts are."

It's hardly typical superstar behavior. The man who bats .398 or gains 2,000 yards or shoots .600 from the floor on a losing team may pay lip service to the organization that falls short of his figures and loses the pennant or title, but more often his attitude borders on: "Well, I did my part. I can't carry all those clowns."

Bird does not see himself as a soloist. As his coach, K. C. Jones, said after the Laker game: "Larry Bird has a high disdain for losing. He takes it very personally. He doesn't treat himself as a superstar. You see him out there diving for loose balls like a rookie. It pains him to see a fast break broken up by a mistake. Even if it's someone else, he takes the blame for it. He takes the game seriously, and he feels his job is to win."

Won't the postgame depressions take their toll? "Naw," said K. C. "He'll be all right tomorrow."

Which is good news. Because if Bird is going to start to blush over his performance, he'll go around the floor like a moving thermometer.

● ● ● ● ● ● ● ● ● ● ● ● ● ● ● ● ● ●

MAY 18, 1973

Wilt, You Can't Win

Once upon a time there was a mythical kingdom called Basketball, and its dwellers were poor and fearful.

The ruler of this kingdom was Emperor Bill Russell, and he ruled in the best of ways – without seeming to.

One day word came that a giant had entered this kingdom and would soon devour it. The giant had come down from a beanstalk in the sky, and the people were frightened and went to Emperor Russell and cried, "Save us!"

Emperor Russell said, "Fear not!! Haven't I always?" But the people cried, "Lo! This giant named Wilt Chamberlain has scored 100 points in a single game, and he averages 50 a night, and Basketball will die in its sleep at his hands!" And Russell raised his hand and said, "How little faith have ye? I will remove the basketball from him."

And it came to pass that Emperor Russell did so, and once the natives had become safe, they became cocky. They jeered at the giant and said, "Ha! You are a paper giant! Your scoring scares no one, for you are at last defeated by our emperor with ease. We fear you not."

And then Emperor Russell retired, and it came to pass that a new giant appeared, and he was more formidable than the first. And the people shook and they went to Russell and cried, "Save us! For this new giant, Kareem Alcindor-Jabbar, is more terrible than the last. He comes to consume Basketball, and there is no one to stop him." And the ex-emperor said, "Tut-tut, look you to Chamberlain." And they cried, "Chamberlain!? Forsooth, he cannot take a basketball from a baby, he can only drop it through hoops."

Nevertheless, they went to Wilt, with faint hopes, and said, "Save us! You are our only hope! Our emperor dawdles in a Gomorrah called Hollywood."

And Chamberlain said, "I will change my methods. I will save you from this scourge." And he stopped dropping balls through hoops and started taking the ball away from the young man who would. Only thus, reasoned the seers of the kingdom, could Basketball be saved.

And so he saved Basketball from the new giant, and the people cried, "Behold! We have a new emperor! Hail Caesar! Chamberlain has saved us! He has turned away the giant Jabbar from the gates!" And Chamberlain said, "This winter can my friends walk in public without embarrassment."

And Chamberlain became the Emperor of all Basketball. And it came to pass again, on the following year, the 23rd year of the kingdom, 1973, that the kingdom prospered and the harvest was good and the giant Jabbar was contained.

And then a more subtle dynasty appeared, calling itself the New York Knicks. And, as it had no giant, the kingdom considered itself not threatened at first, but it watched with growing anger as the new dynasty tied the Emperor Chamberlain into knots. And the people grumbled. "Thee must go to the basket more," they chided him. "Thee must not let these pygmies make a mockery of thee and us."

Chamberlain cried, "But Willis Reed is no giant! Jerry Lucas is not of the stuff that brings down kingdoms! Bill Bradley is no 7-foot brigand! This is not a one-man team that will make the game ruin us! This is only a governing body, not a ruling body!"

The people listened not. They jeered and hooted. "Behold!" they cried. "He is not a worthy emperor!" And they told each other, "Now see, the emperor has no clothes on!" And so they mocked him. "Why goest thou not to the basket?" they demanded. "Why hoard thou thy talent? Why, used you not to score 100 points a night? Fie on thee! Thee have betrayed us!"

And in New York, one of the respected seers of the kingdom, the prophet Dick Young, wrote darkly: "I know I'm in the vast minority on this, but I just can't feel Wilt Chamberlain is a great basketball player. I don't think he's even a good basketball player. He's simply a very big basketball player."

And his own palace guard began to refer to him slyly as "The Load." And the public pointed and scorned, and they mocked him. And they were sorely disappointed in him. For the life of him, the giant Chamberlain could not reason why. "Have I not done what you asked?" he pleaded. "Egad, did thee not bid me change my style, and I did so, and when I did so the kingdom was won? Wherefore now mock me?" But they only sneered the more. "Show us thy strength now, Samson, shorn as you are!" They jeered him.

Moral: No man loves to think he fears, no man pays Goliath, and if you get a chance to devour basketball, do it – or it will devour you.

• • • • • • • • • • • • • • • • • •

APRIL 13, 1962

A Tribute to Cousy

There are some things that just should not happen, and one of them is that Bob Cousy should never have to walk off a basketball court with tears in his eyes.

And the young man who ran out on the court to take a swipe at him as he did the other night should be taken to the woodshed forthwith.

There were more than 15,000 people in the L.A. Sports Arena two nights this week. If there had been room, there could have been 20,000. I don't know of anybody who can take a deeper bow over this state of affairs than Robert Joseph Cousy.

At his age and status in life, you might expect to walk up to Cousy after he had lost a hard game, ask him if it hurt, and get a wisecrack in reply, "Only when I laugh."

But Cousy's approach to basketball – or anything else – has never been flippant. Bob Cousy is one of the finest athletes and finest gentlemen ever to grace any professional sport. The really magnificent thing is that, after 12 years of gallops up and down a hardwood floor, a confused melange of arenas and crowds and dusty buses and 100 nights a year of hearing "Cousy, you're a bum!" Bob Cousy not only still cares, he cries when he loses.

He was still a little sheepish as I braced him in his dressing room the other night, not over the tears but over the fact, he whirled on his tormentor, who was beating him on the back. "It was just a kid," he said wryly. "I thought it was a man, and I felt bad when I turned and it was just a worked-up kid."

Before Bob Cousy, professional basketball had all the class of a traveling band of snake-oil hucksters. Franchises were jerked out from under the league. The Pistons were in Fort Wayne one part of the season and some other place – or two other places – the rest of it. The players moved by bus or creaky old airplanes Eddie Rickenbacker's Flying Circus wouldn't throw their goggles in. The crowds were just guys waiting for the pool rooms to open.

Cousy brought the electrifying drama of the dribble behind the back, the backward pass, the all-court pass off the dribble and any one of a dozen feats of legerdemain that not only hadn't been thought of as possible but hadn't even been thought of, period. For the first time in history, when someone referred to a "dribbling fool," he meant it as a compliment.

Cousy doesn't even look like a basketball player. He looks like what he also is, an insurance agent. He was even cut from his high school team once. His legs are too heavy. He was what the mariners would call "beamy." But basically, his trouble is that he's built too close to the floor. At 6-1 on the skyline of professional basketball, he's a shack.

But there is little doubt the majestic poise of the Boston Celtics derives in large part from the presence of Cousy. He revived the science of playmaking just at a time when it seemed the pivot man and the overworked pituitary would reduce the game to an endless comedic vaudeville – when a player's only future was stooge for the Globetrotters.

He was as canny as he was good. He led the fast break like the lead kid out the door on the last day of school. On court he had a field of vision like a haddock. The Celt player who was daydreaming was liable to find a basketball sticking in his ear from a Cousy pass thrown while Bob had his back to the target. He specialized in whistling a pass close enough to the ears of a rival to make him flinch enough to open a path for a Cousy drive-up.

Many of the Cousy techniques are standard today. They were revolutionary when Cousy tried them. The business of showing a defense man the ball in one hand, like a shill flashing a pea under a walnut, then switching it quickly to the other hand for the layup has flowered under Baylor. But it may have been planted under Cousy.

Basketball is an endless search for the "open" man today. An orthodox pass will never find him. Cousy has practiced the no-look feed so expertly there have been movements to frisk him for mirrors.

The game will be poorer without Bob Cousy. He's the son of French immigrants whose father had to give up a baronial farm, after the Kaiser burned it down, for a taxicab job in New York. But Bob is genial and approachable, and a man who has given unselfish hours to the promotion not of Bob Cousy, but of the sport generally.

He is decent to the core. His own speech impediment (his "r's" come out "w's," which gave the gagsters a field day with his "Roman Meal Bread" commercials) may be rooted in the fact that he had a two-language communication problem at home. But it made him aware of the shyness of people handicapped in the world. His college thesis was "The Persecution of Minority Groups," and he lived up to its high sound in Raleigh, North Carolina, one year when a hotel turned down his Negro teammate, Chuck Cooper. Cooz got tears in his eyes then, too, from anger. So he called for his bag and rode a sleeper back to New York with Cooper.

As elder statesman of the game, Cooz gets certain privileges-a $35,000 salary, dressing in a head coach's office. But among them should be the right to walk off a court dry-eyed with head held high – to the accompaniment of cheers, not punches in the back.

● ● ● ● ● ● ● ● ● ● ● ● ● ● ● ● ● ●

MARCH 2, 1977

Dr. J's Trick Bag

The incident was almost embarrassing. The player wearing No. 6 grabbed the ball at midcourt. He faked two defensive players sideways, spurted to the basket. Halfway through the key, he began his patented soar to the backboard. It was the celebrated Dr. J, the ultimate basket-ball player, the man who scores more air-to-air baskets than any man who ever played the game. Dr. J began his descent at the basket, poised for a slam-dunk. The ball hit the rim, rolled and then dropped to the floor. No basket.

There was a gasp from the Seattle audience. For a moment all 10 players stared at the ball as if they couldn't believe it. It was like Sandy Koufax serving up a home-run ball to Marv Breeding. O. J. Simpson getting tackled in his own end zone. Ali getting knocked down by Henry Cooper, Chrissie Evert missing a Rosie Casals baseline volley, Notre Dame getting shut out, Dr. Schweitzer bungling an operation. Something that's not supposed to happen.

Julius Erving has 100 dunk shots this season. The rest of the league has 107.

You look at any basketball statistic you want, and Julius Erving has to come out in your mind as a guy between 7 and 8 feet tall with arms he has to lift to keep from scraping the ground. He's airborne so much you figure he must have to file a flight plan with the FAA before every takeoff. He must have an extra eye because he can see 360 degrees in every direction. His hands are just smaller than Rhode Island. He picks up a basketball the way you would pick up an olive. He could rebound a bullet. He probably sings bass and eats with a shovel.

When you see the real Dr. J, you want to call the cops. Clearly, this soft-spoken fellow, barely 6-6, who may weigh 200 pounds, cannot be the scourge of basketball. He's too small to be a forward, too polite to be a superstar, and he would need steps to reach the rim. You would guess Julius Erving to be a 10-points-a-night guard whose specialty is bringing the ball up the floor. Instead, he's almost outdunking the whole league, has more than 500 rebounds and more than 1,100 points.

The Philadelphia 76ers are the New York Yankees or the Notre Dame of basketball. The team you love to hate. They have two of every-thing. Everywhere they go, teams lie in the woods for them. Teams that get bored playing the Chicago Bulls or Milwaukee Bucks get as psyched up for the 76ers as they would for a playoff game.

When Philadelphia, which already had George McGinnis at forward, acquired Dr. J, the experts figured these guys would wear out two basketballs a game, and the nets would begin smoking by the third quarter. It wasn't a team, it was an act, a collection of soloists like an allgirl orchestra – Dr. J and his magic basketball. George McGinnis and his high-wire act. It would be playground basketball. The Rucker Tournament had come to the NBA.

It hasn't worked out that way. And for the Philadelphia 76ers to be winning – they're leading their division, and when they do lose it's usually in overtime – is the nicest thing that could happen to basketball. For their games, unlike most of recent years, do not look like feeding times at the zoo. The 76ers play the closest thing to Dr. James Naismith basketball since the pros took over the good doctor's game. It's a graceful, moving ballet, not a dock fight. People who had forgotten the beauty of the game flocked to 76ers games. You could set Dr. J's moves to Tchaikovsky. It's like a figure-skating final when the Dr. is in his office.

"We have a lot of one-on-one players," admits 76ers coach Gene Shue. "We go to the line a lot, and our game has a very good flow to it. We shoot less than other teams but make more. We do seem to play effortless basketball."

Dr. J assents. "This (the NBA) is the best league that ever existed," he insists. "Just look at the quality of ballplayers out of work, guys who can't crack this league. All the best talent in basketball is playing under one sign now. And our team is marked. Everyone wants to beat the 76ers because we have 10 of the best individual players. We sell out everywhere we go, and the crowd isn't always for the home team. We are building up fans."

Julius Erving is the only player in the NBA who can make the crowd boo the home player who follows him. And when he misses a dunk shot, they want someone prosecuted. The basket must be tilted. It's a sacrilege – like Jack Nicklaus missing a two-foot putt. Or John Wayne getting shot by the Indians.

• • • • • • • • • • • • • • • • •

It's Just Chick Chat

"Front court to Nixon. Dribble around Spanarkel. Bounce pass to Magic. He pumps, fakes. Seventeen-footer, no good! Rebound to Magic! Nice hustle! Give to Cooper. Top of the key to Jamaal. He shoots up a prayer! Air ball! Ladies and gentlemen, I don't believe it! Dawkins has him in a wrist lock. They don't call it! No harm, no foul. Rebound to Kareem. Yo-yoing to the baseline. Around Dawkins. Slam dunk! Wait a minute! They call charging?! I don't believe it! Dawkins has set up light housekeeping in the key, brought the family and a tent and everything, and they call charging?! OK, Jones to the dribble. Ladies and gentlemen, do you and your family want to save on a new set of clothes? Then go this week to Sears...."

A man in the throes of a nervous breakdown? The end of the world? Armageddon? A ride over Niagara Falls in a barrel?

No, just another Saturday basketball game with Francis Dayle Hearn at the mike. Nothing serious. Chick's pulse is a nice, steady 68. His blood pressure is normal. He might even be stifling a yawn. But he sounds like a man in terminal dementia, or one experiencing the onset of St. Vitus' Dance.

They don't pay Chick Hearn to be *blasé*. They don't pay him to understand officiating that goes against the home five. Chick is paid to make pro basketball exciting. And he does this better than anybody in broadcasting, and always has.

Chick doesn't really think a March meeting between the Los Angeles Lakers and the Dallas whatyamacallems is World War III. But neither does he think it's the skins against the shirts in a Poly High gym.

Chick doesn't necessarily tell it like it is. He tells it like it ought to be. Wildly exciting. Sports need dramatizing. Two travelers from

141

Siberia might think Chick was talking in code. But around the NBA, they eat it up. Too many broadcasters sound like two Englishmen at a cricket match. Chick sounds like he's inciting a riot.

In 1961, when owner Bob Short transferred the Minneapolis Lakers to Los Angeles, the club was one jump ahead of the sheriff and foreclosure. The Lakers were lucky to draw the rent. I can remember a Sunday afternoon playoff game that drew all of 2,800 people to the Sports Arena. The top salary in the league in those days was $15,000 and Wilt Chamberlain got it. The game got about the same press that high school soccer got. Playoff games were in junior college gyms. Minor league hockey was a bigger draw.

A phone call from owner Short to a fledgling football announcer in L.A. on the eve of the fifth game of the 1961 playoffs against St. Louis changed all that. The National Basketball Assn. went from pass the hat and "Where will the game be played?" ... "Where would you like it?" to a multimillion-dollar industry. As someone has said, "Wilt Chamberlain went from freak to Farouk."

Chick Hearn could talk fast – and think faster. Chick was an embellisher. For instance, he was in World War II, all right. But he did not parachute in and capture Goering, as he used to love to tell the rookies on the long, boring bus rides through the snow. Neither did he force the Japanese surrender by leading the raid on Tokyo, as he might well tell a bellhop or a cabdriver. Chick was a sergeant in special services. But who wants to hear that?

Like a Republican convention keynote speaker, Chick's function was to view with alarm, not to say sheer terror. To Chick, the cup was always half empty. A 116-90 Laker lead with two minutes to play filled him with dread and foreboding. If Magic Johnson sneezes, Chick has him in intensive care. Jerry West played with a broken nose most of his career, and Chick called it with a broken heart.

Chick talked so fast the game couldn't keep up. Most basketball announcers are telling you what happened two minutes ago. Not Chick. Chick tells you what's going to happen.

He's worth 10 free throws a night to the franchise. Twenty years and 2,000 consecutive games have not slowed his tongue nor dimmed his enthusiasm. Chick is paid well but not excessively. He has enriched the language. "Yo-yoing" is a Hearnism. As is "slam dunk," "dribble drive," "fall-away jumper," "popcorn machine." A "tickytack foul" is any one that goes against the home team.

They're giving Chick a "night" at the Forum this Friday. The Lakers will be playing the Seattle SuperSonics, a team not to be confused with the 1961 Celtics. But Chick will make you think it's the Alamo. Not only L.A. should honor Hearn. The whole league should get in the act. Chick Hearn helped all the clubs, not only Bob Short's Lakers.

The team had its lunch in a bag when Chick started broadcasting. It sold for $5.175 million four years later, and it sold as part of a $68 million package four years after that. Chick made the game. Every guy in it making half a million should be there Friday to doff his hat to the man who made it all possible, who brought the game of pro basketball in from the cold.

• • • • • • • • • • • • • • • • •

May 13, 1986

He Has Them in the Palm Of His Hand

If I were an NBA player, the last sight in the world I would want to see is Magic Johnson coming downcourt with the basketball.

You imagine this is the way the captain of the Titanic must have felt when he saw the iceberg.

It's like seeing Babe Ruth coming to bat with the bases loaded and your fastball gone. It's like having A. J. Foyt in your rearview mirror on the back straight with 10 laps to go. The feeling Al Capone must have had when he got on the intercom and they said, "There's a Mr. Eliot Ness down here to see you. He's got three men with him and he says it's important."

It's like seeing a hand come up out of a coffin, or hearing a wolf outside the castle in the moonlight.

He starts out at 6 feet 9 and 225 pounds, which is frightening enough, but by the time he reaches the top of the key, he begins to look to the defense like something you'd call out the National Guard for while evacuating the women and children. Like something you'd send an expedition for if rumors of its existence reached civilization.

See him now as he brings the ball up the middle. He disdains the feeble efforts of the enemy guards to steal or harass, flicking them away contemptuously as though they were flies buzzing around a lion.

The ball is almost an extension of his hand as he bounces it around him. His eyes sweep the floor. You figure this must be the way Caesar looked over a battlefield or a wise old prizefighter peeked through his gloves. He is probing for weaknesses.

When he finds them, he is galvanized into furious action. He may trigger the fast break, that sudden, seemingly out of control dash to the basket that looks like a prison bustout or a raided craps game.

Or he may whistle one of those 80-m.p.h. passes right by the ear of a defender into the hands of an open man. Or he may throw one of those high lobs to his captain and center in the low post. Or, he may just take off and drive the lane, drawing the foul or making the basket – or both. Or he may just stop, pump and throw in a three-pointer of his own.

Whatever he does, he's as indefensible as a riptide. There is a law of physics that says that for every action, there is an equal and opposite reaction. The great counterpunchers have it, and Magic goes into it instinctively. If the defense comes out, he goes around them. If they stay back, he goes over them.

He doesn't play a game, he choreographs it. "He's like a magnet," his coach, Pat Riley, says of him. "He draws players to him like filings."

He draws a crowd like a guy selling vegetable peelers on a street corner. When enough of them are around him, he knows there's a man open. He finds that man.

He has the peripheral vision of a fish. And he throws the basketball around as if it were a grape. He can curve it, slide it, float it or slam dunk it if he wants. Sometimes he just makes it disappear.

There is no question who is in command when he is out there. He is the high command. He should wear a monocle and spiked helmet. He masterminds an attack like the German general staff going through the Low Countries.

He expects uncompromising obedience. His countenance, normally as clear and untroubled as a sleeping baby's, furrows into annoyance when someone is out of position, that is, not where Magic wants him to be. Even the captain himself, Kareem Abdul-Jabbar, has to find his marks and get to them like an actor for a demanding director.

What he does is not always obvious to the casual fan. It's just that every hometown fan knows that everything is going to be all right if Magic has the ball.

Historians of the future may be hard pressed to understand. Sifting through the sterile artifacts of statistics, the point of this guard may elude them.

Before Magic, the great playmaker of basketball history, the man against whom they measure all others was the great Oscar Robertson.

The Big O had gaudier statistics in his prime. The archeologists may pause at Magic's 18.8 average this year, compared to Oscar's 31.4 one year. They may compare his 1,384 total points this year with Oscar's high-water mark of 2,480. Or his 426 rebounds this year with Oscar's high of 985.

But Oscar was a soloist. Magic is a conductor. Magic gives you a symphony, not an aria. Magic is trying to win a war, not a medal.

The things he did to Houston the other afternoon at the Forum should bring the Geneva Convention down on him. He did everything but pull their fingernails out.

It is customary for the point man in basketball to bring the ball upcourt along the sideline. That way, you can be sure one flank is protected.

Magic brought the ball right up Broadway. He defied anyone to stop him. He invited triple-teaming. He made Houston look like a bunch of guys looking for a collar-button in the dark.

They kept showing up at places Magic had just been. They played their little walk-up game with their skyscraper offense, and they used the whole 24 seconds to try to get off an inside shot. And then Magic would take the ball out of somebody's ear and swish it downcourt for a five-second, or less, basket.

The game was kind of a sleepwalking Alphonse-and-Gaston act midway through the second quarter, and Houston had ambled into a seven-point lead, 41-34.

Magic took the game out of idle. Almost before the minute hand made another sweep, he made Houston look like a bunch of guys who had just seen a spaceship. He not only tied the score, he swept the team into a six-point lead at halftime, and Game 1 was over.

Some people have nightmares about tidal waves, vampires, earthquakes or falling from great heights. If I were a Houston player, I would have nightmares about this big, cheerful young man wearing No. 32, coming at me, bouncing a basketball as if he had some good news he couldn't wait to tell me. You should at least get one call to your priest.

● ● ● ● ● ● ● ● ● ● ● ● ● ● ● ● ●

FEBRUARY 4, 1996

It's Basketball Played On a Higher Plane

You go to see Michael Jordan play basketball for the same reason you went to see Astaire dance, Olivier act or the sun set over Canada. It's art. It should be painted, not photographed.

It's not a game, it's a recital. He's not just a player, he's a virtuoso. Heifetz with a violin. Horowitz at the piano.

He doesn't even play the game where everyone else does. He plays it from the air. He comes in for a landing every now and then, usually from above the basket. Then he stays on the runway for a while till the next takeoff. You get the feeling the other players don't know where he has gone till he cups his mouth and shouts down "Up here!" He should probably be wearing a cape and high boots.

What he's doing is making a shambles of the game of basketball, laying waste to the landscape. He's as unstoppable as tomorrow.

Many people were wishing he could hit the curveball. Let pitchers worry about stopping him instead of NBA guards. While he was gone, Hakeem Olajuwon took over. But while Hakeem is a great player, he pretty much plays a ground game. He's infantry. He slogs to the basket. Jordan is more like a stealth bomber. You can't see him coming, and you don't know where he is until you hear the swish of the net.

It's hard to believe this talent wasn't the No. 1 pick in his draft year. You wonder how a general manager could justify passing him up. You get a picture of the GM telling his owner, "Aw, he's just a baseball player. We need somebody to go to the basket – like Sam Bowie. Besides, he's too short."

When you see the numbers Jordan puts up, you might, at that, expect to see someone 7-feet-7 or so, with the steroid musculature of a bouncer, a master of the two-foot basket. But Jordan looks more like a ballroom dancer than a bouncer. His muscles ripple, they don't bulge. He's only 6-6. Until he's airborne, that is. Then he becomes 20 feet. He has to watch out for the rafters, not defensive guards.

He doesn't stand around in the low post waiting for someone to go get him the ball. He goes and gets it himself. He gets more steals than a pickpocket at the Kentucky Derby and led the league in them his last full season.

He came into town Friday night for the most publicized confrontation since the second Dempsey-Tunney. It came out more like the second Louis-Schmeling.

Michael Jordan vs. Magic Johnson was supposed to have all the dramatic impact of the Red Baron vs. Eddie Rickenbacker, or any of the other great matchups of history. But the matchup it resembled at the end was the Titanic against the iceberg. It was as one-sided as a heart attack.

We were supposed to get a clue as to whether Magic could be enrolled in the crusade to save basketball from the ravages of Air Jordan and company.

Not yet, at any rate. Magic didn't even have time to get the number of the truck that hit him. The Bulls put their resident Goldilocks – otherwise known as Dennis Rodman – on Magic. Meanwhile, Michael acted as resident decoy, drawing traps while he casually passed the ball to an open Scottie Pippen, who plays the game at treetop level himself.

The job of stopping Michael Jordan and his Bulls now falls on Olajuwon and Shaquille O'Neal. Anything short of their best, and the league may need an anti-aircraft battery to stop him.

The league may have to resort to drastic Break-Up-Michael-Jordan rules. I mean, here is a team that is 41-3 and hasn't lost in 18 (count 'em) games.

They may want to consider leveling the court by 1) making it illegal for him to make a basket without one foot (or both) on the ground; 2) making it a two-shot foul and no basket for any player to rise vertically more than eight feet above the floor; 3) ruling that any basket made by a player who is horizontal to the floor at the time shouldn't count.

Of course, you could make any Michael Jordan basket count only one point and let him go to the free throw line only if he had to get there by stretcher or on life support. Perhaps they could rule Jordan could have the ball only every other team possession.

They should make these rules retroactive. Anything short of that and the season is over. Jordan's Chicago Bulls are sitting there with a .930 (you heard me) won-lost percentage when the highest winning percentage in the history of the game was .841 by the 1971-72 Lakers.

There are few players of whom it could be said they swallowed the game they played whole. Babe Ruth did it. Bill Tilden. A case could be made for John Unitas, a young Wayne Gretzky.

But the way Michael Jordan is going, there may be nothing left of the game but a loud belch. He and his Bulls are feasting on the league like Henry VIII on a chicken, bones and all.

"Man, they're scary!" Magic Johnson exclaimed as he escaped Friday night like a guy who had just crawled ashore from a torpedoed ship.

If the Bulls can scare Magic Johnson, they're in the wrong arena. We should send them to Bosnia. Maybe the league should find out where it goes to surrender.

● ● ● ● ● ● ● ● ● ● ● ● ● ● ● ● ● ●

MAY 17, 1992

L.A.'s Showtime Becomes Crunchtime in New York

The Lakers called him "Riles." The Knicks call him "Coach."

In a profession – pro basketball – where protocol, for some unknown reason, calls for the coach to dress as formally as a Wall Street stockbroker, Riles goes them one better. He looks as if he's on his way to pose for a GQ cover. His pants are pleated and razor-pressed. He has a contract with an Italian clothes designer. His wardrobe is color-coordinated. His shirts are white-on-white and tailored for him. His shoes are London's best. His tie matches. He exudes dignity.

His hair is slicked back and oiled in the style that hasn't been popular since Rudolph Valentino's time. He is an educated man. He was a (journeyman) player himself, but his conversation is not peppered with the vulgarisms of the locker room.

He is a supremely organized man. Patrick James Riley does not like surprises.

He became a coach by accident. He was summoned from the broadcasting booth (where his dialogue consisted mostly of "Yes, Chick") to be assistant coach when a near-fatal accident befell Jack McKinney, and then he became head coach in the fall of '81 when a player mutiny 11 games into the season deposed the new head coach, Paul Westhead.

Riley was supposed to be an interim coach. Nine division championships and four NBA championships later, he was being hailed as coach of the year.

Still, Pat Riley felt underestimated, unappreciated. The attitude of most was, "Sure, he won all those championships – who wouldn't with Magic Johnson and Kareem Abdul-Jabbar?"

It was never a surface thing, but its periscope was always sticking out of the water. When Abdul-Jabbar left and the Lakers got eliminated in the semifinals of the playoffs, the wise guys said, "See!" But Riley's team won 63 games that year, tops in the league.

He cut the cord himself and drifted back into broadcasting. But the networks wanted him to be a clown, strident, assertive – everything but paper hats and noisemakers. Everything Riley isn't.

Not the Riley style. Riley's image ran more to Father Flanagan than Red Skelton. He was as serious as the secretary of state.

When the rumors began to spread of his putative return to coaching – with the New York Knicks – well-meaning friends thought it was the worst idea they ever heard. Better to leave his record where it was, they advised, than risk it with the unpredictable Knicks.

The Knicks were not a team, they were an embarrassment, a collection of underachievers. Half a dozen coaches had tried to make sense out of them. They had had losing seasons 11 out of 16 seasons, and they were 39-43 last year.

They had one good player, but the evidence was, Patrick Ewing was becoming discouraged, too – to the point where he was trying to implement a clause in the fine print of his contract that would let him become a free agent if four or more players in the league made more money than he did.

Riley let it be known: no Patrick Ewing, no deal. Riley knew the Knicks were a challenge enough. He didn't want to have to change water into wine.

Riley knew that, with Ewing, he had half a basketball team already. He rolled up the sleeves of his $200 shirt and set to finding the other half.

In L.A., Riley's teams were famous for their Showtime glitz and dazzle. It wasn't a team, it was a chorus line. They should have worn net stockings. They came down the court like a Busby Berkeley revue. You could set it to music.

The Knicks were ditch diggers by comparison. They brought the ball upcourt like a load of coal.

So Riley set about to recasting his thinking. He built a team that was as suited to the NFL as the NBA. It wasn't Showtime, it was Crunchtime. The basketball version of three-yards-and-a-cloud-of-dust. The Knicks, so to speak, elbowed their way into the playoffs.

Everyone said the Chicago Bulls would fly through the playoffs without a defeat. They were the defending champions and clearly the class of the league. They had Michael Jordan, who walked to work on the Chicago River every day.

The Bulls had blown the Knicks out of the playoffs last year in straight sets. In fact, they only lost two games in the entire playoffs.

They were supposed to do it again this year.

But a funny thing happened to the Chicago Bulls in Chicago Stadium opening night. First of all, they only scored 89 points – which is 20 below their season average. Ordinarily, Michael Jordan can score that many himself.

And then they lost the game – to the New York Knicks, who hadn't beaten them all year.

The Bulls haven't scored 100 points in any game in this series yet.

The Knicks, who don't usually need 100, got that many Thursday night.

Perhaps you saw Thursday's game. That was vintage Knicks home game this year. The Knicks have reclaimed the sidewalks of New York. For years, it's been a snarly home crowd ("OK, how are youse gonna lose it tonight, ya bums?") No more.

To have taken the Chicago Bulls and the Archangel Michael to seven games is glory enough, even if the brass knuckles don't work one more time today.

Patrick is living the life of Riley again. So when the New York tabloids trumpet that they owe it all to "St. Patrick," don't be so sure they mean Ewing.

● ● ● ● ● ● ● ● ● ● ● ● ● ● ● ● ●

JANUARY 14, 1965

Game Is Russell's

ST. LOUIS – An "All-Star" basketball game is like a John Wayne movie. The only reason you need all those extra people around is because the script calls for them.

It's really a recital for 10 fingers and two legs. All those other guys are spearcarriers who will get shot by the second reel, dress extras who have to turn in their wardrobe by nightfall.

The game of basketball belongs to William Felton Russell. He rules it the way Russia rules Bulgaria – without seeming to. He asserts his might the way a Central Park mugger might. It is to his advantage that you not know he's there until the right precise moment when he can separate you from your senses – and the ball.

Against him, the Big "O" is just a big zero. Wilt Chamberlain is just a pituitary freak. Any guy with a basketball is just a baby with a lollipop, little Red Riding Hood in the forest.

William Felton Russell dominates his sport as no man in history – not Ruth, Dempsey, Jim Brown or Bill Tilden. What they did was spectacular, dramatic. What Bill Russell does is as unnoticeable as pick-pocketing, and just as effective. Sometimes you don't know till you check your pocket you've been had.

Some years ago, in a burst of zeal and arithmetic at an All-Star game, I totted up the best nights of some five basketball players who would be opposite Emperor Russell, and the total came to just under 400. I figured if they showed up sober, they couldn't help scoring at least 200 points. I predicted the game's first 200-point night.

By the time Bill Russell got through with them, they were lucky they could walk to the locker room without a cane.

It is a serious vexation to basketball. If you must have a superhero, it is to a sport's advantage that he be history's leading ground-gainer, or a one-punch knockout artist, or the man who hit 70 home runs a season. Bill Russell does what he does as unobtrusively as the groundskeeper or the guy who knits up the basket. If YOU can see him do it, he's slowing up. Because not even the guy he does it to can be sure. All he knows is that he had it (the basketball) a minute ago. And what the hell happened to it beats him.

To tell the truth, it's not terribly much fun. Bill Russell is playing a recital that can be heard by only a few dogs' ears. It's a subsonic pitch. You never even know he's been there till you see the scoreboard. And then it doesn't take Scotland Yard. His fingerprints are figuratively around the throat of every team that ever took the floor against him.

When Russell was in college some years ago, an eastern magazine that prided itself on having its nerve center in New York but its eyes, ears and fingers all around the rest of the world loudly ignored Bill Russell. "He's averaging only six points a game," they grandly informed their informant. The coach at Bill Russell's university was helpless with laughter when he heard the quote.

When he gained control of himself, he demanded the names of the eastern players who were burning the nets – in this case, Hal "King"

Lear and Tom Gola. "I want to send them 'get well' cards when Russ gets through with them in the NCAA," he announced.

Bill Russell is Wellington at Waterloo, Grant at Richmond, the Russians at Stalingrad. He is where the war ends. In all the slow processes of history, defense always conquers in the end. Bill Russell is The End.

He's almost the first athlete in history to compete in a goatee. He comes on court looking like a figure from a Balkan postage stamp. He could play in the nude and wear a spiked helmet, for all the Boston Celtics would care.

He has changed the game to a point where coaches no longer ask "What's his average?" but instead want to know "Never mind can he make a shot, what I want to know is, can he block one?"

He has driven more people into retirement than old age. He has rattled chromosomes, destroyed confidence, has dammed up more rivers of talent than anyone in sports since Lefty Grove or Christy Mathewson.

He has made more coaches geniuses. Red Auerbach never lights up a cigar until a game is safely in hand, and already his friends are warning him to cut down on his smoking.

He has been responsible for the "goaltending" rule in the game because without it, basketball would go two years without a basket when Russell was playing.

The Boston Celtics had Cousy, Sharman, Ramsey, Auerbach, Easy Ed Macauley and quite a few hard cases before they had Russell. But since Russell, they have made the New York Yankees look like a team of in-and-outers. Basketball's play would seem to be to take up a collection and send him to Elba. Because, with Russell, everybody else is fighting for second place. He is the bewhiskered spider under the basket, he is mischief afoot, he sucks up basketballs like a vacuum cleaner with a beard.

"With Russell," a veteran who doesn't want to be quoted told me, "you only hope he doesn't eat you. Some night, when he's up for the game, they're going to have to count the players."

No one at any time has dominated his profession as W. F. Russell has. He is Henry Ford at an assembly line, Abraham Lincoln at a platform, Babe Ruth with a bat, Jim Brown with a football. He is genius in his BVDs. He has shaved a thousand points a year from a court game that was on its way to breaking down every adding machine in the country until he came along. If he gets any better, they may make him play blindfolded. Even then, he will be 6-to-5 to block 90% of the shots. Even then, the registered superstars of the game will still go around scouring the floor on their hands and knees demanding irritatedly of the referee, "Did you see a ball around here someplace? I had it only a moment ago."

He is Bill Russell, and he owns the game of basketball as no one ever has before and as no one ever will again. He is all alone for his time and his specialty as Shakespeare, Caesar – or Brigitte Bardot. But if you want to see him in action, you better look quick. He doesn't do encores. He is like the shell man at a carnival – or a porchclimber. His wealth lies in his invisibility. He is the only 6-foot-9-inch pickpocket in the country. He doesn't steal a watch. He steals Big Ben with the bobbies watching.

• • • • • • • • • • • • • • • • • •

JUNE 19, 1986

He's More Than a Footnote To the Celtics' Title Season

CARLSBAD – "Hello, I'm Bill Walton of the Boston Celtics," the man said, thrusting out a huge paw and smiling sincerely through his shock of unruly hair.

As if such an introduction were necessary, weren't superfluous, redundant. As if there were another 6-foot 11-inch redhead with size-15 tennis shoes and three-foot arms and the long, loose limbs of a basketball player at large on the grounds of the La Costa Hotel and Spa.

You had a picture of another well-known figure coming up to you and saying, "Hi, I'm Ronald Reagan!" Or, "Hi, there, my name is Adolf Hitler." Or, "Excuse me, I'm Robert Redford. I'm an actor."

William Theodore Walton, who is appearing at La Costa in the guise of a tennis player at a sports celebrity tournament this week, is not the type of guy who has to go around wearing a name tag, like a conventioneer from Dubuque falling out of an elevator with "Call Me Joe" pinned to his lapel.

His is one of the more recognizable silhouettes in the skyline of sports. You don't have to run to a schematic drawing as if he were a D-class enemy destroyer and you were an Air Force spotter. There are not too many human beings of his carrot-topped configuration.

If he were standing under a basket on a parquet floor holding a ball and wearing a green-and-white uniform with 32 on its back, you could recognize him with a bag over his head.

There is a large body of thought in this country holding that Bill Walton, healthy, was the best player of basketball this sport has ever seen – better, when fit, than Wilt Chamberlain, Kareem Abdul-Jabbar, Bill Russell, Larry Bird, Magic Johnson and Dr. J. Certainly, as good.

They base it on some kind of private hocus-pocus of their own, and assouredly on personal observation. Because roundball historians of the future are going to be hard put to reconcile that point of view with the evidence at hand, the cold statistics.

Bill Walton's 10-year point total – fewer than 6,000 – is not only a far cry from Abdul-Jabbar's nearly 35,000 or Chamberlain's 31,419 but also suggests more of a mop-up player or a substitute off-guard than one of the league's all-time best.

The problem is, basketball cannot be played with glass feet, and Bill's were made out of some of the finest stemware this side of a champagne cellar. Crystal by Waterford. You need the underpinnings of a locomotive to be able to chug up and down a hardwood floor every 24 seconds every night.

Had Walton had the metatarsals of a high jumper, he might have had to go to a higher league. When he could stand without grimacing, the basketball floor usually belonged to him.

He won NBA championships 10 years and a continent apart, in Portland in 1976-77 and in Boston in 1985-86. In between, he was in an orthopedic ward. He missed three seasons altogether and parts of most others. He played in 14 games one year and in 33 another.

In the geriatric explosion of 1986 – the Shoemaker Derby, the Nicklaus Masters and the Floyd Open – the reincarnation of Bill Walton, who'll be 34 this year, is almost more remarkable. At least, none of the others had to interrupt a career on five different occasions in recent years.

Walton had given up on the Clippers, and most of the league had given up on Walton, and on the crystalware on the ends of his legs, when the '85-86 season started. The Lakers were uninterested. Only the Boston Celtics would even come to the phone. Canny old Red Auerbach was intrigued.

The NBA operates under a wages-hours-and-working-conditions plan unique in the history of labor relations. It's called a salary cap. It is designed to keep employers, i.e., owners, from doling out to their employees, i.e., players, more than the employers can afford. Employers historically have never had that trouble, but in the wacky wonderful world of sport, where winning is everything, money isn't anything.

Walton and the Celtics had to circumvent the salary cap by having him forgo his free agency and go back on the Clippers' head count so he could be "traded" to Boston for Cedric Maxwell. Walton did.

The Celtics didn't need much. In Walton, they were getting plenty. One of the greatest players of all time would only have to call on his remembered skills for brief stretches at a time, spelling the center, Robert Parish, who had played 159 of 164 games and all but a handful of minutes the two previous years.

With Walton around, Parish never had to pace himself. And neither did the Celtics.

It was Walton who won the pivotal fourth game of the championship final in Houston. Unaccustomedly called into the game in the waning minutes, with the score seesawing back and forth, a time when the young Rockets usually start to overpower tired rivals, Walton took charge.

He plunged after a rebound, rescued it from a sea of red-numbered jerseys, swept out, turned – and threw in the shot that nailed the season for the Rockets. If they had won that game, and without Walton they would have, they likely would have gone back to the Boston Garden with a 3-2 lead. Instead, they went back in their coffins.

Even with a tennis racket in his hand, Bill Walton does not need a name tag – or have to stick his hand out and identify himself like a guy running for office. Anybody with a television set knows who he is now. In Boston, he ranks with the Lowells and Cabots and the cod. The Kennedys might not want to ride in the same car.

Even on the White House lawn, he might not have to introduce himself. If he starts, his greeter will interrupt: "I know who you are. You're Bill Walton of the Celtics. But who's that actor with you?"

● ● ● ● ● ● ● ● ● ● ● ● ● ● ● ● ● ● ●

APRIL 27, 1969

It's a Bird! A Man! A Car! A Bullet! ... It's ...

The first time you see Jerry West, you're tempted to ask him how are things in Gloccamorra. The Lakers didn't draft him; they found him – under a rainbow. Either that, or they left a trail of bread crumbs in the forest and then snapped the cage when he showed up.

There are those who swear Jerry arrives for work every day by reindeer. He wears the perpetually startled expression of a guy who just heard a dog talk. He doesn't walk anywhere – he darts. He has the quickest hands and feet ever seen on a guy without a police record. If they put a cap on him sideways and turned him loose on the streets of London, there wouldn't be a wallet in town by nightfall.

He can hang in the air like Mary Poppins. It would take a week to hang him. He could play Peter Pan without wires. Some night he's going to go up for a jump shot in the first period – and they're going to have to get the Fire Department to get him down.

His nose has been broken so many times, he sneezes through his ears. Cigarette smoke would come out of his nostrils in corkscrew patterns. His septum is so deviated, he's breathing YESTERDAY's air. He goes through life with such a s-w-o-o-s-h that there are only a few people certain what color he is.

Inch for inch, he's the greatest basketball player in the world. There is no more exciting sight in the world of sports than Jerry West dervishing down court with a basketball, eyes and nose flaring, basketball thumping. His shots are a blur.

He's such a bundle of exploding nervous energy that by the end of the season, they don't need a chest X-ray. They just hold him up to the light. If you put a picture on him, you could send him as a postcard. Jerry wasn't born, he was pressed. A steamroller would miss most of him.

He can hit a golf ball 300 yards (with a 2-wood) and be there when it comes down. He would make one of pro football's great defensive backs. He could play the outfield like Willie Mays if they could get him to stand still in one place that long.

He was born to play basketball. If, indeed, he was born. "Cabin Creek, West Virginia" sounds like such a suspicious natal place that some people check to see if there's a flying saucer depot nearby.

He is a nine-year veteran in the league but he always looks like a kid getting his first sight of Disneyland. A guy asked to guard him sometimes feels as if he had spent the night in a revolving door in the dark, but Jerry has never even had a cross word with an opponent. If he has an enemy in this world, it's news to him – and the enemy.

He has arms so long he could drive a car from the backseat. No one has ever caught him asleep. He's as democratic as a panhandler. He chats with anyone. He talks as fast as he runs. When he first came up, his mountain twang was such – spoken so rapidly, he began his sentences in the middle and worked his way to both ends simultaneously – that it was understandable only to hunting dogs, canaries and certain woods animals.

He had a brother killed in Korea and has never been able to find a mere game worth complaining about since, not even in late season when he is so exhausted pigeons try to feed him. He even eats fast. He shops so fast he can get a complete wardrobe and take the same elevator back down. He's supposed to be injury-prone but he has NEVER missed a playoff game. He's so modest, game journalists avoid him after his good nights. "Talk to Jerry and you'll wind up KNOCKING him for an all-time scoring night," a regular once warned.

His play in the opening playoff game against the Celts last week was, to understate it badly, historic. In the presence of a dozen of the game's greatest scorers, one of every four points was thrown in by Jerry West. "It was such a good game I wish I could have seen it!" glowed Jerry afterward, ignoring the fact that he had left smoke coming out of both baskets.

A lot of the Celts assigned to guard Jerry wish they could have seen it, too. Like a lot of people, they figure Jerry is a figment of someone's imagination, like the Easter Bunny, Santa Claus, leprechauns and witches. And, as soon as they can find it, they're going to hide his broom.

● ● ● ● ● ● ● ● ● ● ● ● ● ● ● ● ● ●

AUGUST 10, 1972

Hoosier Hotshot

You picture the man who is, demonstrably, the world's greatest basketball coach, and there comes to view a guy with lots of diamonds on stubby fingers, a Rolls-Royce illegally parked outside the gym with his driver reading a comic book in the front seat. Guys leap to light his cigarettes, the president of the college is on the phone seeking an appointment, maybe so is the president of the United States. He is doing a commercial, dictating a book, getting a manicure, reserving a table at Scandia for lunch, and two 7-foot phenoms from the sidewalks of New York are cooling their heels in the outer office waiting for an audition and/or a scholarship.

Then you meet John Wooden and he is answering his own phone, he clips his nails with a drugstore clipper, his haircut has a faint bunkhouse bowl look to it, his clothes are less Savile Row than bought-with-a-coupon, and the whole thing cries out for a Grant Wood brush, not a shrill sports column.

John Wooden is American Gothic to the collar button. You meet him and you're tempted to say, "All right, what did you do with the pitchfork, John?" You can smell the hay if you close your eyes. Players might call other coaches "The Baron" or "The Bear" but they call John "The Reverend."

His walls are awash with homilies, exhortations of the spirit, words-to-live-by. He's as homespun as calico, as small- town as a volunteer fire department. He doesn't juggle oil wells or cattle deals or tax shelters. He doesn't even own his own house. He has turned down $100,000 contracts to coach the pros.

He looks like the kind of guy you could get to guess which walnut has the pea under it. The eyes are a kind of a guileless blue, and the conversation is sprinkled with "Oh, my goodness!" and "Gracious!" and you bet he could never figure out how they sawed the lady in half, or got the rabbit into the hat. They run carnivals for guys like this, you feel sure. He'd buy a watch from an 8th Avenue auctioneer, or a vegetable slicer from a sidewalk pitchman.

Yet this is a man whose basketball teams have won more than 1,000 games over the years, and who is sitting on the crest of six national championships in a row.

It is a conceit of our times that kids are supposed to be manageable only by their peer groups, that they are in headlong rebellion from any other authority and, the postulate has it, there is no way a street kid from Philadelphia or a blacktop player from Lexington Avenue could relate to a Bible reader from Indiana who coaches by wall motto. In a time when training table mutinies are as commonplace as any other forms of campus unrest, Wooden has managed to put together title teams from elements as diverse as a Democratic ticket. People thought the playground players would take one look at Coach Wooden and say, "Is that a name or a description?" and take the next bus back to where the words on the walls aren't out of Edgar A. Guest.

Wooden built championship teams when he had to practice in dingy second-floor gyms in between the Greco-Roman wrestlers, the trampoline gymnasts, the girls in leotards, and even the glee club practice and the pompom girls. He played in Venice High gyms, on City College parking lots and at auditoriums built for auto shows, not zone presses.

His monument is the 13,000-seat Pauley Pavilion at UCLA. It is also the 10-man squad of alumni who will contest the "Elgin Baylor Pro Stars" at Pauley Pavilion Friday night, a team that will include Kareem Abdul-Jabbar, Henry Bibby, Lucius Allen, Sidney Wicks, Curtis Rowe, Abdul Rahman (ne Walt Hazzard) and a team that might easily win the NBA any year. The game will benefit the Ralph Bunche Scholarship Fund at UCLA.

Someday this empire may fall to a diamonds-on-the-fingers type who will keep a staff manicurist, a bar in the office and a picture of Raquel Welch where the "Pyramids of Success" or "The Tree of Self-Realization" is now framed. If so, he'd better turn John Wooden's picture to the wall – unless he wants to draw that frown and icy glare of disapproval that guys who draw charging fouls or show up for preseason practice with tender feet are so familiar with.

Boxing

• • • • • • • • • • • • • • • •

APRIL 27, 1967

Louisville Loudmouth
Secedes From the Union

There is a stillness at Appomattox, all right. The bugles of Shiloh lie mute.

The campfires on the Potomac have all burned out. The blood in the Rappahannock has all gone to sea.

The caissons no longer rot in the sun at Gettysburg. The trumpets in the dust of Bull Run are silted over.

Muffle the drums of Vicksburg. Bottle the fleets of Farragut. Call the roll of Chancellorsville, Fredericksburg, the Wilderness, Antietam.

Spike the guns of Sumter. Hobble the horses of Sheridan. Listen no more to the ghostly tread of Sherman's marchers to the sea.

Dismantle the gallows at Harper's Ferry. Burn the banners of the noblest cause man ever fought for. Scuttle the ironclads. Drop no flowers in the watery resting place of the Monitor off Hatteras.

Put the torch to Uncle Tom's Cabin. Flog Uncle Tom. It's OK. No one likes him anymore. Set the bloodhounds on Little Liza. Who cares?

Scrap the Gettysburg Address. It's just another piece of Fourth of July oratory, campaign promises, high-blown histrionics. Hang it up, Abe. Nobody's listening. Tell it to John Wilkes Booth.

"The world will little note, nor long remember, what we say here." Right, Abe! "But it can never forget what they did here." Oh? Yes, it can, Abe.

You see, Cassius Marcellus Clay, one of the greatest heroes in the history of his people, has decided to secede from the Union. He will not disgrace himself by wearing the uniform of the Army of the United States. He will not fight "a white man's war."

Not for all the gangrene in Andersonville will he march. From the safety of 103 years, he waves his fist at dead slave owners. Down to his last four Cadillacs, the thud of Communist jackboots holds no dread for him. He is in this country but not of it. His only contact with America is by closed circuit. The devil is a white man. And vice versa.

After 100 years of freedom, he sulks. "We don't own no railroads." The attar of truth perfumes his charges. But only the scent. You buy railroads at the stock exchange the same way you buy silk shirts at the store. Clay has preferred to buy a religion, not New York Central. But don't give us freedom, give us railroads.

So turn off the watchfires of the night. Send OUR sword to Bobby Lee. Tell Jubal Early there's been a terrible mistake. Apologize to the 70,000 dead along the Rapidan. Cover the trenches of Petersburg. Tell those who fell in the "gloomy thickets of Chickamauga," we're sorry. Come back, Gen. Rosecrans. You've been outflanked by a Louisville loudmouth. The Bill of Rights has been mugged.

Wave no poppies for Soldier Clay. John Brown's body may lie a-moldering in his grave, but Cassius' won't. Strip the laurel from the graves of the Blue. Let the willow wave over the GAR and the Gray like.

When lilacs last in the door-yard bloom'd and the great star early droop'd in the western sky in the night, this legatee of Lincoln picked up his sword – and ran it through his country's breast. The last full measure of his devotion. Twenty-five million of his people watched silently. He has posed a dreadful moral dilemma for them. Uncle Toms? Or render the Union again? Serve or smite?

You were right, Abe. "We cannot consecrate – we can not hallow." It is "far above our poor power." The point needs your wisdom: Is it our fault? Or his? Has he dishonored the dead? Or have we? Were we all listening when you said "that from these honored dead we take increased devotion to that cause for which they gave the last full measure of devotion – that we here highly resolve that these dead shall not have died in vain – that this nation, under God, shall have a new birth of freedom"?

One of us wasn't listening. Which is why no leaves stir at Appomattox. But the blood still caulks the rocks at Shiloh.

• • • • • • • • • • • • • • • • •

MAY 4, 1976

The Greatest Show on Earth: Muhammad Ali

Well, I see the Muhammad Ali traveling medicine show and snake oil team has been through town again. As usual, it leaves a whole lot of guys banging themselves on the side of the head to be sure they were seeing right.

I swear, the champ should run his gift with a calliope and a barker proclaiming it the Greatest Show on Earth. Ali is about as predictable as a chorus girl.

You never know whether you're going to get Hamlet or the Marx Brothers. Whether it's going to be sitcom or one of those disaster movies. Ali is one of the world's foremost quick change artists. You can never be sure whether it'll be Edwin Booth or a booth fighter, whether he's going to show up in baggy pants and a nose that lights up, or whether he's out to kill.

It's "The Perils of Pauline" every time he straps on the gloves. Jimmy Young is a heavyweight of considerable indistinction. He ranks in ferocity somewhere between Ali's shadow and the heavy bag. He makes his fight like a guy trying to creep down a fire escape.

Muhammad Ali almost made him the 26th heavyweight champion of the world. Mack Sennett should choreograph Ali's fights. Were the Keystone Kops any funnier? Laurel and Hardy?

The trouble with Ali is, he'd rather be Grimaldi than grim. He'd rather make people laugh than bleed. He really should hit people with rubber bladders. I wouldn't be surprised if he pulled out a seltzer bottle and began squirting opponents in the best traditions of Minsky's some night. Or he might lace on a couple of custard pies instead of mitts.

I can't understand why people take him so seriously. Maybe he should have a laugh track so they could get the idea. Poor Howard Cosell gets shrill with indignation by the fifth round. Dick Young gets hot under the collar. He laughs at all the wrong places. Doesn't anybody have a sense of humor anymore? What does Ali have to do? Stop in the middle of a round and explain, "These are the jokes, son?"

In the first place, Jimmy Young vs. Muhammad Ali is a one-liner already. Getting indignant about it is like getting indignant when all those midgets come pouring out of a clown's car in the circus and want the driver cited.

I guess he'll have to learn to flutter his eyebrows like Groucho or stop and ask the sourpusses at ringside, "Am I going too fast for you?" I would guess Ali's idol would not be Jack Dempsey or Jack Johnson but Jack Benny, Don Rickles. He's like Sid Caesar pretending he's speaking German. Ali is pretending he's fighting, but he's milking it for laughs. It's a comedy dance act.

You take him seriously, he'll drive you crazy. He can be the Killer of Kinshasa against a George Foreman, but against the Lion of Flanders he's Henny Youngman.

I remember one time Ali came to town and took the podium to denounce a reporter in ringing prose for writing something unfriendly. I took the bait, and in a few minutes I was in his room sputtering with outraged innocence, offering to continue to God-knows-what charity if I was wrong.

Ali lay on the bed with round-eyed innocence, then quietly pulled the offending column out from under the covers. It was one written not the week before, as he had indicated, but years before. No matter. He rolled all over the floor, roaring with laughter. He had set the scene up with a room full of his followers, some hiding behind the curtains. He got more kick out of that little game than he did beating Ken Norton the next night.

He's more mischievous than malicious. But he's one of the world's great showmen. Who else could get a fight with Jimmy Young (Jimmy

Young!?) on page one all over the world? He regards an opponent as a straight man, and a fight as a useless interruption of an otherwise marvelous comedic career. The best part of the act is the way everybody keeps getting annoyed at him. That's the very essence of true comedy. Shakespeare would have understood Ali perfectly. But I'm afraid we ringside wretches aren't Shakespeares.

● ● ● ● ● ● ● ● ● ● ● ● ● ● ● ● ● ● ●

JUNE 6, 1996

He Doesn't Look Right – Until He Gets in the Ring

LAS VEGAS – Oscar De La Hoya is too good to be true. I mean, he's more priest than pug, more altar boy than home boy.

Look at him! You ever see a prizefighter like him? Even Dempsey bragged a little. Joe Louis too.

Not our Oscar. First of all, he barely talks above a whisper anyway. He always says the right thing. He seems almost wistful. As if he were smelling flowers or saying his breviary in a monastery. He says things so softly it's almost as if he were in confession.

Anyway, he's too pretty. Not a hair out of place. Smooth skin. Ears not swollen, lips not busted.

Pugs aren't supposed to be like this. De La Hoya even has a good word for guys he knocked into the seats. He's going to fight Julio Cesar Chavez on Friday night at Caesars Palace and, to hear him talk, you'd really think he just came hoping to get his autograph. Julio Cesar is his idol, he tells you. It's an honor to be in the same ring with him. Hell, the same room!

That's no way for a pug to talk. Pugs are supposed to say, "I'll moider da bum!" as Tony Galento used to. They're even meant to say in controversies over referees: "All he has to do is be able to count to 10." De La Hoya, in a similar controversy over judges, only said politely: "Maybe they won't have to vote on a winner." In other words, somebody will knock somebody out. Oscar didn't say who. Oscar shies away from controversy.

Even Muhammad Ali brought opponent-insulting to a high degree, an art form. George Chuvalo was "the Washerwoman," Floyd Patterson was "the Thud at the End of the Third Round," and Sonny Liston was "the Big Ol' Ugly Bear." He said the only thing Chuck Wepner would prove in the fight was that he was type-A. Liston once growled of an opponent, "If he runs, I'll cripple 'im, if he comes to me, I'll kill 'im."

Even though he wasn't given to opponent-baiting, Joe Louis once said, "He can run but he can't hide."

Pre-fight news conferences have taken on the aspects of a dock fight of late. Riddick Bowe even started to punch out an opponent at one. At the very least, the boasting and threatening gets in the high decibels.

Oscar De La Hoya's sound like Geneva peace conferences. No one raises his voice, least of all Oscar. Mutual admiration societies. They should have teacups.

You get the feeling Julio Cesar Chavez would like to launch a few missiles. In fact, does. But since he doesn't speak English, by the time the translation is haltingly made, some of the venom is lost.

Oscar just smiles sunnily. He's almost apologetic about what he's going to do. This-is-going-to-hurt-me-more-than-it-is-you syndrome. The father to the woodshed.

He's younger, prettier, faster and bigger than Julio. What more could you want? So why is all the money pouring into the Caesars Palace books on the eve of their fight here?

Well, for one thing, the odds were attractive – 3 to 1 on Oscar. For another thing, Julio has one edge. And it's a big one – experience.

Julio Cesar Chavez was probably the most damaging sub-heavyweight the fight game has seen since Henry Armstrong. His punches hurt, and he threw them with a will. He was as undiscourageable as an insurance salesman, as hard to hurt as a telephone pole. And he loved to fight.

There is some question Oscar loves it that much. He talks vaguely of becoming an architect. Or maybe archbishop.

He's a traitor to his craft. He has never been hauled up on charges for breaking a barroom mirror. Or a cop's jaw. I mean, who does he think he is, Mother Teresa? So far as anyone knows, Oscar never even stole a Hershey bar. What kind of a record is that for a champion? It's un-American.

The guess here is, he became a fighter because he looked like such easy pickings to the street gangsters. I mean, Oscar probably looked as if he were bringing an apple for the teacher. A Mama's boy.

You love to reflect on what might have happened when those thugs got too close. And got their first samples of the Pretty Boy De La Hoya left hooks and right crosses. You imagine a lot of them were eating through a straw for weeks.

Because, make no mistake about it, whether he likes it or not, Oscar De La Hoya can fight. And one way you know is by his face. It's unmarked. And this is the only American who won an Olympic gold medal in boxing at Barcelona and who has had 21 tough professional fights. Fighters like this used to be called "Baby Face." Jimmy McLarnin comes to mind. Ali used to complain, "I'm too pretty to be fighting these big ol' ugly bears." Gene Tunney looked as if his sport should be crew.

If he beats Chavez, Oscar may not have much more to learn in the ring. Out of it is another thing. He should learn to scowl a lot. Travel around with an entourage. Trash his opponent.

Talking trash has become an American hallmark. It has been a major part of basketball and football of late. It was even brought into the gentlemanly sport of tennis by Connors, McEnroe, Nastase and company. It's part and parcel of the way we compete. Frank Merriwell is dead. Joe Louis saying "Another lucky night" is in the long-gone past.

Oscar doesn't have to work on his jab, his uppercut, but he has to work on his vocabulary. He has to learn his opponent is a bum, the referee a crook, and that bad manners sell tickets. I don't say he has to go to prison, but maybe a few traffic mishaps, maybe a 2 a.m. difference of opinion with a bartender is indicated.

To date, he has had only a few disagreements with managers and sponsors, things that are handled politely by high-society lawyers.

As I say, he's too good to be true. The Chavez fight is the proverbial Battle of the Century. It doesn't need the hype. But wait till he fights some other guy who's good to his mother and helps little old ladies across the street. You can bet the networks will want him to suggest his opponent drowns canaries, robs poorboxes and kicks cats. And Oscar himself has to stop smiling so much. Get a little scar tissue and a dent in the nose and speak in the laryngitic rasp of a Mafia don. Be the kind of guy who will make you want to call 911 when you see him coming.

Oh, yes, first he has to be sure Julio Cesar Chavez doesn't do all of those things for him. After all, Julio's the champion and may do a makeover on Oscar all by himself. He may resent Mr. Goody Two-Shoes stealing his spotlight. It'll be like a bird biting St. Francis of Assisi.

● ● ● ● ● ● ● ● ● ● ● ● ● ● ● ● ● ●

FEBRUARY 6, 1973

A Fiscal Tragedy

Joe Frazier reminds me of a guy who lit a match to see if his gas tank was empty.

In the gallery of serious miscalculations of history, his has to rank with the captain who chose the iceberg route for the Titanic. Or the guy who bought into the market on Oct. 20, 1929.

It's a financial catastrophe the ripples of which become tidal at the outer edges. Joe took a lot of people with him.

His gamble in fighting George Foreman for what was, effectively, 20 cents on the dollar (compared to what he could have pulled down fighting Muhammad Ali) is a fiscal tragedy for Ali, Frazier and Jack Kent Cooke, who now holds the rematch contract on a bout that has depreciated faster than a new car driven around the block – or off a cliff.

Joe torched $20 million. It's like selling a house with oil under it, dropping Man o' War into a $2,000 claimer, trading a diamond in on paste. Frazier discounted the heavyweight championship of the world. His parent holding company, Cloverlay, Inc., now becomes officially "Overlay, Inc." The total assets of the company were one left hook on which delivery was not made. There's not even enough left to auction off. The managing director of the corporation, Yank Durham, made a serious marketing error.

Joe Frazier was made to order for George Foreman, who is what is known in the fight game as a "waiter." Come to Foreman and he will destroy you. Move around and he looks like a guy lost in a blizzard.

One of the best kept secrets of the Philadelphia gym is that Joe Frazier never was what is known as a fighter-who-can-take-it. Frazier, for all his reckless fury, was aground more often than a near-sighted whale. Who can forget the night the late Eddie Machen, out on his feet, out of condition, rubber-legged and noodle-armed, nevertheless chopped in a right hand that made Frazier sag all the way to Machen's ankles, where he saved himself a count only by hanging onto them till the bell rang?

Recall the night a so-so puncher named Manuel Ramos lifted Joe four feet in the air with an uppercut? Did the clumsy Oscar Bonavena put him on the floor twice? What bout the night Scrap Iron Johnson, a human punching bag, staggered Joe? People forget Quarry took the fight to Joe when Jerry might have been a "waiter" with different results. Frazier sometimes has to hang on in a workout with the heavy bag.

There is no doubt Foreman is a massive puncher, but all he had to do in Jamaica was hold his enormous arms out at right angles to his body and let Joe Frazier impale himself on the end of them. Frazier came at him like something swinging off the end of a chain.

I sat with impresario Jack Kent Cooke the afternoon of the fight. The promoter now has the exclusive rights to an attraction about as compelling as frost warnings. "You are going to lose $2 million tonight," I hazard. "I think you're right," Cooke said. "Tell me, why do you think Yank Durham took a fight with a man as dangerous as this Foreman?"

I shrugged. "Some guys put their fingers in the cage at the zoo. Some guys steal alligators, ride sharks or walk across a chasm on a piece of dental floss."

Frazier topped them all. His mother should have pinned the title inside his blouse and said, "Now, Joseph, this is the heavyweight championship of the world. It is worth $5 or $8 million. Don't take it out to bet with strangers on the train or put it up for collateral on a crap table – and don't fight George Foreman. A lot of people are depending on you – program printers, ticket sellers, ushers, theater chains and Howard Cosell."

And Jack Kent Cooke, who is now just another bidder on a Foreman-Ali fight which will be a good one only if Ali wears a bell. Or drops bread crumbs. Otherwise, it'll be more a hunt than a fight. Maybe they should let George bring a pointing dog in the ring with him.

●●●●●●●●●●●●●●●●●

June 14, 1992

She's Why He's A Real Champion

When you think of the heavyweight boxing champion of the world, you picture this swaggering, cocky half-bully, throwing his hate around – John L. Sullivan, pounding on the bar and announcing "I can lick any man in the house!" Muhammad Ali trumpeting, "I am the greatest!"

Sonny Liston glowering, "If he runs, I'll cripple 'im. If he comes to me, I'll kill 'im!"

Then there's the now and maybe future king of the heavyweights, Evander Holyfield.

"He's never raised his voice in his life," says his promoter, Lou Duva. "I've never even heard him say 'Darn!'"

Holyfield never promised to lick any man in the house. Evander lets the other guy do all the boasting, then gets in the ring and gives the guy a lesson in humility.

It is considered axiomatic in the fight game that every fighter, sooner or later, runs into someone he can't handle, someone as tough as, or tougher than, himself. Sometimes it's a matter of clashing styles, but when it happens, a fighter is either made – or fades.

Holyfield met his match very early in life – his mother.

Annie Holyfield would make Jack Johnson look clumsy. She had all the moves. She brought the fight to you. Dempsey could have learned from her. She never took a backward step. She cornered you; she never went into a clinch. Evander remembers. After her, George Foreman was a day at the beach.

Evander was the baby of Annie's eight children and she didn't raise him to be a palooka. Mom threw combinations.

"I was brought up where you couldn't talk back to nobody," says the current heavyweight champion of the world. "We said, 'Sir' and 'Ma'am' to anybody who was older. You didn't say 'What?' to anybody. You said 'Sir?' or 'Pardon me?' You couldn't even say 'Darn!' with my mama. You got a whuppin'. You didn't cuss or do what she didn't think was right. I used to think it was because my mama didn't like me. Then one day I knew it was because she loved me."

Evander couldn't have learned more from Archie Moore. Even in a fatherless home, he learned patience, forbearance, gentility, dignity. Other people were to tell him how to slip punches, how to handle boxers. Mama Holyfield taught him how to slip phoniness, how to handle life.

It may be why Evander Holyfield has so much trouble gaining credibility as heavyweight champion. He doesn't act the part. He walks through hotel lobbies by himself. He doesn't look as if he's leading a parade. He is so polite, it's surprising somebody doesn't hand him the luggage.

When Mike Tyson wanted to fight Buster Douglas for a lucrative payoff in Tokyo, Evander Holyfield didn't scream or sue, even though he had the contractual rights to the title shot. He stepped aside with a shrug.

"What was I going to do – go through a long, expensive lawsuit?" he asks.

Instead, he simply bided his time.

His graciousness probably robbed the fight game of another "Fight of the Century." Holyfield-Tyson would have been Dempsey-Tunney, Louis-Schmeling, Jeffries-Johnson. A big betting proposition, a must-see for corporate and blue-collar America, a pugilistic happening.

It might never happen, because Holyfield took the high road.

On the other hand, it resulted in his becoming champion of the world. After Douglas beat Tyson, Holyfield beat Douglas.

It was Mama Holyfield's influence that made Evander the darling of America's sports fans at the 1984 Los Angeles Olympics. Evander was the victim of the most outrageous heists and blatant injustices in the history of the Games.

It happened this way: During the second round of a light-heavyweight semifinal, Holyfield, with a dazzling one-two combination to the body and head, floored and knocked out New Zealander Kevin Barry.

But the Yugoslav referee, unaccountably, stepped in and declared that he had been trying to break a clinch at the time and disqualified Holyfield, declaring Barry the winner, even though they had to wake him up to tell him.

That decision paved the way for the Yugoslav's countryman to be declared champion and gain the gold medal, because knocked-out fighters such as Barry were forbidden by Olympic rules to fight again for 28 days.

Thanks to his machinations, the referee's homeboy, Anton Josipovic, won the gold medal by default. Holyfield, the best fighter in the tournament, got the bronze.

Barry was embarrassed by the episode. So much so that he raised Holyfield's hand as if to spurn his "victory." But Holyfield simply shook it off.

"My goal was to make the Olympic team," he says. "And I achieved that. I was proud to wear the robe that said 'USA' on the back of it – and when we'd walk through airports in our warmup suits that said 'U.S. Olympic team' on them, that was my victory."

He took his unjust treatment with such sportsmanship that he got more than a gold medal, he got the goodwill and sympathy – and admiration – of the world. He became a folk hero. Even Mama approved.

"Did you do your best?" she asked. "Well, then, you're a winner."

The world agreed with her.

Holyfield doesn't make waves, he makes fights. The last fight he "lost" was that Olympic outrage. He since has defeated everyone they put in front of him.

But the more he wins, the less respect he gets.

"They say I'm too small," he grins ruefully. "They say I'm just a blown-up light-heavyweight. Hey! Nobody's born 6-2, 240 pounds. You grow. I grew."

At 6 feet 2 and 210, Evander thinks he's big enough for anything sub-King Kong.

"You know what they say?" he reminds you. " 'It's not the size of the man in the fight, it's the size of the fight in the man.' "

Holyfield will fight the former champion, Larry Holmes, Friday at Caesars Palace in Las Vegas. As usual, lots of people think the 42-year-old Holmes can win. He is louder. He talks more.

Maybe Holyfield could get more credibility if he went around banging on bars or boasting and bragging, making noises, showing disrespect, sneering at his opponent, belittling his skills.

But Mama Holyfield wouldn't like that. And Evander is more scared of her than he is of Holmes. He should be. She didn't raise him to be a loudmouth. She raised him to be a champion.

● ● ● ● ● ● ● ● ● ● ● ● ● ● ● ● ● ● ●

DECEMBER 6, 1992

A Pro Boxing Fan
Born Every Minute

Fight promoters are, by all odds, the strangest cast of characters in the whole spectrum of sports.

Tex Rickard was a nerveless gambler who could turn over a card that would mean he was $100,000 richer or flat broke without a change of expression. He was the first to put gold leaf in tickets and charge $100 for them in a day when $100 would have bought you a car.

But he was always afraid he had overmatched opponents with Dempsey and even went so far as to beg Dempsey once to take it easy with Luis Firpo – who only knocked Dempsey out of the ring.

Mike Jacobs was a Broadway ticket speculator who got into promotion because fights sold tickets and that was his business. He worked out of his office, and no one ever saw him at a fight camp or even ringside; his connection to the sport was the countinghouse.

Don King is as unlikely a historical figure as any of them, and he sees himself as their spiritual heir.

With his electric hair and long-running monologues delivered in the booming bombast of Moses addressing the children of Israel, King feels he is the apotheosis of the breed. Not for him the brooding uncertainties of a Rickard, the reclusion of a Jacobs.

"I am a showman!" he bellows. "There have been only three great showmen in the history of this country – P. T. Barnum, Mike Todd and me!"

Look, if you were too young to remember the traveling medicine shows or the snake oil merchants of the Old West, take heart.

There's always a visit from King. Be prepared to be sold the Brooklyn Bridge, a gold brick or prime swampland in Florida.

It has been said King could sell sand to an Algerian or ice to an Aleut.

There used to be a saying in Hollywood: "The bigger the flop, the bigger the junket." In other words, a studio with a turkey of a movie on its hands would fly the press to Monte Carlo for the premiere.

King isn't going to fly anybody to the south of France, but he was in town this week in a blizzard of superlatives and hyperbole to promote a fight card at the Mirage in Las Vegas next Sunday featuring Julio Caesar Chavez and Terry Norris and Greg Haugen and Julian Jackson and Michael Nunn and Tony Tucker.

Pretty good slate, you would say? Right.

Only Julio Caesar is not fighting Haugen or Norris. He's fighting Marty Jakubowski, the scourge of central Indiana who might or might not be undefeated in 37 pro bouts.

I say "might be" because King in his checkered past might be called the "fight doctor." Not because he treated fighters, but because he doctored fights.

A heavyweight elimination tournament of King's once proved to have 25 fights recorded that had never taken place and another 80 that probably didn't take place.

The network canceled the tournament. King sued the network.

Julio Caesar Chavez against Marty Jakubowski might be the most lopsided mismatch since the Titanic and the iceberg, but promoter King is having none of it.

Carefully avoiding calling Jakubowski by name (he can't pronounce it), King hints that every fighter of no matter what lean skills is up for a fight against Chavez, whom he identified as the best fighter pound-for-pound in the world.

Jakubowski might be up for the fight, but not for long. By the second round, he will be down for the fight, is the way to bet.

Undaunted, King promotes Terry Norris, who, he tells you, is the greatest fighter "pound-for-pound," if Julio isn't.

He touts his meeting with an unknown named "Irish" Pat Lawlor as a "war." If so, it's the United States vs. Grenada.

Irish Pat is, pound-for-pound, one of the worst fighters in the world. He's probably not even Irish. In the fight game, "Irish" in front of your name is a code word for "white."

Julian Jackson, who might actually be pound-for-pound the best fighter around, will take on Eddie Hall, who isn't. Hall has lost nine of 21 fights. He has been knocked out three times in his last six fights, lost another and got a draw in another.

None of this deters King. He takes it as a challenge, and the adjectives flew. Anybody can promote Dempsey-Tunney, Louis-Schmeling, Ali-Frazier, is his position. P. T. Barnum could sell Tom Thumb. But could he sell Greg Haugen vs. Armando Campas?

Actually, King is a sad case these days. He still owns 2,000 acres of prime land in central Ohio, a Park Avenue penthouse, a fleet of Cadillacs and a closet full of bench-made English shoes.

But, for the first time, almost, since he got out of prison, he is without a heavyweight champion or contender in his entourage. It's kind of depressing.

King is not a lightweight champion kind of guy. His real meal ticket is a heavyweight champion. Unfortunately, his is in the big house in Indiana these days doing three-to-10.

A promoter without a heavyweight champ is like a captain without a ship. But Captain King is not discouraged:

"We are working to get Mike Tyson out. (Alan) Dershowitz expects to not only get him out, but pardoned. When we do, he will be able to beat the likes of Riddick Bowe, then rest for a minute and beat

Holyfield or Lennox Lewis or anybody else."

King will tell you that Tyson's misadventures began with "the second fight" against Buster Douglas in Tokyo.

The second fight!? The record book lists only one – "Douglas, K.O. 11."

King shakes his head. "Tyson knocked him out in the eighth round. The long count. Then Douglas won on an illegal knockout in the second fight three rounds after he was himself knocked out. I mean, how many times you got to knock a man out?"

King's face hardens. "Then Buster Douglas lays down and bays at the moon against Holyfield. He quits like a dog. He cheats the public. He cheats the world.

"We need Tyson to restore order," he says.

In the meantime, the great showman must make do with guys who are too light fighting guys who are too obscure.

King accepts it. After all, Barnum did it with a guy 30 inches tall.

● ● ● ● ● ● ● ● ● ● ● ● ● ● ● ● ●

APRIL 7, 1987

Sugar Ray Shows What Boxing Is All About

LAS VEGAS – It wasn't even close....

Hey, maybe Jeffries couldn't do it. Maybe, Johnson, Dempsey, a half dozen other famous names from out of the past.

But don't put Sugar Ray Leonard in there.

He did it. He came back. Did he ever.

Calling on skills you wouldn't think he could even remember, he put the hurt on Marvelous Marvin Hagler in the parking lot at Caesars Palace Monday night. But that was nothing to what he did to Father

Time. He stopped that old impostor right in his tracks.

You imagine if Peter Pan were a fighter, this is how he would do it. It was pretty, dazzling, daring. He not only turned back the clock, he made the most fearsome pugilist in a ring today look like a clumsy old character in a gorilla suit.

He didn't just outpoint Hagler, he exposed him. He made him look like a guy chasing a bus. In snowshoes. Marvelous Marvin Hagler should have put stamps on his punches. He kept aiming them at places Sugar Ray had left much earlier in the evening. Sometimes, you expected Hagler to tap the referee on the shoulder and say, "Excuse me, did you see a little fellow, about 5-foot-10 with dark hair and a nice smile go by here tonight? I was supposed to fight him, but I guess he couldn't make it."

The moral of the story?

Well, it is this: Never underestimate a man with an obsession.

Captain Ahab had Moby Dick. Sugar Ray Leonard had Marvelous Marvin Hagler.

It might never have happened if Sugar Ray Leonard had retired to the French Riviera, got a yacht, a fleet of Ferraris and went around the world playing polo.

But Sugar Ray became, of all things, a fight announcer.

It was cruel and unusual punishment. He had to sit there and ooh and aah and gush and exclaim over a fighter he knew wouldn't give him much more trouble than a heavy bag or his shadow.

It must be awful watching someone with your title, your money, your place in history swaggering around society, doing commercials, going on talk shows, taking bows. All the time knowing that, if you tap the world on the shoulder and say, "By the way, I could lick this guy 12 rounds to none," they would turn on you and snarl "Sour grapes! Shame on you! Your day is gone, kid. Have the grace to forget it!"

Sugar Ray couldn't take it.

The world thought he was crazy. Obsessed people frequently are.

Captain Ahab, you will recall, had a wooden leg. Sugar Ray Leonard had a game eye. A torn retina.

He was Don Quixote. He had an impossible dream. He saw things that weren't there. He would never get away with it, they told him. He would go blind. He would get punchy. He would be selling pencils in arena lobbies.

Hagler was a certified killer, they warned him. Just look at that shaved head, that menacing glare, those muscles on muscles.

To Sugar Ray, he just looked slow. It would be like fighting a statue.

It tormented Sugar Ray to think an eye gouge had robbed him of his rightful place in history. He must have seen himself in his sleep throwing a shutout at the lunging, graceless Hagler.

You have to remember boxing is a speed sport. It's not a strength sport. It belongs to the Sugar Rays of the world (the original and Leonard), to the Muhammad Alis. Those big slow guys were duck soup (literally) to Ali. And the burly, muscular Hagler was to Leonard what George Foreman, Sonny Liston and all the George Chuvalos in the ring turned out to be: Instruments on which they can give a concert. Bells they can ring.

Leonard-Hagler was in that genre. It wasn't even a good fight. Leonard repeatedly beat Hagler to the punch. When he did, he hit harder. He hit more often. He made Hagler look like a guy sweeping snow off a windshield most of the night. Sugar Ray Leonard couldn't have ordered a fight that would have better suited his skills. He seduced his opponent into doing every awkward thing he had seen him do in his dreams. He made Hagler into what he had perceived him to be throughout his career – a brawler, a swarmer, a man who could club you to death only if you stood there and let him. If you moved, he was lost.

It is a landmark event in boxing history. This is not "Rocky V" or "Golden Boy" or Errol Flynn defeating John L. Sullivan. This was in a ring, not a sound stage. But it was another affirmation that brute strength does not rule this sport no matter how cruel it becomes.

It belongs to a little bright-eyed, curly haired kid who conjures up

images of Little Orphan Annie, Skippy, Bugs Bunny turning his opponent into an outline on a cement block fence. It is like a boy with a dog
and a fishing pole outwitting the town bully, the outlaw gang.

Sugar Ray kept his eye on his obsession. He ignored the advice. He
dismissed the notion that inactivity can overlay even genius.

He knew Hagler was his. He could see it in his dreams, he could see
it in the ring. He could not rest until he proved it. To himself. He could
gloat, now. But it's not likely. The man he proved it to is the man who
needed no proof. The one he had to show was not the world, it was
himself. And like all magnificent obsessions and magnificently
obsessed, he knew it all along.

● ● ● ● ● ● ● ● ● ● ● ● ● ● ● ● ●

SEPTEMBER 23, 1962

Stop, Look 'n' Liston

CHICAGO – The first look you get at Sonny Liston, you only hope it
don't bite.

You get the idea Floyd Patterson shouldn't fight him, Clyde Beatty
should. Patterson should bring a whip, a chair and a gun that shoots
blanks in the ring. Or one that shoots bullets.

Liston would be an 8-5 favorite over the Marines. He already has
beaten more cops than Perry Mason.

You go out to his training camp at an abandoned racetrack in Auro-
ra, and when he comes in, you panic – because you think someone has
forgotten to hold a rope around his neck. I never thought I would see
anything like it when I was awake. And if I was asleep I would wake up
screaming. You half expect it to roar. Two people saw him doing road-
work one morning and called the circus to see if any of their cages had
been vacated.

If I were Patterson, I would make bloody sure Sonny had eaten before he went in the ring. If Liston gets hungry in the middle of the fight he may not even throw the bones away.

Someone has dug up an old part of the archives to find out that if a man is knocked out of the ring, he gets 20 seconds to get back. But from the look of Liston's hands, Floyd may need a cab to get back. Instead of knocking him for a loop, he may knock him in to The Loop. If Liston knocked me out of the ring, I would be inclined to let it go at that. I wouldn't get back in the ring if they gave me a week. I would take a fast inventory, and if I had all my vital parts I would go take in a show. The man has such a fantastically long reach he could jab Patterson from the second row of ringside. He may score a few jabs from his stool.

The prevailing opinion in Chicago is Liston may knock out Patterson in 2 minutes and 9 seconds of the introduction. They brought a hypnotist into the camps, presumably to hypnotize the champion against pain. But when the hypnotist got a look at Liston, they had to revive him.

The late Arthur Brisbane, a journalist, used to always boast that a gorilla could lick any fighter but up to now I never thought we'd live to see it done. But Sonny Liston is such an awesome specimen that even though you know he can't read or write, the big shock is that he talks.

His fist is so huge his boxing gloves look like saddles. Patterson's manager is holding out for a brand of gloves he knows won't even keep Sonny's hands warm. He should throw in a pair of handcuffs.

The betting around town among people who saw Liston is not whether Patterson will win or lose but whether he will show up. There are those who think Sonny can knock him out even if he doesn't.

Liston's camp is a lighthearted place – for everybody but the sparring partners. When they go home in single file they look like the retreat at Dunkirk. Sonny broke Big Jim Robinson's ribs. If he ever hit him on the head he's henceforth be known as "Little Jim Robinson." Lou Bailey tried a couple of rounds and left the ring, the camp and ultimately the state. He complained his head still hurt two weeks later –

but those who saw the workout say he was lucky he had one left to hurt.

They're allowed to take pain pills, but morphine would be more humane. In fact, the best guess is that the hypnotist was really going to work on the sparring partners. Sonny ran out of them so fast he would have had to take his workouts to the Chicago Zoo to find opponents. But the Society for Prevention of Cruelty to Animals would have stalled that.

His chest, neck, fist, thighs, wrist and calf are all one to four inches bigger than Patterson's. If you saw his footprint in the snow in the Himalayas, four expeditions would be launched to capture him. As long as he lives, man can believe in the Abominable Snowman.

He has been celebrated in print as one of the few guys who ever could think of anything to do in Philadelphia after dark. He chased a woman off the highway with a red light and a fast car and was surprised she didn't know he was joking.

He is the best argument I know for schooling. He never had any, and if he wins he's going to be stuck with all those millions of dollars and not even know which salad fork to use. Tunney read Shakespeare, but Sonny has a tough time with a "No Smoking" sign.

He is so sure he is going to be champion that his only fear is Patterson will get hit by a streetcar before the fight. He got his jaw broken by a fighter named Marty Marshall one night because he was laughing at Marshall. "I never laughed in the ring since," he explains. He might add he seldom does out of it, either. "They say I look evil and mean. If you got your jaw broke you'd look the way I look," he told me.

Patterson's speed bores him. "We ain't gonna race," he explains. He is of the opinion the only way Patterson can survive the fifth round is by hiding under the ring until the sixth.

● ● ● ● ● ● ● ● ● ● ● ● ● ● ● ● ●

JANUARY 26, 1962

A Job for Joe

In the kitchen of his home, the greatest heavyweight champion of his time, perhaps of all time, sat staring at the television screen flickering before him.

It was too early for television. The sun was not yet up high enough to shine in the lifeless eyes of the two stone lions guarding the massive front door. But it was too wet for golf. And Joe Louis didn't have anything better to do.

"I get up at 7:30 to watch it," he admitted, indicating the screen, which was alive with deafening action. "Tomorrow I got to fly to Kentucky. Got to cut a ribbon for a new supermarket."

He paused for a moment, studied the picture critically, then turned to a companion. "Turn it off," he instructed. "I seen it before."

He directed his attention to a newcomer. "What can I tell you?" he wanted to know.

The newcomer studied him. The hair was graying at the sides of the temples. The face was puffy from sleep. But the eyes had the same impassive steadiness that used to reduce ring opponents to masses of gibbering fear. The gaze was level and honest. The Brown Bomber had a gray casing, but it was possible in the mind's eye to still see the sleek, destructive outline of fury that had made this man the most celebrated athlete of his decade.

Joe Louis is a man who looks without surprise on life. And sometimes without much interest. He has seen it all before. His youth was spent in such a pitch of constant excitement and swirl that it is possible now to be bored enough to start watching TV at dawn.

I have always thought Joe Louis the most honest athlete in the history of any sport. His phrases had the simple, uncomplicated sincerity of the child who sees no need to lie or the adult who sees no fear to make him want to. In a chorus of politicians' patriotic fervor, it was Joe Louis' simple declaration, "There's a lot wrong with our country, but nothin' Hitler could fix" that bolstered the resolve of a whole generation of his people.

"We are on God's side" was more eloquent than a coast-to-coast line of posters. When he was old and awkward and knocked out by the young bull from Brockton and his dressing room was awash with the tears of his friends, Joe shrugged. "I knocked out lots of guys." He had a simple dignity about him a king might envy. He hit with the explosive detonation of a dynamite cap, but even in losing fights, he stepped back when an opponent lost his footing.

He left his cruelty in the ring. He ripped Carnera's mouth into a Niagara of blood, knocked Paolina Uzedun's gold teeth into the press row, but helped them to their feet and ever had a generous word for the courage of any foe. "Another lucky night" became his post-fight interview trademark.

It is a wrench to see this great champion scuffling for something to do – not so much for money, because the government, bad advice and bad friends have made money as meaningless a part of life as a gold belt. As an economic entity, Joe Louis disappeared into a hole years ago and pulled it in after him. He cannot tunnel out in his lifetime. He owes the United States more than some European allies.

"It all began with that first $98,000," he told me the other morning, with that crooked grin that seems to light the whole Louis face with merriment. "They got that 50% penalty, and it's not hard to double and triple what you owe as the years go by. I could have paid that first $98,000, but my accountant advised me to let it go by. "The bigger it gets, the quicker they'll settle,' is what he told me. Pretty soon it got so big there was nothing to settle.

"If I were to live another thousand years and have 250 oil wells, I couldn't catch up to it now. It was over a million dollars when the government finally stopped the penalty. With the penalty, it was growing like a weed. But they didn't stop the principal. You know how long it would take you and how much you'd have to make to clear a million dollars?"

Louis was victimized by more than tax accountants. Sport should have hidden its head when it found Joe Louis forced to referee the comedy of wrestling or to appear in court for Jimmy Hoffa to pay off a favor to people he shouldn't have had to go to in the first place.

Joe wants to promote boxing in L. A. now. His right to do so is under attack by resident promoters Aileen Eaton and George Parnassus. As usual, Joe can see their side of it. "You know how it is: People have something so long, they hate to give it up. I don't blame them."

But if Joe Louis had been a different kind of person, there might not be any boxing today. The game owes him something. The country owes him something. It's times sports stopped dumping its great champions into a pile of boredom, stopped sweeping its heroes under a corner of the rug. It's time somebody showed concern when Babe Ruth dies a lonely, bitter, bored man; when Ezzard Charles winds up broke and neglected two years after he quits the ring.

It's time Joe Louis was too busy to be watching television at seven o'clock in the morning and too hard at work to be cutting ribbons in Kentucky. There should be room for two boxing promoters in L.A. If there's room for any. If there's no room for Joe Louis in boxing, there should be no room for boxing, period.

· · · · · · · · · · · · · · · · · ·

MARCH 16, 1962

The King at Home

Archibald Lee Moore, the box-fighter and unfrocked light-heavyweight champion of the world, has been fighting for money ever since he was old enough to understand what it was.

His first opponent was a streetcar conductor, and the purse was a fistful of change swiped from a coinbox. His next opponent was a policeman. It was one of the few times in his life that Archie was overmatched.

In the St. Louis of the '30s, a bright Negro boy had two choices of a career. He could go into the ring or into vice. That was a time when vice, as Almena Lomax used to say, was a Negro's Wall Street. The real Wall Street was open only to the graduating classes of Yale, Harvard and a few other cloisters Archie didn't even know existed.

Archie Moore chose the ring, the hard way to make a buck, and began a long 26-year peregrination through the jungles of fistiana. He rode the rods, hitchhiked, tussled for donut money, fought anybody who would pay him. Word of his prowess spread through the better gyms, and the word was "Keep away. He'll hand you your head, fighting one-handed." History periodically swallowed him up in places like Tasmania, Montevideo, Bahia Blanca and North Adams, Massachusetts. Archie always came walking out of the brush again, sporting a goatee, a win streak, a roll around his middle and the greatest left hook in the business.

He got an ulcer and a heart condition, not from fighting but from trying to get fights. Uncle Sam made him 4-F, but so far as the ring was concerned he was 1-A, a two-fisted traveling train wreck.

He coaxed champion Joey Maxim in the ring with him only by giving away the purse and agreeing to take on the champion's manager, because everyone quite understood that climbing in the ring with Archie Moore was tantamount to giving him the title. The fisticuffs were such a formality that Maxim's concentration was survival, not victory. Archie got the title and cab fare home.

He couldn't get a main event in New York until he could bring the championship with him. When he did, he dazzled the trade and revived the sport as an art form. Archie was the Rembrandt of boxing. A little dab here, a touch of color there, and soon his opponent was immortalized on canvas. He was as good copy out of as in the ring. He showed up for weigh-ins in tuxedos, then had to shuck down to the buff to make the limit. He wore Bermuda shorts and tails on the street. No one dared laugh. He didn't hold press conferences, he granted audiences.

He ruled as well as he had served. He changed from a sullen, suspicious refugee from the squalid tenements of St. Louis into the gracious patriarch of a savage kingdom. He lost as well as he won. He didn't acquire class; he always had it. He merely got in a position in life where he didn't have to be ashamed of it, where his friends were the first citizens, not the thugs, connivers and perjurers of what one writer called "Tin Ear Alley."

I saw the end result of the strange odyssey of Archie Moore this week, the monarch at his home and at his camp called "The Salt Mine," a Spartan hermitage in the Poway Valley of San Diego, so remote a bloodhound would get lost, and so rugged it has all the comforts of a convict hell ship of the 1700s. The last sight a guest saw on leaving was Archie busily bathing under an outdoor shower with cold water.

His house in San Diego is a $150,000 showplace of used brick and mahogany on the far side of the city. Archie pours money into it because he has seen the disastrous results of other fighters pouring money into businesses they knew nothing about. The view is not sensational, a freeway on one side, a warehouse on the other. The lot beneath is perhaps not worth the guest house or the swimming pool. But what is important to Archie is not that it should be in Bel-Air but that it is Home, almost the first he has had, full of warmth, hospitality, a pretty wife and four happy kids. Bel-Airites should be so lucky.

He sat on his flagstone fireplace and oozed pride with his guests and family around him. It almost seemed a wrench for him to discuss his upcoming prizefight with Alejandro Lavorante at the Olympic March 30. His encyclicals ranged the spectrum:

On his unfrocking: "A mistake. Harold Johnson will not be champion until I say he is. I will fight him as soon as he proves he is able to draw anything besides his breath. If he wins the championship they might as well create a new division. No one will pay any attention to that one."

On Sonny Liston: "His biggest drawback is his reluctance to meet the public. Would I fight him? What would keep me from it? He had his jaw broken and fought on five more rounds. I dare a man to let me break his jaw and keep on fighting one more round."

On Lavorante: "I saw him fight Von Clay for two rounds. I only need 30 seconds to study a man, so I had five minutes to let my attention wander."

On his age: "I am two years older than I was two years ago."

On his future: "I would have retired this year except they tied up my purse for the Rinaldi fight – $86,000. A man can't leave that kind of money lying around."

The greatest fighter he ever saw: "Henry Armstrong. Positively."

It was the first time that day Archie was wrong.

● ● ● ● ● ● ● ● ● ● ● ● ● ● ● ● ● ●

AUGUST 3, 1972

Here We Go Again

Let's have a game of charades, right?

Now, the most stupefying athlete of our times, OK? Two words.

First I'll make a circle to show I'm doing the whole thing, not syllabifying it. I run out to the center of the floor with my hands covering my eyes in fists that I peer over. Then I topple backward onto the floor on my back and shake my head to clear cobwebs.

Give up? Wait a minute. Now, I'll don a beard and smoked glasses and tiptoe out of town. No! NOT Judge Crater! Now watch. I make a fist and I extend it out and leap like a kangaroo toward another. How about if I just lie down here in a corner? A CORNER, get it?! Wait a minute! How about if I pick a fight with a 98-pound Boy Scout? You got it?! Right! Floyd Patterson!

If you saw the headline out of New York the other day, you know Falling Floyd is going to fight Muhammad Ali sometime in September. The mind reels. It's almost like reading "Joe Frazier to Meet Jim Jeffries," "Ali and Jim Corbett Matched," "Dempsey and Tunney in Line for Title Bout." They should stage the fight in a museum.

Floyd Patterson reminds me of one of those seriocomic movies where the gang plots the murder of an unaware boob. They push him off a cliff. And he comes climbing back up complaining they should be more careful. They drop him in a river – and he's on the dock waiting for them when they come in. They throw him out a hotel window, and a few minutes later he's pushing the buzzer. They give him poison – and he asks for a second cup.

The most destructible of fighters in the ring, he's the most indestructible out of it. He's the little man upon the stairs. He wasn't there again today. He's like the stagehand who keeps wandering through the set. He's Charlie Chaplin being chased by history, which keeps missing him.

Do you realize when Floyd Patterson first challenged for the heavyweight championship, the Dodgers were in Brooklyn, Vince Lombardi was a coach at West Point, Sonny Liston was in prison and Muhammad Ali was a Louisville teenager named Cassius Clay?

This is a man who has fought for the heavyweight title 14 times. He is like a pitcher with an ERA of 12 who keeps starting World Series, a quarterback who fumbles getting the Super Bowl starting job, a passer who throws interceptions, a card player who bumps a busted straight, a yachtsman who keeps sinking at the starting line – and he keeps suiting up and going in there.

"I'm hooked on fighting," Floyd admitted in a recent issue of the Police Gazette. "It's my trip." He's 37 now. He never was much more than a bloated light-heavyweight. He has the instincts of a monk, foreswearing sex, family and city life for months before a fight. As a kid, he used to hide in tool cupboards on the side of New York subways. He would climb trees for days. Life is a bat cave to Floyd. He speaks in whispers. He's as apologetic as a clumsy waiter. He is America's Stranger. He seems to feel he's intruding on the world.

Some guys fight out of a crouch. Floyd would fight out of a funk. He has several flaws as a fighter, not the least of which is, he hates to hurt anyone.

You would hope that would include Floyd Patterson, but Floyd announced in New York last month that, in a couple of years, he should be a great fighter. All he needs is experience, he says.

He expects to beat Ali this time. He was too inexperienced (he was only 30) last time. "Fear made him a great fighter," he says of Ali. "You don't develop that fantastic defense unless you're afraid of getting hit."

Unfortunately, Floyd never minded it. And if the commission picks up his license, he may get a job in a carnival letting people throw baseballs at him. He won't duck.

• • • • • • • • • • • • • • • • • •

MARCH 15, 1970

Sugar Ray's Comeback: A Punch, a Prayer and a Plea

In France, they called him "Le Sucre." In Germany, he was "Der Zucker."

Sugar Ray Robinson went through life like syrup over a waffle. The world looked to him like a two-pound palooka with a glass chin. Nobody ever saw him frown. He went through $4 million with a wave of his hand. He filled the Polo Grounds, the Garden, the Earl's Court in London and the Palais Des Sports in Paris. He browbeat promoters for top dollar, then left it to the world as a kind of a complicated tip.

He loved crowds. And colors. He drove a fuchsia Cadillac, and he wore clothes you could read by in a cave.

He came out of the streets of Black Bottom in Detroit dancing. He was a street kid. He knew more gangsters than J. Edgar Hoover, but nobody ever questioned a Sugar Ray fight. It would be like doubting a Rembrandt. Sugar Ray raised boxing to a high and holy art.

It was hard to hate him. He could charm a shark. When you saw him fight, you could forgive him everything. Often there was a good deal to forgive.

One day, he came home to find the music had stopped. A quarter of a million had disappeared from the restaurant till; Ray didn't know where. He never was any good at tracking down small change. His dry cleaning establishment had dry-cleaned him.

Life began to crowd him. And a crowding fighter always gave Sugar Ray trouble. Sugar Ray, who had once gone to Europe with such a large retinue it looked more like an immigration than a tour, was suddenly down to last year's clothes and yesterday's shirt. He owed the government more money than France, and he tells in his book, "Sugar Ray," which he wrote with Dave Anderson, of the night he came home from his testimonial with the trophy inscribed "To the World's Greatest Fighter" – and had no furniture in the apartment to put it on.

They say you can never tell about the great ones until they hit the floor. It's how you make your fight with your eyes cut, your head spinning, your stomach aching and your nose bleeding that tells a champ.

Pound for pound, Ray had been the world's greatest boxer, but dollar for dollar he was its gaudiest pauper. Still, the towel didn't come fluttering in. The toast of Paris, the lion of London, the rage of Rome was suddenly fighting in Steubenville, Ohio, for $790 against kids who stammered, "I can't tell you what a thrill it is to meet you" – even after they beat him up. "It's a new experience for me, too," Sugar Ray told them sadly, pocketing money that wouldn't have paid his tailor in the old days.

As a kid, Ray danced for pennies and played craps for dollars in the streets of Harlem. He wasn't a high school dropout because he never made it to high school. He led the neighborhood in hocked watches he won in "amateur" fights all over New York and New England. But he never made a police lineup or a hot list. He never drank; he came full of the wine of life. He was raised by his mother and two adoring sisters, and it was a reverend who first jerked him off his knees in the ghetto where he was crouched over a pair of dice and marched him to the gym and told him to make life his punching bag.

The Sugar Ray Robinsons bring out the cynicism in the graceless, the frustrated, the bitter, the losers. Ray's mistakes were, by and large, joyous mistakes. His victim, after all, was Ray Robinson. When he fought charity fights, they said, "What's his angle?" The only thing he ever did alone was fight and pray. He would duck into any church that was open. He was as ecumenical as the Bible, but when he would profess faith from the ring, the press row winked broadly and sneered. "Sugar Ray Religion." Lots of people disbelieve because they think a person who believes in God has to look gloomy.

Sugar Ray is making a comeback. I don't mean the ballroom four-rounder he has with middleweight champ Nino Benvenuti of Italy at the Beverly Hilton March 23. That's only an exhibition. His winner-take-all fight is with the corrupters of our youth.

The "Sugar Ray Youth Foundation" (for whose benefit the Benvenuti fight is being staged) may indeed be a match for that champ. It has a good left, a wicked right. It is 49 years old, but it can still make the weight, its stomach flat, its face unmarked, its teeth white and smiling. Lord knows, it has style. It already has 175 lifetime victories and has never been knocked out.

"It looks to me as if the count has reached nine for this country when kids are dying on the street from dope. It is time somebody took a few punches at this thing," say Sugar Ray, boxing shadows, skipping rope to get in shape.

As a foe, it looks as tough as La Motta, as dirty as Zivic, as slick as Gavilan, as indefatigable as Basilio. Let's just hope it's clumsy, or open to a left. If it is it will lose its title.

• • • • • • • • • • • • • • • • • •

The Mike Tyson He Knew Showed Humor, Not Bite

All right, Miss B., take a letter to Mr. T. That's right, Mr. T., the quondam heavyweight champion. Boxing's Dracula. Half-pug, half-vampire. The Tooth Fairy.

"Dear Mike,

"I guess I go back with you as far as any other journalist. You remember, we rode to the Roy Firestone show in a stretch limo a few years ago. You were the up-and-coming heavyweight hope and you poked me in the ribs as we got in the car and you grinned 'You know, if I were around a limo like this five years ago, I'd be stealing the hubcaps.' You seemed to have an appealing sense of humor behind that frightening exterior and those bulging muscles.

"I don't want to say I defended you to many of my friends, but I did tell them I saw another side to the brute they perceived in mid-ring.

"I knew your co-manager Jimmy Jacobs well. He had been world handball champion and a world-class fight buff who collected boxing films all the way from the days of Thomas Edison's early kinescopes.

"I knew your other co-manager, Cus D'Amato. A man of dignity and probity, he also was the most paranoid fight manager I ever knew. I drove him and Floyd Patterson to the Olympic Auditorium one night (Floyd fought a man named Jimmy Slade) and I thought Cus was going to have a heart attack when I made a wrong turn. He suspected me of being Sammy the Bull. "Who are you?! Where are you taking us!? I have told the police to be on the lookout for our kidnapping!" he shrieked before I could calm him down.

"But in spite of these derangements, you were in good hands, Mike. Cus kept you on a pretty tight leash. Because he knew you needed it.

Jacobs inculcated a love of boxing history in you and you were the only guy I ever met who knew more boxing lore than I did. (You stumped me on Mickey Walker-Pete Latzo, remember, Mike?)

"When Jacobs and Cus died, you put your career in the hands of guys who would let you do anything you wanted. They were afraid to say no to you. They were as scared of you as Peter McNeeley was. Afraid of offending by offering even good advice you didn't want to hear. "Sure, Mike!" was their idea of guidance. You were a cash cow to them. Jimmy Jacobs never needed cash, and Cus D'Amato had almost no interest in it.

"You were on top of the world, Mike. Or thought you were. Don King used to chortle you were 'the baddest man on the planet Earth' and if you weren't, you were getting there.

"The rape of Desiree Washington was the signal to the world you were out of control. You thought you were a law unto yourself. Athletes get that way. All the adulation, the publicity, the hype. You get a false sense of your own importance. It's called 'How dare you turn me down?! Don't you know who I am?!'

"Yeah. You're about 87 cents' worth of zinc, iron, calcium and water like everyone else. A ranch mink is worth more than you skinned.

"Prison is supposed to be about rehabilitation. There are social scientists who think you could put a man-eating shark in prison for a year or two and, with 'help' (buzzword for therapy), he will come out a goldfish. Maybe so, but don't get in a pool with one, especially if your nose is bleeding.

"I don't know how you came out of prison mentally, Mike, but it looks as if you went right back to the same sycophants, leeches and manipulators with which most fighters surround themselves.

"The inevitable happened. The one dignity you had left was your athletic prowess. When Evander Holyfield robbed you of that, you couldn't deal with it. You became obsessed with revenge. It would make everything all right. I mean, how dare Holyfield? Didn't he know with whom he was dealing?

"When it became obvious by the second round you weren't going to make everything all right, that it was deja vu all over again (as Yogi says), you burst your moorings. Your eye was bleeding, you couldn't hurt Holyfield, I think you would have killed him if you had a knife. You did the next worst thing, something that was the most disgusting thing I have ever seen, not only in a prize ring but anywhere else. Maybe Jeffrey Dahmer did it, but they didn't sell tickets. It wasn't on pay-per-view.

"I don't know whether you couldn't handle fame or fame couldn't handle you. You want to be allowed to fight again? Why, Mike? So you can get the rest of his ear? So you can punch out more cops, spit at more customers, encourage more lobby riots?

"I don't think so, Mike. We've kind of lost the capacity for indignation in this country. Forgiveness is the 'in' thing.

"But boxing shouldn't forgive you. You made it seem like a citadel of depravity. As a student of its history, let me ask you – do you think Joe Louis would ever behave like that? Rocky Marciano? Dempsey? Jack Johnson? Ali? Lord, even Sonny Liston? I don't think so.

"Letting you back in the ring would be like letting Hannibal Lecter in a prom. If you fight Holyfield again, what are they going to release it as – 'Jaws, the Sequel'?

"If we want to see things get bitten, we'll go to a cockfight. So wipe the blood off your teeth. I wouldn't go to see you and Evander Holyfield again even if you wore a muzzle and he wore earmuffs."

Golf

● ● ● ● ● ● ● ● ● ● ● ● ● ● ● ● ● ●

FEBRUARY 22, 1976

Baby-Face Bomber

Ben Crenshaw has the biggest feet, the babiest face and the longest swing ever seen on a golfer 5 feet 9 inches tall. He looks like he should be just learning to ride two-wheelers, not win golf tournaments. For the rest of golf, it's a little like getting shot at from a baby carriage.

Most golfers' swings are 380 degrees. Ben's is at least 580. It starts somewhere between his knees and navel on the back swing and goes around three or four times before it hits the ball. Sometimes Ben himself seems to spin around twice, like a propeller. When he hits the ball, it goes screaming out of there almost into orbit and comes down glowing. The power of the swing is such that Ben has to screw himself into the ground like a posthole digger to keep himself from flying after the ball. If he ever misses, he won't come down for five minutes.

He looks as if he came direct from a Christmas pageant. The face – cherubic, blue-eyed, pink-cheeked – looks out of place without a halo over it or wings behind. The tour is used to blond hair, but Ben's looks as if it still might have cradle cap. He's 24 years old but looks like someone who just got a new bike for Christmas. But he's already won three tournaments, which is, for instance, three more than Arnold Palmer had won at that age and two more than Johnny Miller.

Crenshaw takes a crack at the ball the way Dempsey would hit a chin or Larry Csonka a line. They'd call him Belting Ben if they were still into nicknames. Sometimes, of course, the ball curves foul. And when it does, you need two men and a dog to find it. Not since another Ben – Hogan – has anyone 5-9 driven a ball so far.

Despite the fact that he looks like someone you'd like to take to a parade and buy a balloon, Ben came into golf under more pressure to succeed than anyone since Jack Nicklaus – or St. Nicholas. So much was expected of him, you'd think he was found under a burning bush. He had absolutely scattered collegiate golf, winning the NCAA title three years in a row. They spoke of him in Texas as if he changed water into wine on the side.

When people saw where his drives landed, they hung around expecting to see King Kong emerging from the woods. Ben won the first pro tournament he entered. He got his pro card by beating the qualifying school field by 12 strokes.

The way old-timers in Texas talked about him, it seemed unfair to have him wait to go to the Hall of Fame, and unfair to the rest of golf not to have him give shots. Most guys can sort of "feel" their way into the tour. Ben came in on a sedan chair to the sound of trumpets. But the crown came down over his eyes at first.

Ben played golf as if it came wrapped in tinsel. He could have won half a dozen tournaments, but he never hit a commercial shot in his life. He went to the flag, the horizon, first place, not the cut or the top 60. He threw roundhouse rights at the course, never clinched with it. Naturally, a few shots got away in this kind of toe-to-toe exchange, but little Ben shrugged, teed up another ball – and hit it just as hard.

He walked up on a green as if he intended to arrest it. Hands on hips, a confident, almost swaggering, rolling gait of a Texas Ranger on his size 11½ shoes, out roping rustlers.

Ben Crenshaw never crept through a round of golf in his life. He shot an 82 or a 62 with the same boyish enthusiasm. He never ran around tinkering with his swing or begging for an explanation for a bad round. When the course knocked him down, he got up swinging like Dempsey. He'd come home all beat up – but so would the course.

Ben is the newest rising star of golf. What Palmer was in '55, what Mickey Mantle was in '51, what Dempsey was at Toledo or O. J. Simpson at his first Rose Bowl, Johnny Bench in his first World Series, Crenshaw is – the hope of an entire sport.

He's not going to win his third tournament in a row at the Glen Campbell L.A. Open today, but when someone observed "that kid's got a great future if he keeps his feet on the ground," the answer came back, "With that swing, he's got to keep his feet on the ground. If he ever doesn't, he'll look like the world's biggest divot. And when they say 'Crenshaw just landed in a trap,' they'll mean it literally."

● ● ● ● ● ● ● ● ● ● ● ● ● ● ● ● ● ● ●

APRIL 11, 1971

America's Tomboy

She was America's tomboy, a hoyden in high heels, freckle-faced, gum-cracking. You were sure if she emptied her pockets, even when she was being presented at court, they would have a live lizard, a slingshot, a sack of marbles and some sticky licorice in them.

They didn't make the game she couldn't play. She could jump higher, run faster, hit harder than any girl who ever lived. She was as extroverted as a puppy in a store window.

She thought she was the luckiest girl in the whole world. But her life was as sad as a Bronte novel, wall-to-wall melancholy. It only lasted 45 years.

She once won a track meet all by herself. She got cheated out of a gold medal in the Olympics with a grin. She tied for first in the high jump but was disqualified for a western roll technique that was ruled legal before the next Olympics. (She got a "silver" medal, half gold.) She won two others, all gold and all hers.

If she ever said a bitter thing in her life, no one heard it. Her confidence was effervescent. She once struck out Joe DiMaggio, won a tennis tournament two weeks after she bought her first racket, threw a baseball 272 feet on the fly, threw the javelin to an Olympic record with torn cartilage in her right shoulder, won the British Women's Amateur golf championship with bone chips in her right thumb.

She was the daughter of Norwegian immigrants, Hannah Marie Olson and Ole Didrikson, and they christened her Mildred but everyone called her "Babe."

It was 18 years ago this week that Babe Didrikson Zaharias entered a hospital in Beaumont, Texas, for an operation called a "colostomy" which is a medial euphemism for a catastrophe. As usual, Babe expected to make a two on the 18th hole.

As it was, Death had a terrible time closing her out. The match went several extra years. Babe kept making impossible recoveries from the rough. For instance, she won the Women's Open by 12 strokes only a year after her colostomy.

Life was a downhill 90-foot putt with a double break for Babe Didrikson almost from the start. Incredibly, she became a fine seamstress, cook and rose gardener even though most of her childhood was spent jumping hedges, climbing trees, throwing rocks at cans, hitching rides on streetcars, breaking windows with swatted baseballs. Her best sport was basketball. Still, she was no Amazon, standing a little over 5-feet-6, weighing barely 135 pounds.

Athletics is a mournful prowess for a young lady, if the truth were known. It is basically unacceptable to the human male, an irritant. It is a matter of consummate indifference to the human female. Women envy women who went to Bryn Mawr or married royalty or made the Blue Book, not the sports page. They want glass slippers, not steel cleats.

Babe Didrikson married a wrestler. Her finishing school had no lorgnettes, no ballet slippers. She didn't play the piano, she played the harmonica. But she found – and brought – happiness wherever she went. Life looked like a two-foot tap-in to Babe Didrikson Zaharias.

She died still a laughing girl going over the hedges. Even when life became a match-play tournament with Death, Babe used a driver off the tees. She went for birdies to the last, died still trying to hit to the pin.

Around the first tee and the 18th green at Augusta this week will be a rumpled old party with eyes that have been sad for 16 years.

George Zaharias still looks as if he had been hit by a train. The ex-wrestler has a cauliflowered heart. For him, a legend wasn't born, a love affair was ended.

Or maybe it hasn't. At Easter, the lesson that life is a fragile flame even in the best, the swiftest, the strongest, is renewed. Still, the Babe will never grow old, never know what it is to choke over a putt, walk around a fence or read with glasses. She died on the fairway, a competitor to the last. She never asked for strokes. She climbed on the operating table herself, winked at the doctor and said "Keep it in the middle, Doc, it looks like a long par five." The cancer was the only unplayable lie she ever had in her life.

● ● ● ● ● ● ● ● ● ● ● ● ● ● ● ● ●

JULY 31, 1997

Divine Course for Disciple of Golf

My late wife always used to say, "If Jim ever gets to heaven and Ben Hogan isn't there, he ain't staying."

We all laughed. But you know something? I hope today they have in heaven this little 18-hole golf course with trouble on the right, narrow fairways, maybe a par three with this sand trap in the middle of the green, a long par five or two that requires a one-iron second, a finishing hole uphill against a sloping fairway to weed out the ribbon clerks and identify the champions.

You see, I'm assuming Hogan's there and I have this fantasy in which God is waiting for him and he says "Ben! We've been waiting for you!" and he shows him the course, which looks suspiciously like Riviera in 1948, and the Lord says "Look! Hogan's Alley!"

And I don't want to be blasphemous, but I would then visualize the

Lord saying, "Now, what do you say, Ben, we have this little 18-hole four-ball tomorrow? St. Peter and I will stand you and Jay Hebert, who just got here the other day too."

Then the Lord will say, "We'll play at full handicap, one low ball, play it as it lies and I'll promise no miracles."

But Hogan will say, "Wait a minute! No disrespect but you may need a couple of miracles, Sir. I'm really on my game and Jay is putting well. How about we give you three shots and two miracles a side and we'll adjust at the turn?" And the Lord will say "Fine, automatic presses, $20 four ways and we'll flip for honors at the first tee."

God is a golfer, every weekend hacker is sure. Probably a five handicap but maybe scratch. But Hogan, of course, will have to find out before they arrange the bets.

And the Lord will say, "Ben, I'm actually a plus-two these days, but I've got a new putter in the bag that needs breaking in – what say we play even?"

And my fantasy continues where they have this wonderful match – kind of like that storied foursome years ago at Pebble Beach in which Hogan and Byron Nelson played Ken Venturi and Harvie Ward, two amateurs then, for all the guts and glory. It'll come down to the last hole all even, and it'll be like Riviera's 451-yard 18th uphill, and St. Peter will drive the green and the ball will go in the hole, but Hogan and Jay will protest, "You already used up your last miracle back on 15!" And the Lord will agree "You're right," and make St. Peter go back to the tee where he will then, out of miracles, hit it out of bounds left to lose all four ways.

And the Lord will say, "Same time tomorrow, Ben? This time we get one a side?"

Hogan left us the other day for greener fairways. A goodbye as he would have wanted it, without superlatives, by a man of God in his own church in Fort Worth before an audience of his contemporaries and the flower of American golf. A proper goodbye to a man who was a part of our youth, a source of our pride. A man on whom even a breath of scandal never touched, who never did an unworthy thing in his life, whose friendship was as rare as rubies.

For what Hogan meant, it's the old story. For those who know golf, no explanation is necessary. For those who don't, no explanation is possible.

He died as he had lived, in the care and arms of his lovely Valerie. My wife, Linda, and I went to see her after the services this week, talked into the afternoon with her about bygone days, never-dimming triumphs, the legend that was Ben Hogan, her husband of 62 years.

"I was holding his hand and kissed him," Valerie whispered, "when the nurses came in and said 'Mrs. Hogan, he's gone. He's been gone several minutes.'"

Ben hated to leave her, as usual.

All I can say is, I hope they have a lot of par fives where he is today. And God better not give him too many strokes. Or all He'll hear all day is "You're away!"

●●●●●●●●●●●●●●●●●

APRIL 15, 1986

A Masterful Performance At Augusta

Well, we're all 20 years younger today.

You always want Jack Nicklaus to win golf tournaments. The way you always want Ruth to get homers, Rose to get hits, Dempsey to get knockouts, Koufax strikeouts and Mays fly balls at the fence.

It brings a sense of order, stability to our world. The rest of it may be in ferment, change and chaos, but you think, "Well, it can't be too bad. Jack Nicklaus just won the Masters." It's 1963 again and there's no Kadafi, inflation, Central America. We're all right, Jack.

It's something to cling to. The recognizable, the reassuring. We're back with the familiar, the comfortable. Tomorrow is going to have to hold off for a while.

What does the old song say? "I'd Give You a Million Tomorrows for Just One Yesterday"? Well, Jack gave us one more yesterday. Tomorrow can wait. He is not going gently into that good night. He's going to eagle it.

Jack's been winning this thing since the days when we didn't need bifocals and didn't go around wondering why people didn't speak up anymore.

I remember the first one he won. We were very annoyed at him. Here he was, this little fat kid – he was 23 – beating Ben Hogan and Arnold Palmer, to say nothing of Sam Snead and Tony Lema. Plus, he was so damn good. He had no idea how difficult this game was.

You have no idea how depressing it was to follow a golfer who thought every putt should go in the hole, every drive 300 yards, every iron onto a green and who wondered why they put all those funny little sand traps around a course when they didn't come into play.

I mean, it was all too simple for Jack. Birds fly, fish swim and he made threes.

One of the things I liked about the 1986 Masters was the way other golfers appeared human, playing the game on occasion the way you and I play it. Seve Ballesteros, supposedly the next Nicklaus, pull-hooked a ball – and the green coat – into the water on 15. Greg Norman slid that four-iron into the customers on 18.

You never used to see Jack Nicklaus do that. At least, none of us ever remember it. Just as we never remember seeing Roberto Clemente throw to the wrong base or Willie Mays make a last out.

Jack got beat. But somebody always beat him. Somebody ran down a seagoing putt. Lee Trevino hit the pin with a shot that was on its way to the Firth of Forth.

We can remember Hogan snap-hooking it off the tee at 18 at Olympic in 1955 to lose a playoff to Jack Fleck, or Arnold Palmer scattering a seven-shot lead on the back nine in the '66 Open there like a sailor on leave leaking money.

But you had to beat Jack Nicklaus. He didn't do it for you.

Jack had his bad tournaments. Sometimes he finished as far down as fourth. But he never threw a tournament away on a final round or a final hole.

Winning is an art in itself. And, apparently, it's like riding a bicycle. You never forget how. Not if you're Jack Nicklaus.

He played golf better than anyone else. But, so, they tell us, does Ballesteros.

Winning one out of every five tournaments he ever entered worldwide, one out of every six on the tour, stamps Jack Nicklaus as an athletic marvel whose like we shall not see again. Winning 20 majors out of a possible 96 is stupefying.

Someone once said that the really astonishing thing about Jack Nicklaus was that he won so many tournaments that he didn't care whether he won or not. It's interesting that the last five tournaments he won were the Open, the PGA, the Colonial, the Memorial and the Masters.

That's three majors, and you have to know that the Memorial is Jack's own tournament, which makes it a major in his eyes, and that the Colonial is a course where you measure yourself against Hogan.

Jack can still play. But he can't win on the interest of his talent anymore. He has to dip into the capital.

Was the 1986 Masters his most satisfying win? I doubt it. Jack has always found it galling he didn't win more British Opens, a tournament he rescued from a downslide by his constant appearance in it. Jack won three and was second an incredible seven times.

The Masters was not that hard to win in the early days. It was a tournament you got invited to, like a cotillion in the Confederacy.

It was a happy hunting ground for venerable former winners, foreigners and amateurs, and it was not till a few of us began pointing out the inequity of inviting a foreign player like Gary Player and not a native-born tour winner like, say, Charlie Sifford, that the Masters' braintrust wrote a rule that tour winners get invited.

Still, despite the heavy concentration of legal aliens, the Masters has become, sort of, America's tournament, the Dallas Cowboys of golf.

It has the tried and true, the recognizable on its leaderboard. The star system, which works best at the box office, on video or in person, is alive and well. You never see "Unknown Wins Masters" in the Monday paper.

But no one is as known as Mr. Jack Nicklaus. Mr. Golf. God must be a fan. Ballesteros had to hit the ball into the water, Greg Norman had to hit the ball into the crowd and Tom Kite had to leave two straight crucial putts short. He knew that Nicklaus could take care of the rest.

As the poet said, with Nicklaus winning the Masters, God's in his heaven and all's right with the world.

• • • • • • • • • • • • • • • • • • •

NOVEMBER 14, 1996

To Some, He's Always A Champion

Before there was a Tiger Woods, and after there was an Arnold Palmer and a Jack Nicklaus, there was a Greg Norman.

Golf's Job was a sight to behold on a fairway. The shock of cotton hair, the flashing blue eyes, out-thrust jaw, he was a combination Fearless Fosdick and Frank Merriwell. Wasp-waisted, broad-shouldered, he had the eyesight of a circling hawk and the boldness of a bank robber. They didn't make the hole he couldn't eagle, the course he couldn't drag home to the cave with him. He was predatory. He got his nickname, Great White Shark, not so much for the fact that he used to hunt sharks with a kitchen knife but from the fact that he looked like one on the spoor of first money in the tournament.

Nobody ever played the game with more confidence. That was just the trouble. Norman didn't know the meaning of the word patience – or defense, for all of that. He was like a fighter who throws crazy rights and moves in. He never wanted to decision a course but to knock it in the seats. He and Palmer were the most exciting players ever to pick up a one-iron and go for it.

He was also the unluckiest golfer who ever lived. Every great golfer has been visited by Aristotelian "undeserved misfortune." It's the name of the game. But no one to the extent Greg Norman was.

Do you realize that, if the Scots had decreed a "tournament" to be 54 holes instead of 72 – or even if they had settled on 63 – Greg Norman would have won seven more majors than he did? He was in the lead coming into the final nine in all of those tournaments.

Only two players in history have been in a playoff for each of the major championships – the Masters, U.S. Open, British Open and the PGA. The two are Craig Wood and Greg Norman. Neither won a single one of those playoffs.

Norman was second in the Masters three times, second in the U.S. Open twice, second in the British Open twice (he won it twice) and second in the PGA twice.

Talk about star-crossed! Greg Norman has been a target of the fickle gods of golf. The most enduring mental picture you have of Greg Norman is of his looking skyward as an "impossible" shot goes over his head as he is standing on a green with a short putt to win but watching as the miraculous (not to say malicious) shot goes in the hole to beat him – like a pitcher watching a home run soar over the fence to beat him out of a World Series.

They had pummeled him for years, those evil invisible deities, but they saved their worst indignity for this year's Masters.

You know, in the long annals of the game, the most famous – or infamous – "blowup" was held to be the Sam Snead eruption in the 1939 U.S. Open. Sam, who was to win more tournaments than any golfer who ever lived, came to the 70th hole that year needing only two pars to win his Open. He bogeyed 17 but still could have won with a par on 18. He took an eight. Ocho. What the college boys call a "snowman."

It was No. 1 on golf's all-time catastrophe list – until this year's Masters.

Greg Norman had his accustomed 54-hole lead as he teed it up with Nick Faldo on the final round. He was six shots ahead. Six! Prevailing opinion was, he could have won it with a rake and a shovel and a ball-marker.

He still had a two-shot lead going into the back nine. The things that happened to him should have happened to Jack the Ripper. By the 18th hole, seasoned golf galleries couldn't look. He was in more water than a U-boat. He went from six shots ahead to five shots behind. It made Snead's one-hole blowup look like a hiccup.

But in a funny kind of way, it made Norman a sort of national hero. We're supposed to be a society of front-runners, addicted to winning, scornful of being second best.

Not so. I sat with Greg Norman the other day out at Sherwood Country Club in Thousand Oaks, where they're holding the annual Franklin Templeton Shark Shootout. It pits 20 of the best golfers in the world in a tournament for Norman's favorite charity, the National Childhood Cancer Foundation.

"You know, I used to be a cynical individual," said Norman. "I won't say I expected the worst in people, but I counted my change, if you know what I mean. I kept my own optimism but I kept my distance. But I honestly believe – no, I know – the outpouring of letters and calls I got from people all over the world really changed my outlook."

There was not a single instance of gloating by anyone, he recalls. Even Nick Faldo, the beneficiary of his implosion, appeared embarrassed, even tearful.

"I was touched," admitted Norman. "I took out newspaper and magazine ads here and in Australia and England to thank the people. It made me feel good there are so many caring people out there."

It wasn't sympathy, it was empathy. "They know," Norman says with a smile. "You know, golf has been good to Greg Norman. It doesn't owe any of us anything. I won a tournament in Australia in 1980 or '81 and won 69 pounds (about $105). Today you get $1.6 million. To be part of that is lucky, not unlucky."

Norman is now the patron saint of every guy who ever missed a three-foot putt to win the 20-and-over flight at his home club, every guy who ever shanked a three-wood into a living room window of a fairway condo, everyone who fanned a tee shot or hit a ground ball in a pro-am with the whole world watching or hit it in the water to lose four ways to his brother-in-law.

And, to every kid with cancer, he's their master champion every year.

● ● ● ● ● ● ● ● ● ● ● ● ● ● ● ● ●

JANUARY 20, 1991

Whatever It Was, Arnie Still Has It

I guess everything will be all right as long as Arnold Palmer is playing golf. That way, we'll never get old. It's always 1964 or so. Things were better.

Look! Mickey Mantle isn't hitting curveballs into the seats anymore. Willie Mays isn't hauling down three-base hits in center field. Rod Laver isn't blasting anybody off Centre Court at Wimbledon.

But Arnold is still out there, with his shirt hanging out, a glove peeking from his back pocket as he hunches over a putt with that peculiar knock-kneed stance, face contorted with effort, concentration in every line. He still comes on TV wincing in dismay and rolling his eyes heavenward as a 35-foot putt fails to drop. He still has that Army out there, trampling down small trees, spilling the beer out of cans and imploring, "Go for it, Arnie!"

Oh, maybe the hair's a little gray, the feet probably hurt, the back aches. He doesn't buzz the fairways in his private jet anymore.

But he still remains the most exciting player ever to take up the game. America has had a 30-year love affair with him.

No one knows exactly what it was about Palmer. He had the kind of chemistry some movie stars have. He lit up the screen. There was no higher drama in any sport than Arnold Palmer on the spoor of first money in a major.

I'll never forget my first encounter with the man who was to symbolize golf for his generation. It was at a tournament in Tijuana, of all places. I was covering it for a magazine. I got separated from my wife because I was following a golfer named J. C. Goosie (I wanted to see if there was such a person).

That night, she came to me, all enthusiastic.

"I have just been following the most exciting player I've ever seen," she said. "He makes everybody else look like malted milk. His name is Palmer."

"Oh, yeah," I told her. "I know. Big shock of jet-black hair. Kind of short. Compact swing. A North Carolinian."

I was thinking of tour veteran Johnny Palmer, who was a second-echelon pro in the ratings, but the more famous Palmer on the tour at that time. My wife frowned.

"No," she said. "That doesn't sound like him. This guy plays like something they just let out of a cage. This guy doesn't tiptoe. He charges."

It was the first time I had heard that word applied to Palmer, although it was to be used many times in the years to come. I went out to see this wonder who could attract the attention of even non-fans.

I was hooked, too. Palmer on a golf course was Jack Dempsey with his man on the ropes, Henry Aaron with a three-and-two fastball, Laver at set point, Joe Montana with a minute to play, A. J. Foyt with a lap to go and a car to catch.

He never hit a safe shot. He tried to make two on every hole. Sometimes he made 12. That was Palmer. They loved him for it.

No one ever quite commanded the rapport with a gallery Palmer did. Players hated to play with him – or in front of him or in back of him. The audience was Palmer's, and they were legion.

Part of it was, he swung like they did. Palmer went after the ball like a guy beating a carpet. It wasn't pretty, but it was effective. He won 62 tournaments but always managed to look like a refugee from the truck drivers' flight at the local municipal.

He was the greatest long putter who ever lived. He didn't lag them. He never finished up on the same side of the hole as he started. Palmer's putts were either in – or five feet past. He attacked the game of golf like a cop busting a crap game.

He ran down so many 40-foot putts in one tournament that when he came up unaccountably close, within three feet, on one hole and took out his putter, his playing partner, Dave Marr, remarked wryly, "You've got too much club, Arnold."

He hasn't won a tour tournament in 18 years. He hasn't won a major in 27. He threw away more tournaments and more money than a sailor on shore leave. He never learned to play commercial golf. He only won one U.S. Open, but he was in a playoff in three others and in one of them threw away a seven-shot lead with nine holes to play.

He had the physique of a middleweight boxer, the hands of a bricklayer and you didn't have to watch the shot to see where it went, you could tell by Palmer's face. But he never cried. The grass was never too long, the greens too hard, the weather too bad and, once, when he made a 12 on a hole at the L.A. Open and someone asked him what happened, Palmer replied, "I missed a short putt for an 11."

In a sense, he made golf in the early TV era. If Palmer didn't play, people didn't watch. If he didn't win, it was a non-tournament.

And he pumped so much life into the senior tour that it now outranks the ladies' tour – and, sometimes, the men's.

A few of us were on the phone to the aging idol the other morning. He's getting ready for the annual Senior Skins Game, a modification of the great game that has caught the imagination of the public and that, fittingly enough, came into public favor because it had Arnold Palmer on screen live and on the attack again.

This year's Senior Skins Game, which will be played at Mauna Lani on the big island in Hawaii on Jan. 26-27, will be a fivesome – and everybody knows why. Chi-Chi Rodriguez has earned a place in the traditional foursome, having won $729,788 on the senior tour last year. Arnold won only $65,519. He's in the field because he's defending champion. But he's also in the field because he's Arnold Palmer. We play five, gentlemen.

In looking back on an illustrious career, Palmer is asked if he had any regrets, any things he wished he had done differently. How about the seven-shot lead he threw away in the Open at Olympic in 1966?

"Nah," said Palmer. "I had a seven-shot lead. I was trying to make it 11.

"I did it my way."

He still does. It's what keeps us young.

• • • • • • • • • • • • • • • • •

JANUARY 9, 1969

Sifford Made His Way With Par, Not Politics

Before Charlie Sifford, if a Negro walked on a golf green in this country, chances are he was carrying someone else's clubs and/or a wet towel to wipe somebody else's ball.

If he was in the grille room, he was carrying somebody else's coffee. He came to fix a shower, not take one.

Golf was not a game for the ghettos. Neither did it leave any time for carrying picket signs, joining demonstrations, or running for office.

Charlie birdied, not talked, his way through society prejudice. He broke barriers by breaking par. His weapon was a nine-iron, not a microphone. Charlie stands as a social pioneer not because he could play politics but because he could play golf.

Golfers, you have to know, have to be single-minded human beings. Ask one of them what he thinks of Richard Nixon, and chances are, he will frown and say "Too much right hand" or "He's bringing his right shoulder through too fast." The golfer doesn't know his politics, just his handicap.

Prior to Charlie, pro golfers had the effrontery to have a "Caucasians only" clause in their bylaws. It was the recreational arm of the Ku Klux Klan. Charlie came out of the darktown alleys of Carolina, packing for the rich folks, but practicing his own swing by moonlight. He "looped" for the hotheaded Clayton Heafner, with whom he gypsied through the tournaments. He hustled the hoods of Philadelphia. Charlie putted for his supper. He played nickel-and-dime games with the same skill and enthusiasm as $10 Nassaus. Charlie learned how to save strokes around the green and around the first tee, too.

The singer Billy Eckstine got him out of nickel cigars and nickel putting contests, and together they began to apply the abolitionist movement to golf. The first breakthroughs were – and, I have to think, were intended to be – token. When they were backed to a wall, golf tournaments would let Negroes in – and then sit back and watch them shoot 80. "See? It's not their color, it's their score," they would contend.

Charlie doublecrossed them. Charlie could play this damn game all right. Charlie was competition, buddy.

His swing was nothing to get drunk over. Off the tee, Charlie ends up with his hands crossed, his legs crossed, and sometimes his eyes. He looks like a guy who has just fouled off a low, outside 0-and-2 pitch. But when Charlie gets around the green and smells money, he's like a surgeon.

Charlie is the only Negro to have won a tour tournament. He made the field – and the cut – in five National Opens. He has been in the top

60 money winners every year since they let him in – 1961.

They kicked his ball out of bounds in some Southern tourneys, but Charlie held his temper. No Uncle Tom, neither is Charlie a minstrel Negro. He's as dour as Hogan on a course, as serious as an undertaker. He doesn't like his back slapped any better than his face. Charlie is his own man; the face around the cigar frequently is scowling. He doesn't like anybody standing in his line – on or off the course. Getting a weekly threatening letter from some mental case in Florida, as Charlie does, hardly promotes a sunny outlook on one's fellow man anyway.

But Charlie, who tees it up in the L.A. Open this week, has now played in every tournament in America save one – the Masters. This August Augusta tournament has a complicated formula for selecting its field. If you come from Formosa, it's easy to get in. If you come from a cotton patch in Carolina, it's impossible.

The one avenue open to Charlie isn't really open at all. Past winners of this tournament can vote in a man who, either because he wasn't lucky enough to be born in Formosa or to have had one bad round in the Open, does not otherwise qualify.

In the past two years, Charlie has played this game about as well as anyone on the circuit, certainly as well as anyone in the Masters. The past Masters selected Mike Souchak and Tommy Jacobs.

Pretty soon Charlie found people driving into him from the front tees. "Sure I was disappointed. Sure I know it's the only tournament Negroes have never played in. Sure I know that most of those Masters winners come from Texas or the Deep South. But I find letters putting words in my mouth to get at Jones (Bobby) and the Masters. So I get this letter from Bobby Jones telling me to stop threatening him. I don't threaten any man. I GET threatened. But I felt that, when I finished 25th in the money list, or won that tournament, or took third in the Canadian Open, I was entitled to some consideration. I have never disgraced anybody – with a golf club or with a salad fork."

It is a feeling of this 22-handicapper that the Masters ought to send a car for Charlie and, considering he's the only guy in the field who couldn't get started on his golf career till he was 33 years old or his tournament career till he was almost 40 because it took democracy so long to catch on in this country, maybe they ought to give him two a side. If they do, I'll guarantee you Charlie will be voting on the invitee next year.

● ● ● ● ● ● ● ● ● ● ● ● ● ● ● ● ● ●

OCTOBER 23, 1966

Like Old Man River, Snead Keeps on Rolling

CARLSBAD – There is a game sportsmen like to play called "Where Are They Now?"

Take 1936, for instance. That was a good year. Carl Hubbell started the World Series. Gehrig, Dickey and Lazzeri ended it. Joe DiMaggio was in his rookie year. James J. Braddock was heavyweight champion. Arthur Tracy, the Street Singer, was very large on the airwaves. Sandy Koufax was six months old.

And out in the hills of West Virginia, a skinny-framed kid, Samuel Jackson Snead, with forearms like anvils, a bushy head of hair with a widow's peak, a length of string and a cork in his pocket so he could catch his supper, a pair of shoes with four spikes in the left one and only three in the other and paper where the soles should be, shot a 61 in golf and won the Closed Pro Champions of West, By God, Virginia.

Where are they now? Well, Gehrig and Lazzeri are dead. James J. Braddock is gray and sad and sings Irish ballads in an old man's quavering voice at fight parties. Hubbell is scouting ballplayers. DiMaggio, the rookie, hung up his bat and spikes 15 years ago and can barely remember what a curveball looked like up close.

Samuel Jackson Snead? You'll find him on the fairway – and the scoreboard – at the Haig Scotch Mixed golf tournament at La Costa. He's still shooting birdies and eagles and uncorking 280-yard drives. The widow's peak is gone. So is the rest of his hair. He gets his fish a la carte now. He doesn't need a gun for a turkey dinner. And he just won the West Virginia State Open again with rounds totaling 199.

The legend of Sam Snead defies belief. It smacks more of a sound stage than a fairway. It's not a career, it's an eon. It is now running neck-and-neck with the Ice Age as an historical era. He's a living fossil. He should be home wrapped in an afghan with his feet in a tub and a hot-water bottle under each arm. He should creak, be able to tell when it's going to rain by a twinge in his toes. He ought to be lipping snuff or keeping his teeth in a glass. He shouldn't be golfing, he should be whittling.

But he still has the kids on the tour talking to themselves or cursing under their breath as he screams one-irons and 250-yard green-splitters dead on line to the pin. He can still burrow a ball through the wind, around a tree, over a creek or through the sand with anybody on the tour. He is still so loose-jointed, he could comb his hair with his toes. He's got 12 spikes on each of his shoes now, his clubs don't have pieces of adhesive tape on the shafts anymore, his eyesight is so good he could see a penny in the dark. His step is so jaunty, Jim Ferree says, he "could walk on eggs and not break any." Adds Ferree: "If he's not the world's greatest athlete, I'll take him and give whoever is two shots a side."

Snead, last summer at a creaky old 54, led the game's second most prestigious tournament for two rounds, and might have made it four except for a hip injury. He is easily the most durable specimen in the long history of games.

To find a precise comparable accomplishment, you would have to imagine General Pershing being in charge at Vietnam, Spencer Tracy playing a college kid – or DiMaggio finishing second in RBIs or stealing third in a World Series.

The swing is still so fluid and uncomplicated – as it was in the days when he used to hum the "Skater's Waltz" to keep it rhythmical – that he may become the first man in history to birdie a hole posthumously. Look for a news story 45 years from now that goes:

"Samuel Jackson Snead, 99, died on the 14th green at Humidity Hollow Golf Course yesterday. This seriously affected his short game, but he still managed to par in the rest of the way for a net 69 – 53 living and the rest posthumous. If rigor mortis doesn't set in, he will still be an odds-on favorite at tee-off tomorrow."

When you talk of the greats in any line of endeavor, you usually deal in the past. I saw Cousy play basketball, Ruth play baseball, Joe Louis box. I heard Pinza sing, Muni act and Paderewski play. But all that is left of them is an echo. I SEE Sam Snead play golf, a link with the past, Old Man River himself in a palmetto hat and 24 cleats. It's eerie. Like watching Nagurski shredding lines, Don Budge crushing Wimbledon opponents, hearing Roosevelt on the Red and Blue networks.

As Jerry Barber once said, "Sam Snead fell out of bed with his swing." And he'll fall into his grave with it. But don't wait around. That should be around $400,000 from now, and someone will say, "Look, Ma, that's Sam Snead. He was playing way back when Koufax was still pitching."

• • • • • • • • • • • • • • • • • •

JUNE 15, 1986

Shark May Have Bitten Off More Than He Can Chew

SOUTHAMPTON, N.Y. – You might want to strike the ball like Ben Hogan. You might want to putt like Billy Casper, approach a green like Miller Barber, swing like Sam Snead.

But I imagine if there's a golfer you'd want to look like, it would be Gregory John Norman. The sloped shoulders, the wide back, the tiny-to-invisible waist, the great shock of white-blond hair, you imagine a statue could look like this.

Greg Norman could walk into a room full of middleweight prizefighters, weightlifters, gymnasts or flamenco dancers and not be embarrassed.

You know how most golfers look – department-store Santa Clauses, Irish bartenders, streetcar conductors, staff sergeants. They look in poor light like your brother-in-law. Plumbers have to be in better shape.

Not Greg Norman. You wouldn't mistake him for anything but what he is – a top athlete.

You could chop wood with his face. You could win a war with his backswing. He doesn't look like a guy you'd want to cheat at cards or make a pass at his girlfriend or steal his wallet. He'd look at home slicing through white-water seas grinding up everything that came in his path. Golf's Jaws.

They say the great white shark is the most perfect eating machine ever created, a scavenger so awesome it attacks ships, de-limbs sailors.

The great white whale is equally mythic, but if there ever was a Moby Dick in cleats, it is this sleek platinum creature from a black lagoon Down Under. Greg Norman looks like something you'd radio for help for in a small boat.

If there is a Captain Ahab in this 86th U.S. Open at Shinnecock Hills this week, it is Lee Buck Trevino. This relentless old mariner of the links has been stalking terrors of the deep on golf courses for almost 25 years.

If it weren't for Lee Buck, Jack W. Nicklaus would have long since surrounded this game even more than he has.

Every time you think you might just as well hand the game over to Jack, there's Lee Trevino banging shots off pins at the Firth of Forth or the Main Line of Philadelphia and saying "Wait a minute, Jack, what about me?"

Lee didn't learn his game in the cloisters of a university or junior golf at pater's country club. Lee learned it the way guys learned to live stealing hubcaps or hawking candy. Lee scuffled, hustled, faded you, raised you, lived by his swing and wits. Nobody bought Lee Trevino a matched set of monogrammed clubs and a gold money clip when he was growing up. Lee got his irons out of a barrel, and his woods had cracks in them, and he played you with a taped soda pop bottle if the bet was right.

"Pressure is not playing in the U.S. Open for somebody else's money," Lee Buck has said. "Pressure is playing for $50 with a guy with a scar on his cheek when you only got $2 in your pocket."

Pressure is playing for the rent money, not the yacht money or Lear jet money. Lee Trevino has played for both. He's big trouble at either.

He doesn't walk around a golf course, he swaggers around it. Lee always looks like a guy trying to scare up a game or press a bet. You get the feeling he could beat you left-handed if the price was right.

The 86th U.S. Open looked like just another shark bite for the great white Greg right up till about 5:10 p.m. Saturday. Lee Trevino took that little fadey swing of his out of the bag on hole No. 13, a tight little 377-yarder the locals call "The Roadside" (they name holes in this tight little isle the same as they do on that one in Scotland).

Greg Norman, the golf player who looks like a Garden main eventer or a refugee from a surfboard, was enjoying a three-shot lead and a walk in the park up to the time he sent a mid-iron soaring over the teardrop green. From there he was looking at a double bogey.

It was the only opening Trevino needed. Lee is a guy who can count the aces, who knows when to bet his play and bump the raise. He fired one of his patented soft left-to-right shots that you could land on an umbrella without breaking it, and it came down two feet from the hole and stopped.

Greg Norman was now looking at a Trevino birdie. Lee tapped it in and gave Norman his sunny, "You're pressed!" look as if to say "Match that around New York!"

It was a three-shot swing on one hole. Trevino gained one, and Norman lost two.

I would not like to see Mario Andretti in my rearview mirror on a racetrack. I would not like to have to go down and check a noise in the cellar in a castle in the Balkans. I would not like to find a rattlesnake under my bed.

And I would not like to go into the final round of a U.S. Open with a one-stroke lead over Lee Trevino. The bleached bones of guys who have tried it line every cattle trail in Texas.

You'd better have carfare home in your shoe when you take on the Mex at his own game. Jack Nicklaus found that out at Oak Hill in 1968, Merion in 1971, Muirfield in 1972.

Lee Trevino is 46 years old. That's not old enough. That has nothing to do with that little sweeping wheel through the ball that has been emptying wallets and piling up trophies and winning 27 tour tournaments since 1967, when he showed up at an Open and had to walk to the course in his cleats or sleep in his car to make ends meet. It may take more than a shark to scare Lee Buck. Where he comes from, they give sharks two-a-side – and the first bite.

● ● ● ● ● ● ● ● ● ● ● ● ● ● ● ● ● ●

JUNE 21, 1987

The Guy Sure Looks Like Tom Watson

SAN FRANCISCO – Once upon a time there was this young golf player who looked as if he had just arrived by raft from the Mississippi River. He had this red hair and freckled face and a gap-toothed smile that made him look as if he had just stepped out of the pages of Mark Twain. He looked out of place with shoes on. You wanted to sift his pockets for live lizards or balls of string and ask him where he put his fishing pole. You wanted to ask him if his name was "Huckleberry."

His name, of course, was Tom – but Watson, not Sawyer. All he lacked was Becky Thatcher.

But "The Adventures of Tom Watson" became an American classic of its own sort.

This barefoot boy from Stanford University played a game they never heard of in Mark Twain lore – golf.

He played it about as well as it could be played. He had this violent, thrashing swing that seemed to create its own wind currents. He seemed to spin for five minutes after he hit the ball and he slashed at it so hard he seemed to recoil like a man who has just fired a heavy cannon.

He rushed into a vacuum in the great game. The Arnold Palmers and the Sam Sneads were just beginning to disappear, and this Tom Watson seemed to be cut from their same cloth.

He went after golf courses like a guy charging a machine-gun nest. He had a take-no-prisoners attitude. His club quivered for five minutes after he hit a ball.

At first, he had the usual talented overeager rookie problem. He either made a two – or a 12. He was either in the cup or in the water.

He had a touch around the greens that bordered on the obscene. He could apparently stop a golf ball rolling down a flight of marble stairs, and he could make his irons do anything Gregory Hines could do.

Legends grew around him. They told of the time when he was 15 and Arnold Palmer came through town and this little redheaded kid reared back and hit the ball 20 yards past him. He almost won the first U.S. Open he was in – or at least he was leading after three rounds. Then he soared to a 79.

But the golf world figured he would win plenty of Opens. And he did. British Opens – five of them. He won Masters and he won 30 other tournaments and, in 1982, he finally won a U.S. Open, snatching it from the bag of Jack Nicklaus on the world's toughest Open track, Pebble Beach.

It was, everyone assured themselves, the first of many.

Then a strange thing happened. This player disappeared. Vanished, without a trace.

In his place, someone had the nerve to use his name and his qualifications on tour.

It was a clumsy forgery. It was as if an Arnold Palmer lookalike had showed up using a four-iron where a three-wood was called for.

What someone should have done was drop four balls in a semicircle around a hole 20 feet away and challenged the impostor to put them in. If he missed one, he was a fake.

Rich Little would have been ashamed of the impersonation. The best guess was, the real Watson was a prisoner in a locker room somewhere. This one couldn't putt, couldn't chip, couldn't hit a fairway, make a cut, never mind win a tournament. They didn't know whether to give him strokes or call the cops. They didn't know whether he was sick or phony.

He hit bottom this year when he was in 12 tournaments and ended up 56th on the money list. He missed three of the last four cuts. The tour was ready to arrest him for vagrancy, and when he came to this 87th U.S. Open at Olympic this week, most people thought he was cluttering up the field. When you said "Watson" in connection with a tournament, you meant Denis. Tom would need strokes. He was playing to a "4" on the tour. He wasn't supposed to be a factor.

Golf is this kind of a game: Just when it begins to look easy, it drifts out of reach – like a coquettish female. It usually strikes just when the player begins to get complacent. It's an invisible barrier the player crashes against.

Some never pick themselves up, and the truck collects them and deposits them in a club-cleaning job someplace in Ohio.

That's what they thought had happened to Tom Watson. He had found out how tough the game was. He was like a mountain climber who suddenly looks down, the deep-sea diver who notices the sharks for the first time.

In the days when he was winning 20 tournaments in three years, a hallmark of Tom Watson's game was tenacity, an almost irrational belief in his own invincibility.

He never lost that. Whatever other qualities this Watson lacked, the sure optimism the next shot would be an ace, the next hole a birdie never left him.

On Saturday afternoon at the Open, the field ventured out on the no-man's land that is Olympic's 18 holes looking like 70 guys who have been asked to break up the Mafia, swim to Iceland, fight Dempsey in a closet.

No one attacked. They were busy trying to defend themselves. They were hoping the course wouldn't notice them. A kid playing an unpressured early-morning round had steered it around in 64 before the course was fully awake, and it looked as if he wase going to get the Open lead all to himself by default.

But Keith Clearwater probably never heard of the real Tom Watson. The Watson who disappeared without a trace three years ago, the Watson who played with the confidence of a guy who knows the next card is going to be an ace.

Only that Watson could have kept the course – and Clearwater – at bay Saturday.

The Watson who rifled mid-irons to guarded greens, the Watson who rolled in putts through three breaks and a foot of spike marks, was the real article at last.

If he shows up today, the field will be playing for second place just as in the old days.

If he disappears again, he may never be heard from again and the game may have to settle for the bad copy it's had to put up with for the five years now since he won his only Open and the three years since he's won anything. He's got a one-shot lead. For the real Tom Watson, that would be about three more than he would need.

• • • • • • • • • • • • • • • • • •

NOVEMBER 28, 1996

Can't See Trees for the Woods

Golf is now a five-letter word. It's spelled "W-O-O-D-S."

Tiger Woods is no longer merely an athlete. He's an industry.

It's already beginning. The headline writers know where their readers are coming from. The headline reads: "Tiger Woods Finishes Fifth, Greg Norman Wins Australian Open."

And that's Greg Norman! Imagine if it had been some rinky-dink tour journeyman. He'd have been lucky to make paragraph eight.

We haven't seen that kind of skewed headlining since the early days of Arnie's Army when the banner would proclaim "Palmer Bogeys 18. Unknown Wins Masters."

All across the country, editors didn't care who won a tournament if it wasn't Palmer or Nicklaus. Without them, the story hit the agate – along with "Fights Last Night" and high school soccer scores.

It's happening again. A tall, smiling kid with the charisma of a movie star, a smile like a sunrise, a swing as sweet as a banana split and the confidence of a riverboat gambler with his own deck has come along to rescue the game from the brink of anonymity, saved it from being won by people named Jones or foreigners whose handles you can't even pronounce.

It was easy to believe there is no such person as Tiger Woods. They made him up, right? Everything about him is too perfect. They sent down to Central Casting and they came up with the right guy for the part. Best bit of casting since Clark Gable as Rhett Butler. It's John Wayne on horseback, as heartwarming as a Lassie movie. Beaver Cleaver with a two-iron.

Tiger was the American Dream, perfect ethnically for the United States in the 21st century. The cavalry to the rescue. The guy in the white hat.

He did everything right. He won three U.S. Amateurs. Only Bobby Jones had done that, winning four. He won two of the first seven tournaments he entered after turning pro. Nobody had ever done that. Or maybe ever will.

He won his first pro tournament at 20. Nicklaus won his at 22. Palmer won his at 26. Hogan was 27.

Americans loved it – Instant Legend. He wasn't going to have a career, he was going to have a ticker-tape parade. He was going to eagle life.

Most people are allowed to slip into stardom, dip a toe in the water, test it, deal with it, maybe pick up a rookie-of-the-year award or so before they start getting measured for Halls of Fame. Tiger dived in headfirst off the high board. The spotlight was on him before he got his first set of clubs. The microphones were under his chin as soon as he could talk, the cameras were trained on him by his first practice swing. The agents were on hand throwing truckloads of money at him, waving contracts as he came off the 18th tee.

It was good for golf, good for TV. Was it good for Woods?

I went out the other night to check this out on our newest national resource. I thought I better get a look before they put him up on Mt. Rushmore.

He was at the family home in Cypress, had just come back from the Australian Open where he had upstaged Norman and the flower of Down Under golf. A spot in a Tiger Woods threesome is a good place for a guy on the lam to hide out. No one will notice him there.

He came home to get in a little of Mom's cooking and Dad's advice (Tiger now lives in Florida), but, as usual, he was surrounded by the pomp and circumstance of his messianic existence.

I was there running around with a notebook and pen, ABC's TV cameras were there to film him for the halftime show on "Monday Night Football," Mom was trying to prepare him Thai delicacies, and Dad, Earl Woods, was trying to catch the football game. A neighbor was suddenly at the door with her 4-year-old son in tow wondering if

Tiger would mind posing for a picture with him. Tiger didn't mind, but Dad had to come up with the camera. This Is Your Life, Tiger Woods.

Everyone wants a piece of him these days. A tournament without Tiger is a non-event. And this weekend, at Rancho La Quinta golf course, he has turned a made-for-TV Skins game, ordinarily a "trash sport," into something as eagerly awaited as a U.S. Open playoff. This is because it will be Tiger matching tee shots with none other than John Daly, the ex-Golden Boy of the tour.

Fans are expecting a golf version of Dempsey-Firpo. ABC expects to buck weekend football. "Hold that Tiger!" doesn't mean a goal-line stand anymore, it means Woods' shots.

Tiger is taking it in stride. Tiger takes everything in stride. Tiger is almost nonchalant about his talent.

Still, he's carrying the weight of all golf on his 20-year-old shoulders. Two of the greatest players in the game, Fred Couples and Tom Watson, will be almost straight men, sidekicks in Saturday and Sunday's drama.

Given that kind of pressure, is burnout an option? His father, Earl, scoffs. "Tiger has been handling the media and publicity since he was 2," he explains. "I taught him. I was the public information officer for the Army at Fort Hamilton in New York. And I told Tiger, 'Always tell the truth and just answer the question asked.' He's as at ease with the media as he is over a two-foot putt."

What about when he finds out putts don't have to drop, balls slice or hook, or go out of bounds, or when he learns why they call bunkers "hazards"?

What then?

Tiger hoots.

"Hey!" he says. "I was the wildest player off the tee you will ever see. I played some courses sideways. I had to invent trouble shots all the time!"

Earl agrees: "You know why Tiger can handle adversity? Because when he goes bogey-bogey-double bogey, I laugh! I always have. He used to look at me and think, 'Well, it can't be the end of the world. Dad's laughing.' That's why he can go from double bogey to birdie, from 79 to 66."

And that's why he can go up to the game of golf these days and say, "You're away!"

Horse Racing

● ● ● ● ● ● ● ● ● ● ● ● ● ● ● ● ●

MAY 7, 1978

It's Affirmed: The Best
In the West is THE Best

LOUISVILLE – It was supposed to be the race of the mid-century. It was to make everybody forget whatever happened on a racetrack before. Compared to this, Noor-Citation was a schottische. Dempsey-Firpo was a debate. Man o'War and John P. Grier were underbred.

This was going to be a ride like Paul Revere's. It would go right into the history books. Poems would be written about it. It would be a celebration of the horse. No Canonero II, Dust Commander, no quarter horse. This field had the look of eagles, all right. These were the kind that won the wars, settled the West, delivered the mail. These kind caught Geronimo, beat Montezuma, conquered Peru and almost saved Lee.

But sometimes great expectations sour. You expect Dempsey-Firpo and you get Dempsey-Gibbons. You want a Super Bowl and you get Harvard-Yale. You get two Hall of Fame pitchers and they're both chased by the third inning. "Carmen" is announced but "Naughty Marietta" is performed.

Well, you can pump up the trumpets for the 1978 Kentucky Derby. Pull the stops, wave the flags. A great, marvelous, well-mannered colt, as gold as bullion, as orange-red as a Canadian sunset, put away a blue-chip field in the Derby as easily as Too Tall Jones might drop a quarter-back or Musial pull a fastball off the fence.

He beat a blue-ribbon panel without really appearing to have to reach in to take out the capital of his talent.

Impeccably trained by a Cuban who appears to be able to talk to horses, skillfully ridden by an unexcitable 18-year-old who looks as if he should be sweeping chimneys in 19th century London, Affirmed won a picture-book Derby. One for the lithographs.

There was one undefeated colt, three bums, a mystery colt, a couple of so-whats? and four very real runners in the race.

You can never tell about colts. They make eggs look sturdy. But Affirmed looked every inch a colt for the lithographs. He went about his work with the bored efficiency of a Joe DiMaggio getting under a line drive, Sugar Ray working his man into a corner, Dempsey measuring a palooka. He looked like Bobby Layne picking a defense apart, Nick the Greek betting a pat hand.

He did what he had to do on the day he had to do it – as the great ones always do. This was the seventh game of the World Series, the fourth quarter, the main event and the 15th round. It doesn't matter in this game what you do at Pimlico next week or Arlington Park next summer. The Kentucky Derby is a grueling mile-and-a-quarter rock-pile a chain gang should work on.

Lazaro Barrera, the trainer who has been acting all week as if the colt told him he would win and by how much, sent out a dead fit animal, trained down so fine his ribs were showing.

Not since the immortal Swaps has anyone seen such a well-behaved horse on a track. More than 130,000 people were screaming, three bands were playing, helicopters were hovering overhead and Affirmed acted as if he were in church. Lighting candles. A monk could not be more tranquil.

He did not spend his condition in fruitless bouts with the rider, the lead pony, the track. He got into his stall as quietly as a burglar. He gave his backers an honest count for the $1,242,322 they bet on him.

It was the seventh time Affirmed and Alydar ran one-two and it was the fifth time Affirmed was one and Alydar, two. Alydar should try another wheel.

In a corner of the jocks' room after the race, the little rider with the Cantinflas mustache and the glistening eyes toweled himself off and tried to answer cruel questions. Jorge Velasquez should be used to chasing Affirmed around racetracks, but this was a race his colt seemed to be trying to get out of. Alydar and Velasquez had only one colt beat going into the first turn. Jorge either thought he had a bunch of Caliente horses in front of him or the clock in his head was busted.

"He could not handle the track," Jorge said sadly as he pulled on his purple shorts and searched for his Brut and embroidered shirt. "I could not get him to run till the final eighth. The track was too hard, and he was slipping and sliding."

Across the room, little Stevie Cauthen, the rider out of Charles Dickens by Walt Disney, shrugged. "Were you satisfied with the time?" someone wanted to know. Cauthen's eyes bugged. "What did you want him to do?" he demanded.

Trainer Barrera was even more expansive. "Against the opinion of almost everybody, my horse was the best," he said. "They said, 'Well he's from California so maybe he can't really run.' But it doesn't matter. He's a great horse. He can run anywhere, China, even."

Added Barrera: "The other day, I put him on the track for a slow workout. Then I wanted to see if he could handle the cuppy track. I told the boy to work him the last eighth. It was the best work I ever saw on a horse. He got the last eighth in 11.1. I said, "The party is over."'"

Would the longer distance of the Belmont be more trying for Affirmed? "We can go five miles and it's gonna be the same result," insisted Barrera. "You saw what kind of horse he is. He comes back from the race like he is just coming from the beauty parlor. We just have to find a horse somewhere who can make him go fast. Then you will really see something."

It was an all-star production that could play Broadway or the RKO circuit. "Carmen" was announced and "Carmen" was performed. The first team showed up. Affirmed beat his competition the way Jack Nicklaus does. On a par five over water, which is what Churchill Downs is after a week of rains.

The vintage years are few in Louisville. A Cavalcade. Citation. Count Fleet. Whirlaway.

Steve Cauthen has now won exactly as many Kentucky Derbies at age 18 as Johnny Longden did, although he tried till he was nearly 60. Only two black riders before the turn of the century and Bill Boland on Middleground in 1950 were younger.

But Affirmed was The Star. A golden glow of a colt. A matinee idol. If he were human, he'd be Robert Redford. He looks the part. The Champ. If you're going to win one race, it should be the Kentucky Derby. If you're going to win one golf tournament, make it the Open. You have to win the one they remember. Affirmed didn't shank, strike out, get thrown for a safety or miss the rim. He turned over his hole card – and it was an ace.

● ● ● ● ● ● ● ● ● ● ● ● ● ● ● ● ● ●

MARCH 2, 1986

Eddie Arcaro Usually Found A Way to Win

When you start talking about great race riders, you begin with George Edward Arcaro. He could do anything on horseback that Jesse James, Tom Mix, Buffalo Bill or the Lone Ranger could.

He rode in the days before they had cameras stuck every step of the way. And he rode in the days when they did. Nobody could snatch a saddle cloth, lock a leg or lug in on a passing entry any smoother than Arcaro.

Lots of guys can whip horses. Eddie could whip jockeys. It was not considered smart to get too close to him in a stretch or to crowd him on a turn, for that matter. Eddie used whatever was available to him.

He never pulled a horse in his life. If you wanted to lose, Arcaro wasn't your man. His book was titled "I Ride To Win." When Eddie got "days" (racetrack-ese for suspensions), it was not for what he did to a horse, it was what he did to jockeys. He once got a year on the ground for whipping not only another horse but another jockey and putting them both in the infield. He was also ready to take on the owner, trainer and members of the Jockey Club before he cooled out. "I shoulda got life," he admits today.

They wrote poems about Earl Sande, they built statues to Sonny Workman, but when a trainer had a good horse, he wanted Eddie Arcaro on him. What Vince Lombardi was to football players, Michelangelo to statues, Eddie Arcaro was to horses. They ran for him or else. A horse moved up several lengths with Arcaro on. The theory was, he was trying to get away from that son of the whip on his back.

He might have been the greatest money rider who ever lived. He won two Triple Crowns. Nobody ever did that before. Or since. He won five Kentucky Derbies. Only one other rider has ever done that (Bill Hartack). He won six Preaknesses and six Belmonts. No one comes close to having done that.

They didn't make the horse he couldn't tame, the track he couldn't solve. In 1941, Calumet had a colt who could run a hole in the wind and break every clock in Kentucky, but he was such a headstrong rogue that Arcaro recalls, "you couldn't keep him between the fences. He'd get five lengths in front and head for the grandstand. He'd pull you off his back."

Trainer Ben Jones wanted Arcaro for this brute. Two other people didn't. One was Arcaro. The other was owner Warren Wright.

Ben Jones threatened to quit if Arcaro couldn't ride the horse. The owner relented. In the contest of wills that followed, Eddie flogged Whirlaway into one of the great Kentucky Derby triumphs of all time by eight lengths. Then he won the Preakness with him by 5½ and the Belmont as easily. Eddie didn't want to ride the outlaw, but he figured as long as he did they were going to do it his way.

Actually, the only rider in America who could beat Eddie Arcaro in those days was Eddie Arcaro. Eddie rode in the first Santa Anita Handicap ever run, 51 years ago, and he would have won it but he got outsmarted by the only guy on the track who could do it – himself. He passed up the mount on Azucar, who won it, to take the one on Gusto, who won eighth place.

But that was nothing. Eddie took himself off a Kentucky Derby winner in 1942. He liked the chances of Devil Diver. And took himself off Shut Out. Shut Out won. Devil Diver struggled in sixth.

Eddie was never without an opinion – or sometimes without a glass – in those days. The morning of his first Kentucky Derby win – on a longshot named Lawrin – trainer Jones took him on a pre-dawn tour of the rain-soaked track. Eddie was pretty well soaked himself. He hadn't really been to bed. "He walked me around that track twice, pointing out the mudholes by the fence. 'Don't run him there,' he told me."

The trouble was, on race day, Eddie couldn't run anywhere else. The rest of the field apparently had the same instructions, and since he had the No. 1 post, he had nowhere to go but straight. "I never went outside a horse all day." It was a good thing. He very quickly saw, through bloodshot eyes, that the 100-degree heat had dried the inside lane so thoroughly that "all those holes he showed me weren't there. It was the best place on the racetrack to be." He won the race by 2½ lengths but estimated he ran about 3½ lengths less than anybody else in the race. "Everybody thought I was a genius. If I could have gotten out, I might not have beat a horse."

The secret of race riding is to make a horse confident or afraid. Eddie Arcaro was good at both. "It's a question of who's going to be boss," he explains. Eddie expects everyone to give his best. When he rode the great Nashua in the '50s, he found it hard to say something nice about him. The trainer, Jim Fitzsimmons, was not so sunny that day. "Why do you keep knocking the horse when all he does is win?" he demanded. "Because he ought to be 15 lengths better than he is," Arcaro snapped.

Arcaro always figured the bettor deserved the team's best. Although still a young man (45) by racetrack standards, he even took himself off the track in 1961. "I was getting good horses beat. My shoulder was paining me." Eddie Arcaro didn't believe sore riders belonged on the track any more than sore horses. He scratched himself out of the game.

Jockeys have suffered all kinds of terrible injuries on a track. Eddie Arcaro is probably the only one who almost drowned. It was in New York, and he got tumbled off a fractious colt named Black Hills into the homestretch slop. The photographer who came out to take his picture noticed his head in a pool of water and lifted it out. "I was actually drowning, they told me later," Arcaro recalls.

Eddie, who rode in 15 of them, is at Santa Anita this weekend for the 49th running of the Santa Anita Handicap. He won this race on Talon and on Mark-Ye-Well, but it was the scene of one of his greatest disappointments. It was in 1950 and Eddie was aboard the great Citation, whom he had ridden to the Triple Crown two years before and whom Eddie regards as not only the greatest horse he ever rode but maybe the greatest anybody has.

"We had a three-horse entry in the race. And it was my stablemate, Two Lea, that blocked me off at the head of the stretch. Johnny Gilbert wouldn't give me, his own stablemate, room. Noor won it, but Citation should have."

It was a week later that Noor beat Citation again in the greatest stretch run that maybe anyone has ever seen on a track when Johnny Longden, on Noor, kept Steve Brooks, on Citation, pinned against the rail all the way to the wire, and he couldn't whip. There were two jockey's agents, neither of them Arcaro's, leaving the track that night. "Arcaro wouldn't have got that horse beat," one of them said. "Arcaro would never have let that good a horse get beat like that."

It's probably as good an epitaph as any for him. Eddie Arcaro never got the best horse beat. Unless someone else was on him.

● ● ● ● ● ● ● ● ● ● ● ● ● ● ● ● ● ●

FEBRUARY 14, 1988

Looks Are Deceiving In This Case

Charles Dickens would have loved Chris McCarron. So would Walt Disney.

Eyes as blue as Galway Bay, framed by ringlets of flame-red hair, he looked like a cross between Oliver Twist and Bambi. Racing's Little Boy Blue. It didn't seem as if he could ever be a match for the 1,200-pound willful brutes they'd load him on in the starting gates around New England, where he began his career.

The contest between horse and rider is the most uneven since the Christians and the lions. It makes Notre Dame vs. Harvard look like a toss-up. The horse has a 1,000-pound pull in the weights, his instinct would be to bite or kick that creature on his back if he could and the last thing in the world he wants to do is run in a straight line.

If he could, he'd head straight for the barn. He'll sulk, jump shadows, lug in, lug out, prop. All he really wants to do is eat. He'll never go between horses or on the rail. He'll run too fast or too slow if left on his own, he's a bundle of nerves from inbreeding and a blowing hot dog wrapper can turn him into a hysterical mass of quivering horseflesh apt to do anything. Some horses you have to wrap a bag around their heads to get them to run at all.

The well-known sports surgeon Dr. Robert Kerlan no less, once said that jockeys, pound for pound, inch for inch, had to be the greatest athletes in the field of sports given the one-sidedness of the competition. They have less body fat than timber wolves and come as tightly wrapped. But their only advantage against a half-ton of horseflesh is their hands – and their brains.

That was enough for Chris McCarron, who was as good as anybody

239

who ever tied himself on one of these runaway causes. Like Sam Snead, he modeled his swing after an older brother's and, like Snead, he got better at it than that brother. McCarron, Chris, fit his style to the horse rather than vice versa.

You measure a rider not only by how many races he wins, but what kind. Some riders get horses to run the same way thunderstorms do – out of sheer terror. Others coax performance out of them. Anyone can ride Man o' War. Warra Nymph is another matter.

McCarron was as at home on horseback as Geronimo. He was only 18 years old when he won his first race, and he went on to win a staggering 546 races his first year in the saddle, a record.

But in the pecking order of racing, young riders – even precocious ones – have to wait their turn at the classic horses. Chris won races – he led the country in 1974, '75 and '80. He won money – he led in earnings in 1980, '81 and '84.

But in the Kentucky Derby, he got on 40- and 50-to-1 shots like Esop's Foibles and Cojak. When he finally got on a middling good horse – Desert Wine in 1983, Bold Arrangement in 1986 – he finished second. He rode John Henry in his Horse of the Year campaign in '84 but disclaims credit. "Easiest horse to ride I was ever on – all you had to do was not fall off. He was like a smart old fighter, an Archie Moore who knew what to do to win and did it."

But what sets Chris McCarron apart is an extraordinary ability to look a fact, even an unpleasant one, in the face.

Usually, when a rider comes back after a disappointing race, he is able to find someone or something to blame – the horse didn't care for the track, the horse didn't run his race, the horse was bothered by the crowd, the horse next to him, the start, his post position, sunspots. "He didn't fire up, when I asked him to run, he didn't have it," is a favorite. English translation: the horse let you down.

When Chris McCarron lost the Belmont on Alysheba last June, the letdown had to be cosmic. It would have made him instant history. Only 11 horses have won the Triple Crown and only 10 riders. Great jockeys have never won it – Bill Shoemaker, Laverne Fator, Lafit Pincay, Angel Cordero, Sonny Workman.

All he had to do was beat a field he had beaten twice – at Kentucky and at Maryland.

He ran a shocking 14 lengths behind a horse he led home twice. He finished a puffy fourth in a nine-horse field. He took a lot of money with him. He went off at 4-5. The winner paid 8-1.

If ever there was a motive to go find someone to blame, Chris McCarron had it.

He found someone to blame – Chris McCarron.

"I blew it. I called a bad game out there, you might say. I used bad judgment, I tried to spot the horse at the quarter-pole between Gone West and Cryptoclearance and I stopped him pretty good. Regardless, I rode him poorly. The fact is, I didn't ride a smart race, I didn't let him run. The first time I tried to ease him off the pace, he spit out the bit and I had difficulty getting control.

"You know how a John Elway can have a great career and then in one Super Bowl game, he throws interceptions? That's what I did. I don't use the word 'choke' because that's not what it is. You just make mistakes and get thrown out of your rhythm and can't get it back."

McCarron got Alysheba intercepted, too, all right. The Racing Form lists the race laconically as "rough trip," but McCarron remembers he got the horse discouraged by plodding around in the caboose of the race while the winner, Bet Twice, was having everything his own way on the front end.

It wasn't as if the distance of the race (mile and a half) was daunting – Chris McCarron had won the Belmont only a year before on Danzig Connection, besting the Derby winner of that year, Ferdinand, under a hand ride.

The race was clearly pilot error, McCarron insists. It's an attitude that may get him thrown out of the Jockeys Guild, but he offers as proof the fact that Alysheba only lost by a fast-closing neck to Bet Twice a few weeks later. Later Alysheba won the Louisiana Super Derby by daylight.

It is considered an axiom around a racetrack that, in any contest of champions, the older horse will win it – and that proved to be the way to bet when the 1986 Kentucky Derby winner, Ferdinand, beat McCarron and the 1987 Derby winner, Alysheba, in the Breeders' Cup. By a nose.

But the two are shaping up as the racing version of Dempsey-Tunney, Ali-Frazier, heading for another title fight in the Santa Anita Handicap.

If Alysheba loses again, one thing is for sure: You will get an explanation, not an alibi. "I rode him like an orangutan" is not outside the realm of possibility.

The experiences have aged young Master McCarron. Where once he looked like something you would take to the police station and ply with ice cream cones if you found him wandering around, he now looks more as if he just missed the school bus, or lost his bike.

But if he ever gets to a Triple Crown again and just misses, you can bet one thing: It'll be the horse's fault this time. Chris McCarron admits mistakes; he doesn't repeat them.

● ● ● ● ● ● ● ● ● ● ● ● ● ● ● ● ● ●

MARCH 16, 1976

29,203 Races Ago

It was April 20, 1949, Golden Gate Fields was conducting the 23rd day of its race meeting, and the starters were loading a field of $3,000 plating horses in the gate for a six-furlong dash.

Trainer George Reeves, who had one of the horses entering that race, also had a problem. Shafter V had beaten this same company a couple of weeks before, and figured to again. George Reeves needed a price more than he needed the purse. Shafter V would go off the favorite unless he could change the conditions slightly to cool the bettors. So he took veteran jockey R. J. Martin off her and substituted an exercise boy.

Shafter V went off at 10-1 and won by three lengths. George Reeves got his price. And launched a legend.

It was probably the last time anybody shopping for a price put Bill Shoemaker in the irons. That was 29,203 races ago. Shoe has won 7,000 races since then. But nobody thought the rider had anything to do with the result that day 27 years ago, least of all the stewards, who called Reeves on the carpet. The trainer had a dead fit horse on his hands who could have won with a fat Indian aboard, but they wondered why he took a chance with a kid who had been in only two races up to that time.

The stewards never did like the way Bill Shoemaker rode a horse. For one thing, he never hit one of them. When they won, they won with their ears pricking, which meant they were still full of run. When they lost, they lost with their ears pricking, too. So the stewards were constantly upset. They liked to see a horse going over the finish line with its tongue hanging out, staggering and lathered in a foamy sweat.

Arcaro, Westrop, Neves, Atkinson, all the great riders of the era used to bring a horse home in filets, 1,500 pounds of frightened, bullied flesh. Atkinson was known as "The Slasher." Shoemaker brought a horse home as if it were a date.

"That boy rides him like it was a bus!" the stewards once protested to George Reeves. But when Shoemaker won a record 218 races that first year as an apprentice, the criticisms slowed. Many years later, I talked to George Reeves about those early days:

"The first horse Shoe ever rode, Ike's Glory, was quite a bit overmatched, so Shoe didn't persevere much with him," he recalled. "Shoe had an awful habit of sitting still on a horse. It was hard to get him to whip a horse at the finish. He figured the thing to do was to hold him together and hand-ride him in. The stewards hated it. But the horses loved it. I was constantly being called in by the stewards, once when I had a horse called Butter Wafer who was close three or four times in races. I got hold of Shoe and said, 'Bill, this horse is a little faint-hearted.' Bill didn't say anything, but he took the horse and won by a nose. In the stretch, Bill never moved. The stewards almost had a stroke. This horse was a favorite, and it looked like he wasn't trying. They called me in. 'Supposing this horse got beat?' they yelled at me. 'That boy didn't make a move on him!' I said, 'Well, how many times has this horse lost close ones? He loses by a nose with a boy whipping and jumping all over him. Maybe this is the way to ride a horse.'"

It obviously was – and is. Bill Shoemaker is clearly the greatest race rider ever to get on a horse. His career is a lesson to everyone who ever thought he had to slug or claw or shout or snarl – or lash – his way to success.

Riding a racehorse is a little like playing a grand piano. You've got to have the touch of a concert artist. The only communication between horse and rider is through the hands and reins. A horse can tell a great deal about a rider by how he jerks and cramps a rein.

The late George Reeves always thought this was where Bill Shoemaker had an edge on every jockey who ever lived. "He never put a horse in a gate with a heart popping and sweat pouring out of him. You can almost feel the horse thinking, 'Hey, this guy ain't gonna hurt me.' His horse is more apt to be standing still and ready to run than the whole field, and to get out of the gate fast and straight. Then he always knows when to give a horse a breathing spell, usually abut a hundred yards from the wire. You got to know just when to do this, because if you get beat that way, you catch hell from the judges. Shoe is a master at giving his horses a breather."

In short, when maestro Shoemaker sits down to play his horse, he gets the "Moonlight Sonata." Lesser riders get "Chopsticks." Shoemaker gives a recital, an artist in the saddle, Horowitz in a concerto, Koufax in a no-hitter, Hepburn playing a schoolmarm. He does what he does without conscious effort.

"He rides a horse as if it were a swan," the late Hy Schnider used to say. "He can go on till he's 80. He makes everybody else look as if they were driving a truck." If you win one out of every four races you ride over 27 years, you wonder why the rest of those guys don't ship their whips and romance their horses, too.

● ● ● ● ● ● ● ● ● ● ● ● ● ● ● ● ●

JUNE 12, 1977

It's a Fairy Tale Finish

OK, move over, Black Beauty, Flicka, Trigger, Tony, Silver. Dust off those old scripts that have the white horse carrying the cowboy out of a burning building or fanning him with his hat.

Get the Disney people on the phone. We got a story that's upbeat, wholesome for the whole family, rated "G" and has this marvelous animal in it. All it needs is a dog.

Yes, Virginia, there is a Seattle Slew. Fairy tales do come true. For once, in real life, the prince didn't put the glass slipper on the wicked old stepsister. Little Red Riding Hood gets to eat the wolf. Cinderella was a documentary after all. Santa Claus lives. The wicked witch ends up in the oven again.

The Brothers Grimm would have loved the story of Seattle Slew. So would Hans Christian Andersen. It's that well-known staple of fairy tales – the ugly duckling that turns into a swan, the frog that turns into a prince.

It all began in the little eastern Washington town of – get this! – White Swan!. As we open on the scene, we see little Mickey Taylor, a poor but honest logger, rolling logs down to Yakima or wherever the sawmills are. In the background is the beautiful damsel Karen. She is in love with Mickey, but he is too busy with his logs. Heartbroken, she goes off to be an airline stewardess. Mickey goes to Santa Anita.

There, with mud all over his cowboy boots, he goes to the window and carefully counts out his dusty old bills and places a bet on a horse that has no chance. But Mickey doesn't know that because – well, what do they know in Yakima?

Except the horse wins, and pays 100-1, and Mickey suddenly has more money than the rest of White Swan put together. He goes around buying up timberland, he sends for Karen and they get married and live happily ever after.

The only thing Karen wants for a wedding present is a horse. She wants one to ride to school but Mickey wants one you can bet on. If she had wanted a car, he probably would have bought her A. J. Foyt's – but they go to Lexington and begin betting on the blueblooded Kentucky stock.

The next scene would bring tears to your eyes. In the auction ring is this lop-eared, fiddle-headed forlorn cayuse who looks as if he has just been liberated from a Wild West raid. And he's got this kind of clubfoot. He doesn't look as if he could keep up with the Rose Parade. But the Taylors are young and sentimental, and to them he's just a puppy in the window that no one wants. Besides, their vet, Jim Hill, tells them he comes from good people and might be a sire. If not, he can always haul logs.

So they buy him for the kind of money, $17,500, that usually gives you a horse you can use to pick up the mail on the farm.

The Taylors call their pet "Seattle Slew." They later say the "slew" is a misspelling of a Florida "slough" or swamp. Anyone familiar with the word "slew foot," then the appearance of this Slew's right foot, doesn't buy it.

They hire a trainer. Now, there are a lot of society trainers about, as well as a few Kentucky hardboots who know more about horses than Getty did about money. But the Taylors pick this tall, skinny kid with the lightest blue eyes and the reddest curly hair you ever saw. Billy Turner looks as if he just walked off the cover of the Saturday Evening Post. He looks like a guy on his way to buy the Brooklyn Bridge, or a watch off a guy with an overcoat full of them.

Nobody pays any attention to horses named Seattle Slew. Great horses have names like Twenty Grand or Count Fleet or Bold Ruler. And they're not owed by ex-apple pickers. And their feet certainly all point the same way.

Seattle Slew didn't impress anybody. All he did was win. "Well," they said, "he didn't beat nuthn'." "Well," they said, "all them other horses were 200-1 shots. Who couldn't of beat them?"

Everyone knew that when the classic races came around, races would once again be won by horses owned by the Mellons or the Galbreaths or the Whitneys or the Vanderbilts – or by somebody that came from Long Island and not the Yakima Indian reservation.

In Florida, a funny thing happened. The Gold Coasters began snapping watches on Slew in training – and suddenly the barns down there began to empty. Trainers wanted to get as far away from Slew as they could. They bobbed at up Oaklawn Park in Arkansas, at Santa Anita, New Orleans, Chicago – anywhere Slew wasn't. You half-expected them to wire their owners to say, "Is this far enough?"

Slew was a compassionate horse. He never beat anybody more than he had to. He was like a poker player who lets you keep your watch and carfare home.

But when he got to Kentucky, after winning the Wood Memorial in New York, he still hadn't convinced anyone.

Even when he won the Kentucky Derby, Eddie Arcaro, the great jockey, who should have known better, harrumphed, "Well, I'd like to see him do *that* again!"

So Slew did it – in the Preakness. The detractors were only half convinced. It appeared they wanted Slew not only to win but to disappear at the finish line – or perform card tricks back in the barn – or maybe win in leg manacles.

All this story needed to wipe out "Ol Yeller" or "The Adventures of Tom Sawyer" or "The Wizard of Oz" at the box office was a socko third act.

Seattle Slew gave it to them at the Belmont Saturday. He routed the bad guys, outran the posse.

The lumberjack types from Toppenish and White Swan had beaten the Great Gatsbys at their own game. The Ballad of Seattle Slew had a happy ending. Tiny Tim got his Christmas goodie. Only in America.

I ask you, is that Picture? Will that sell popcorn? Do they make movies like that anymore? Release that in living red, white and blue. Why, this might bring back Andy Hardy. The Horse-Nobody-Wanted. I tell you, it would play the Music Hall for four years. Set records on the Continent. Without subtitles. Why, it'd make "The Sound of Music" look like "Hamlet" – or one of those Swedish movies that look as though they're filmed in the dark.

● ● ● ● ● ● ● ● ● ● ● ● ● ● ● ● ● ●

JUNE 7, 1973

Racing Holds Its Breath Over Secretariat

Just five weeks ago, 28 horse owners were ready to buy a rope and go after a lady who had sold them a horse.

Mrs. Penny Tweedy didn't look much like a David Harum, but selling 28 guys the same horse was a pretty good start.

That wasn't the worst. She charged them $5,320,000 for it and kept four points for herself. Jesse James would have whistled in admiration.

The horse had all its legs and eyes and could pull a plow all right, but that afternoon in April he had just run down the track to a stablemate and a West Coaster who had just gotten off a plane from Santa Anita, which, as everyone in New York knows, is a track that runs downhill.

Twenty-eight guys had just paid $190,000 apiece for the stud fees to a seven-furlong horse. Now it wouldn't even be able to get a blind date.

Well, that was April. Now it's the week of the Belmont Stakes, and Secretariat, the horse, has been on the cover of Time, Newsweek, The Blood Horse, Sports Illustrated, and he looks like a $6-million steal. His stud book will be busier than a sultan's. If he loses the Belmont, he's going to take more money with him than a bank president absconding to Rio.

He's scared everybody out of the race except poor old Sham, his faithful old companion, who's chased him across three state lines now.

The horse writers have pulled out all the stops. To hear them tell it, you'd think this horse talked, or could pull babies out of burning buildings. They named him Horse of the Year when he was only 2 years old, which is like making an outfielder from Peoria the MVP.

The Triple Crown (Kentucky, Preakness and Belmont races) has been harder to win than a crap game on the waterfront, or a fight with your wife, and any horse who wins it immediately becomes Babe Ruth. Eight horses have won it, lifetime, and each of these races is now 100 years old or better.

All racing will be holding its breath as Secretariat heads for home Saturday. If his leg snaps in the stretch, or the boy falls off, the Jockey Club puts a wreath on the door. Or moves the Belmont to Juarez.

One hundred years they've been improving the breed, and all they turn out is hemophiliacs. The Hapsburgs could have told them that. It's good for any society to have the daughter elope with the milkman every now and then, or marry a guy who doesn't need a monocle.

Still, an examination of the fine print shows the Triple Crown not to have been all that difficult. Since Citation last won it in 1948 several have flunked out. Does anyone doubt Native Dancer should have won it in 1955? That was one of the Great-Mistakes-in-Sports-History, ranking with Sam Snead not winning the Open, Ernie Banks not playing in a World Series or John Barrymore never winning an Oscar. The Kentucky Derby was the ONLY race Native Dancer ever lost.

Tim Tam should have won in 1958, but he had only three legs by the head of the Belmont stretch. Damascus probably should have won in 1967, but came up to the Derby short on conditioning and lost to a 30-1 shot that he easily disposed of in the other two "Crowns." Gallant Man should have won it in 1957. He was easily the best in the Derby until Bill Shoemaker, like a bus rider who misjudges his stop, got off too early. He didn't contest the Preakness, but lumped Bold Ruler and the rest of his company again in the Belmont.

In all, seven horses have come up to the Belmont with two-thirds of the Triple since Citation. And at least two other horses (Nashua, Damascus) won the wrong two.

Well, let's hope there's nothing hiding in the hedges that will uncrown Secretariat Saturday. Much is made of the fact that there were only about 5,000 foals in Citation's natal year that he had to beat, while Secretariat was one of 25,000. I don't buy that.

Whenever you've got 25,000 of something, you can bet me it ain't as good as something there's only 5,000 of. That goes for horses, money, marbles, diamonds, paintings, books – and people. And words too. The Gettysburg Address, remember, fits on an envelope.

Auto Racing

• • • • • • • • • • • • • • • • •

MARCH 29, 1984

His Worlds Run Together In Long Beach

What makes Mario Andretti unique is that he's the only guy who ever won the American driving championship, the world championship and Indianapolis. That's like winning the Cy Young Award and the Triple Crown award in baseball, like playing both ways in the Super Bowl. Throw in stock-car racing, which Mario also excelled in, and you have a decathlon of motor racing.

Mario is the original "If it's Tuesday, this must be Belgium" driver. There are times when he has to stop not for gas but for directions, or to say "Let's see, can I turn right in this race or am I in Trenton?" He pulls into the pits not for tires but to see what language they're speaking. He's usually in either a car or an airplane.

Some people call downstairs in the morning to see what time it is. Mario calls to see what day it is. He crosses the international date line as regularly as the sun. Some people can't remember what city they're in. He can't remember what continent.

Mario is the most successful Italian export since pizza. He came to this country from the displaced-persons camps of northern Italy after World War II, a boy whose family lost everything in the Nazi occupation. When they said they slept "three to a room" in the camps, they didn't mean people, they meant families. The only place young Mario got any privacy was in the front seat of a car.

The first guy who put a steering wheel in Andretti's hands should go down in history with the guy who first put a bat in Ty Cobb's. Most teenagers' first love interest is their homeroom teacher or Sandra Dee. Mario's was a Hudson Hornet.

Most people think a car is a car, a track is a track and if you can drive a school bus, you can drive anything. In reality, the three forms of driving are as different as golf and tennis.

In Europe, the tracks wind around the forests of Germany or the shores of the Low Countries or the vineyards of France, and the thrill is you might hit a cow or a tree or a guy eating ice cream on a bale of hay. In America, you hit a wall. You have to remember you can only turn left. They used to cant the cars in that direction as a reminder. If the car went right, you went to the hospital. Or the morgue.

The Andretti family settled in Nazareth, Pennsylvania, (an uncle lived there), where Mario met and married his high-school sweetheart. Dee Ann never had to worry where he was at night. He was in a sprint car. When he dreamed at night it wasn't of pneumatic blondes, it was of turbocharged roadsters. Mario never wanted to be anything but the world's greatest race driver.

When people say of most immigrants, "He speaks English like a native," they mean a native of Krakow, but Mario spoke English like a native of, well, Nazareth. And the first thing he found out was that, no matter what you did as a race driver, if you didn't do it at Indianapolis, it didn't count. "I won the national driving championship as a rookie," he said, "but when I went on TV, this impressed nobody. Then the announcer said I finished third and was rookie of the year at Indy, and they gave me a standing ovation."

So it was a big decision for Andretti after he had won Indy in 1969 to go racing in Europe and the world venues. The winner at Zandvoort never got on the Ed Sullivan or Johnny Carson shows.

Andretti took on the crowned chauffeurs of Europe on their own turf. In part, it was a promise he had kept to himself. When he was a child in Lucca, Italy, his idol had been Italy's Alberto Ascari, and his dreams had been of winning at Monza or in the Mille Miglia.

He kept his cars in the Indy series, too. He was never to win Indy itself again. At Indy, you arrive at the Speedway on May 1 or sooner and you spend the whole month crawling in and out of engines at Gasoline Alley trying to dial one more mile and hour out of your machine. You practice endlessly, sleep on a floorboard and spy on the other garages. It takes this to win.

Mario couldn't. He had to fly back and forth between Europe and Indiana, preparing for the Grand Prix races at the same time. Once he had to have the car qualified for him by another driver. "This is possible at Indy," he points out.

The result was a schizophrenic existence. Andretti didn't know whether he was on Meridian Avenue or the Bois de Boulogne, whether to call the waiter *garcon* or Mac.

• • • • • • • • • • • • • • • •

MARCH 10, 1974

A. J. and the Volcano

The thing about Anthony Joseph, or A. J., Foyt, is, you might call him "the terrible-tempered Mr. Foyt" – but first, his disposition would have to improve 100% before his temper could merely be called "terrible." Calling what Foyt does "terrible" is like calling the sinking of the Titanic "unfortunate."

Foyt wasn't born mad, but he made up for it.

People just seem to get on his nerves. He wins the pole in the temper derby by 20 miles an hour. If they named a car after him it would be called the Volcano.

Some guys run on methanol. A. J. runs on rage. He drives as if he were sorry there are no pedestrians.

A. J. plays no favorites. He bullies the car, the track, his own pit crew, mechanic, the stewards, starters, press and public with equal fervor. Anyone who would go down to A. J.'s pit at race time would go into a lion cage at feeding time.

A. J. just wants the world to keep off his rear wheels. He doesn't want society tailgating on him. If he can see you in his rearview mirror, you're too damn close. He's as irritable on race day as a guy whose pants are too tight. When he won at Indy on closed-circuit TV one year, they shoved a glass of milk in his mouth, and A. J. sprayed it all over the ground and made a face that would have soured the milk.

He doesn't fraternize with the other drivers. "I don't trust nobody," he grumbles. He likes a nice distance between him and his competition, on and off the track.

When asked when he was going to retire, A. J. growled, "When I do, I'll just drive in and park it and say 'To hell with all of you.'" He once ran half a mile from a parked car to punch in the mouth a rival driver whom he thought had shut him off.

He considers himself a better mechanic than anyone he could hire, and the arguments in the Foyt garage frequently drown out the carburetion tests. He has run through more mechanics than Zsa Zsa Gabor has husbands. "Either A. J. or the engine is snarling," his crewmen say.

He bristles when someone suggests the car is more important than the driver in his sport. "It's just a dumb piece of iron," shoots back A. J. "Do you give credit to the baseball when somebody hits a home run? Do you cheer the racket in tennis? A bad driver cannot win even in a good car. But a good driver cannot win in junk."

To be sure, he does not get in junk. A. J. spends more time around the garage than a drop light. "He's either in a car – or under it," his crew admits. There are times when they wish he'd take up polo.

Still, he just may be the world's greatest race driver. It's for sure he's America's. At an age (39) when most of us are afraid to get in our nice, big, two-toned and two-ton Continentals and venture on the freeway, A. J. is still taking on the kids in those open-cockpit, 200-plus-m.p.h., winged speedway brutes and sliding through the corners so high and low in the groove the customers can't bear to look.

When A. J. started racing, engines were in front, you could have all the fuel you could carry or store, and cars were cars and didn't need wings to hold them on track. It was wheel-to-wheel, not clock-to-clock, driving, and there were no flameproof suits or plastic face masks.

The first Indianapolis race he was in, 12 of the 33 drivers in it since died in a race car, including one, Pat O'Conor, who was to die that day (1958). Of the others, A. J. is the only one still racing. Jimmy Reece, Jud Larson, Al Keller, Short Templeman, Eddie Sachs, Johnny Thomson, Ed Elisian, Jerry Unser and Art Bish all died on or because of the track.

Mad Anthony is on the pole at Ontario in the California 500 today. He's been on dozens of poles. He's won three Indys and more championship points than any driver alive. He won't announce his retirement, he says, because "four or more of my friends who said they were going to run one more race or two more races died in those races."

Death is always on the pole in this game. No 500-mile guarantee comes with these cars. Neither car nor driver has a warranty.

It could happen to A. J. as it did to so many of the company he started out with. He has walked away from cars on fire and on a stump of an ankle. He has been lifted out of stocks with his back broken.

It's unthinkable to A. J. he would go to join that ghostly company from the starting grid of the 1958 race. But if he does, I'll tell you one thing: God's going to get an awful earful.

● ● ● ● ● ● ● ● ● ● ● ● ● ● ● ● ● ●

APRIL 6, 1989

Even His Career Was a Fast One

He was, as one longtime associate put it, "a race driver's race driver." He was the last guy in the world you'd want to see in your rearview mirror with the race on the line and two laps to go.

His name went into the language. Every wife in the country would turn to her husband as he was driving too fast down the freeway and observe, "All right, Parnelli, you can slow it down now. You qualified!"

It was estimated that he moved a car up two laps just by being in it. He drove in seven Indianapolis 500s. He won one, should have won two more. He was on the pole twice and never started farther back than the second row. He was almost the last guy to win without extensive factory or corporate support.

He used to go back to the Speedway with automotive cayuses known affectionately as "Ol' 98" or "Calhoun." They were front-engine roadsters that weren't exactly held together by glue and baling wire but neither were they the computerized marvels Roger Penske puts on the track today.

His mentor was the late J. C. Agajanian, an improbable character who made his money in garbage and who showed up at the Speedway in a ten-gallon hat with a rattlesnake band on it, a diamond stickpin and reptile boots.

Rufus Parnell Jones was probably as good an athlete as ever sat behind the wheel of a race car. He was fearless but not foolish. He was daring but not desperate. He had eyes like a cat and the reflexes of a crouched lion. He could see the whole track at a glance.

It was just about impossible for him to go slow. In the 1962 race at Indy, he lost his brakes with 50 laps to go, and his crew had to stop his car coming into the pits by throwing tires in front of it. He didn't win the race but he finished it. In fact, he finished four of the seven races he drove there. He caught fire in one, lost a wheel bearing in one and had a bearing fail in a third.

He was the first to go over 150 m.p.h. at the Speedway. He won the pole and the race in 1963. He was second in 1965 and, to all intents and purposes, had the 1967 race won in a revolutionary turbine car when, three laps from a coasting finish, a $6.98 bearing burned out – taking about $600,000 with it.

And then he walked away from it.

No one could believe it. It was as if Mike Tyson announced his retirement over the fallen body of Frank Bruno, Magic Johnson hung it up after a playoff. In all of sports history, only one other man, also a Jones – Bobby – had ever quit at the height of his powers in this way.

People thought it was a grandstand stunt. Parnelli was only 34 years old. Parnelli would be back. An Indy 500 at the time without Parnelli Jones was as unthinkable as a U.S. Open without Jack Nicklaus. Parnelli was a part of auto racing lore, the kind of driver they made movies about. How could he park the Offy and go away and leave the game to A.J. Foyt, the Unsers, the foreigners? It was un-American.

That was 22 years ago. I had lunch with Parnelli Jones the other day. The flat fighter's face is still the same. The eyes still take in everything without glasses. The stomach is flat. He still looks as if he belongs on the pole.

Parnelli did not give up racing altogether. He drove the occasional off-road race, a few Trans-Ams. But he never stepped into an Indy car again after 1967. Why?

"It was a combination of things," he said. "The danger? I don't think so. You learn to live with the danger. Danger is exciting. You know, people who live with danger tend to appreciate the other things in life more. They see how quickly it can all be taken away.

"I think it was more that I was winning that 1967 race so ridiculously easy – yet I did not really savor the feeling. My first win was like the highest moment of my entire life. I couldn't sleep the night I won. This time, it was like, 'Well, I've done this before.'"

Was the fact that he lost the race so shatteringly a factor in his decision?

"Well, I'll tell you: the race had been called by rain after 18 laps. It was re-started the next day with the parade lap, pace lap and all the warmups. That bearing quit with only three laps to go and I figured, without those extra re-start laps, it would have held together for the checkered flag."

Had the turbine won, would he have remained in racing?

"I suppose. I would have been defending my championship. But I was anxious to get on with my business career. Agajanian and my partner, Val Miletich, had put me in real estate deals. I had my tire business. I stayed in racing. I just didn't stay in a car."

Did he miss the adulation? Wasn't 34 too early to become a part of the past?

Parnelli laughs. "I was speeding on the Pomona Freeway once and a cop stops me. He comes up to the car and he says 'Who do you think you are – Parnelli Jones?' I had to admit, that was a hoot."

He recalls that he "stayed in just enough racing to keep the guys respecting me. They couldn't be sure I wouldn't return in a fast car. Nobody was ever quite sure he could write me off."

Parnelli, who got his nickname when a friend fixed him a fake ID under the name Parnelli Jones so he could race when he was only 16 years old, resisted the lure of the track even though contemporaries Foyt and Al Unser still tee it up at the Brickyard in or near their 50s.

Parnelli will be on the track at Long Beach this month but not in the Grand Prix. He will drive in the Toyota Pro-Celebrity Race on Saturday, April 15, the day before the main event.

Parnelli will take the wheel against a field of disc jockeys, running backs (Walter Payton), anchormen, movie stars and the sons of race drivers. One of these will be Parnelli Jones' son, P.J.

The race is 10 laps or about 190 fewer than Parnelli was used to, and it will be 16.70 miles, 484 fewer than his rides of more than 20 years ago.

The pros have to give the celebrity drivers a 30-second head start, which means they will get to see one of the most terrorizing sights on a racetrack – Parnelli Jones in their rearview mirrors. Not to worry. He won't be there long. As the Indy racers of the '60s could tell you, pretty soon they'll be in his.

• • • • • • • • • • • • • • • • • •

MAY 27, 1991

Sweetheart of a Ride
From First to First

INDIANAPOLIS – Rick Mears won the 75th Indianapolis 500 Sunday. In a Roger Penske car.

And the earth is round and water's wet. Coal is black. Kansas is flat. And dog bites man.

It's not exactly stop-the-presses stuff. Rick Mears is to auto racing what the old Yankees used to be to baseball, Notre Dame to football. Dempsey to boxing. Rick Mears with a race car is Babe Ruth with a bat, Magic Johnson with a basketball, Sinatra with a song.

He made it look hard Sunday, but longtime Mears-watchers weren't fooled. It was vintage Mears. He just toyed with his field. Waited for the opening, then landed the right, played the ace, went to the whip.

Rick Mears treats race cars the way you might treat a beautiful girl. He romances them, cajoles them, coaxes them. He flatters them. Even talks to them. It was the way Shoemaker rode racehorses, Billy Casper played golf or a riverboat gambler plays cards.

Rick Mears knows an Indy race is 500 miles long. This would seem an obvious piece of information to most people, but it's surprising how many race drivers seem to think they have to win the race in the first turn.

Rick Mears started this race on the pole for the record sixth time. But he really only led the race for the first 12 laps – and the last 12. Mears doesn't really care who leads the race between laps 12 and 188. Mears spends those hours trying to establish a rapport with the car, make it his sweetheart, get it eating out of his hand, not biting it. "With race cars, you have to find out what their personality is," he explained to the press after the race. "You have to find out what they want, what they can do and what they will do."

Most race drivers prefer to find out what their cars will put up with.

Mears' ride Sunday was a marriage made in heaven. But it didn't start out that way. Mears preserved his pole position to Lap 12 when what seemed like the whole Andretti family jumped him. Patriarch Mario and oldest son Michael shuffled Mears back to third, then fourth, then fifth.

Mears didn't panic, raise his voice. He did what any good newlywed should. He went to work placating his mate. "There was some understeering, some changes that had to be made in the wings," he noted. He was patient. He made sure he kept the competition in view, but the car happy. "Basically, the car stayed together. The problems we had, we sorted out together."

The car crept up on the gaudy front-runners. His teammate, Emerson Fittipaldi, flashily took the lead and ran hard-hitting, front-running laps till he burned out a clutch.

Mears moved up from sixth, to fifth, to fourth, to third. He was always lurking. He even took to talking to his car. He wouldn't reveal the dialogue, but it's not hard to imagine him purring to it "OK, sweetheart, just a few more laps now." An A. J. Foyt line might run more to "Don't die now or I'll kick you all around Gasoline Alley!"

The opposition was dropping off like swatted flies as Mears cooed to his racer. Mears finally pitted on Lap 169, took on tires and fuel. He proposed to finish the race with it. It was a calculated risk. Forty gallons of fuel are not a cinch to make 31 laps at Indy. His principal competitor, Michael Andretti, pitted on Lap 166 and therefore had to re-pit on Lap 183. It probably made the difference.

The last 30 laps were reminiscent of the old Clark Gable racing movies. Young Andretti and the veteran Mears were practically in a wheel-to-wheel duel. First, Andretti would slingshot around Mears and sweep to what seemed to be a commanding lead.

Mears just talked to his car, whispered sweet nothings in its fuel gauge. He swept around Andretti at Lap 188. He was home free.

Rick Mears on the front end is like jockey Johnny Longden used to be. A rival once said of Longden, "You can get to him, you can't get by him."

Rick Mears was not about to let anything get by him. When he gets you in his rearview mirror with five laps to go, you stay there.

A driver has won this thing from the pole only 13 times. Three of them, the driver has been Rick Mears.

It's getting so it'll be a bigger story if he doesn't win Indy. He ties A. J. Foyt and Al Unser in lifetime victories with four. But Foyt has run in 34 Indy races, Unser in 25. This was Mears' 14th.

The race was typical Indy. The cars got clear to the first turn in the first lap before Buddy Lazier crashed. They got 17 more laps in before Roberto Guerrero crashed into Kevin Cogan and part of the debris hit and knocked out Foyt's car.

Only 11 cars were running at the finish. One of them was Rick Mears'. One of them is always Rick Mears'. He has finished nine of 14, unheard-of durability for Indy.

In horseracing, they handicap proven winners. Instead of letting Rick Mears ever again start on the pole or in front of the field, they should perhaps move him back automatically in the starting grid. Say, about to Terre Haute would even things up. Otherwise, "Mears Wins Indy" is going to be as standard a headline as "Iowa Goes Republican" or "Taxes Go Up."

● ● ● ● ● ● ● ● ● ● ● ● ● ● ● ● ●

JUNE 12, 1988

King Richard Has 32-Tooth Trademark

If I were a rival race driver, I think the thing that would unnerve me most about Richard Petty is that smile. Richard always looks as if he has just heard or seen the funniest joke of modern times – and you're it.

Richard smiles on his way to the race car, he smiles when he's getting into it, he smiles when he's racing it. He even smiles when he's crashing it.

The racing world thought Richard had finally exited smiling at Daytona this year when he found a new way to come down the main straight – somersaulting like an Olympic gymnast. Any judges in the world would have given Richard four 10s and a 9.9 for the way he put his car through a series of backflips, barrel rolls and headstands. Nadia Comaneci's floor exercises were never more spectacular.

People always said Richard Petty could make a car do everything but sing "Carmen," but this was ridiculous. The car bounced, thudded, crumpled, slid and disintegrated. If it had gone over a cliff, it couldn't have been more mangled. It looked like a tank that had just taken a direct hit, two tons of twisted, smoking, burning metal.

The man they called the King had finally crawled into one race car too many, the crowd was sure. There was so little left of the car, how could there be anything left of the driver?

When they got to Richard Petty, he was smiling.

"Don't try to talk," they warned him. "Why," he asked. "What's there to talk about?"

And he gave them the full 32-tooth trademark grin for which he's famous. He hadn't even lost one, didn't even scratch his gums. He stayed in the car for the moment because parts of it, including the tires, were still raining down. Richard did not even have a nosebleed.

"My ankle hurt," he admitted.

So did his pride. If there's one thing Richard Petty doesn't do, it's total a car. Around the South, they say Richard Petty could drive a race car through the Johnstown Flood without getting it wet, or a forest fire without getting it singed. You don't win 200 stock car races if you're hard on machinery.

When you talk of great streaks in sports, you usually begin with Joe DiMaggio's 56-game hitting streak or Lou Gehrig's 2,130-game consecutive-game playing streak or Byron Nelson's 19 tournament wins in a year or 11 in a row.

Richard Petty once won 10 stock car races in a row and 27 in a season. Today he will be driving in his 493rd consecutive race, the Budweiser 400 at Riverside. It will be the 1,055th of his 30-year career.

Given the time spans – DiMaggio's hitting streak lasted from May 15, to July 17, 1941, or eight weeks; Gehrig's consecutive-game streak lasted from 1925 to 1939 – Petty's streaks, 10 weeks of wins and 17 years of showing up, are, so to speak, in the ballpark. Since Nelson, like Petty, competed in a once-a-week – vs. a once-a-day – event, the great golfer's year, 1945, is more directly comparable to the great driver's. And a standoff, anyway you look at it. Nelson won more in a row, but Petty won more in a year.

It seems safe to say no one will ever break the streaks of any of them.

When Richard Petty first began knocking around in a stock car, his father, Lee, was already a champion in the sport. Which meant his fame spread, oh, clear up to Durham.

The only "modification" in the stocks in those days was that you took the moonshine out of the trunk. Your "crew" was a wrench, and you drove from race to race in the car you raced. On your good nights, you made from $85 to $100. You didn't have to buy your own gas, but you bought your own tires.

"Only about five guys did it for a living," Petty recalls.

The rest of them pumped gas or changed tires or repaired wrecks during the week.

It was during this period of not trying to bring the car home in a bag that Richard evolved his driving style.

Petty has the same style in a car as Nelson had over a putt or DiMag under a fly ball. Since he competed against guys named Fireball, Speedball or Smoky, or even Crash, you could see where they were spotting him two a side or letting him deal without cutting the cards to begin with.

You ask Richard Petty what the racer's edge is, and he smiles and tells you, "Common sense." Other drivers talk of the boost, the stagger, the wings, the setup. Petty tunes in the mind.

Even his winless streaks are larger than life – 118 at the moment. But Richard can be patient. Any guy who can come down the main straight on his nose, and live to smile about it, cannot complain about luck.

At 50, Richard still has all his teeth and hair and skills and, if I were a driver and I looked in the rearview mirror and saw this big wide smile in it, I'd stand on it. Because that would either be a very large crocodile – or Richard Petty. You won't want to wait around for either one to catch up.

• • • • • • • • • • • • • • • • •

OCTOBER 15, 1976

A Profile in Courage

The thing about Indianapolis champion Johnny Rutherford is that if Hollywood wanted to make the story of his life, there'd be no need to send for Paul Newman. Rutherford is better looking.

If you called Central Casting and said, "Send me up a romantic race driver type," they'd pick Rutherford out of a crowd. Stage and screen lost a good bet when they put Rutherford in a race car instead of a school play. He looks as if he had just stepped out of the pages of "The Great Gatsby" or a collar ad. You're pretty sure no one consulted the young ladies before they put that profile out where it might get involved in a flaming wreck.

If Rutherford were just another pretty face, if all those blue eyes and dimples kept finishing 29th, the racing crowd could have written him off as just another Sunday driver, a guy who got into race driving because the polo field was shut down.

At first, John Rutherford contributed to this impression. In his first six rides at Indianapolis he finished 29th twice, 31st once, and got clear up to 27th and 25th two other times. Once, he only made two laps. Other drivers figured Johnny lost interest right after the parade lap.

There's no law that says race drivers have to look like Mafia hit men to be successful – the late Peter Revson used to appear with Miss Worlds on his arm everywhere, and Dan Gurney looked like you'd imagine Apollo did. Still, no one ever gave A. J. Foyt any screen tests, and when a driver was (a) good looking and (b) unsuccessful, the suspicion was he would never go too deep in a corner for fear he'd get his hair mussed or his profile dented.

Actually, Johnny had gone into corners with the best of them and had the skin grafts and reset bones to prove it (race driving has done more for burn surgery and orthopedic techniques than the German army). Johnny had both arms broken, had been upside down in a skidding race car and, in the horrendous Eddie Sachs-Dave MacDonald crash at Indy in 1964, had driven through the inferno. MacDonald's tire tracks were found across Rutherford's car as it came out of the crackup glowing like a coke heap.

Rutherford gypsied around the country in the '50s, barely earning enough from racing for peanut-butter sandwiches. He and Jim McElreath used to sleep in the cornfields in Iowa en route to the little dirt tracks of the Midwest. "Did you know you can hear corn growing on hot nights?" Rutherford asks.

Johnny's problems at Indy were not his innards but the car's. As soon as they got Johnny a car that didn't start to melt at 150 m.p.h., he began making the other guys look as if they were driving buses. In 1970 he was only .008 of a second off the pole in qualifying. And he and polesitter Al Unser were the first to go over 170 m.p.h. at Indy.

In 1973, in a new McLaren, the best car Johnny ever had, he came within a wheel turn of 200 m.p.h. when he gained the pole and set the Indy record (which still stands) of 198.413.

But what Rutherford did in 1974 established him as one of the great race drivers of all time. He won the Indianapolis 500 from the 25th position, which had long been considered impossible. Indy is rarely won by anybody behind the third row of starters unless there's a 20-car pileup, as there was in 1966. Even then, with 13 cars out of the race before it started, the winner, Graham Hill, was in the fifth row. Rutherford won from the ninth row. He was first by the 20th lap. This year, Johnny won his second Indy, joining a select company of only three other active drivers who are multiple winners.

Rutherford, who is in town for the International Race of Champions at Riverside Sunday, the second leg of a series of races in which 12 invited drivers compete in cars (Camaros) they draw lots for, the notion being this kind of racing will develop the best driver rather than the best car, is now the Numero Uno of his sport, like Jack Nicklaus or Jimmy Connors, the one to beat in every tournament.

At 38, Johnny still has his matinee-idol good looks. But this is lost on 32 other drivers who wish he'd take his dimples and do commercials with them. To them, he looks like Hitler. But, of course, they only see him from the back.

● ● ● ● ● ● ● ● ● ● ● ● ● ● ● ● ● ●

MAY 26, 1989

He's Following Dad But Wants to Pass Him

INDIANAPOLIS – It is the fondest wish of most fathers that sons follow in their footsteps, take over the family business, maintain the tradition.

Few do. Ministers' sons often become world-class playboys or tango dancers.

Parents try everything. Take the boy down and show him the family factory, the office with the rug on the floor, promise him the good life. "Someday, son, all this can be yours," they whisper seductively. He can, they assure him, have an expense account, condos in Florida, a yacht, he can be a pillar of the community.

He doesn't want it. He may even run off to join the circus. He'll sell the family business to the first corporate raider and go off to the south of France and play baccarat the rest of his life.

Great authors and painters never seem to replicate themselves. You don't find any Hemingways on the best-seller lists. Only one Rembrandt hangs in the Louvre.

There aren't any Ty Cobb Jrs. on the base paths, Jack Dempsey III's in a ring.

But then it comes to auto racing, and the older generation can't keep the younger generation away with a club.

It's boggling. You close your eyes and imagine a father taking his son to the nearest grease-filled garage with gaskets all over the floor, a naked girl on a calendar, more drain oil than West Texas, a pile of retreads. "Someday, son, all this can be yours," he tells him, waving his arms over the mess. The kid is thrilled.

Then he takes him out to the nearest dirt-track or high-speed oval and says: "Just think, someday you can break an arm or shatter an ankle here. You can burn, crash, get heat prostration. The possibilities are limitless. When you're not in a race car, you're in an airplane. Raises hell with your home life. You'll get bored doing anything under 200 miles an hour. You'll be breathing methane for the rest of your life."

And the kid can't believe his good luck.

There's no love affair in the world that can match one between a young racer and his car. Not Romeo and Juliet, Camille and Alfredo, Scarlett and Rhett. It's more than a romance, it's an obsession.

Young Al Unser is the prototype of the breed but not the only one. There's a grandson of a race driver who is the son of a race driver in here. This sport deals in royal families. Billy Vukovich's grandfather died on this race track at Indianapolis before he was born. He is Billy Vukovich the Third. His grandfather won this race twice before he was killed. His father drove it 12 times. Gary Bettenhausen's father died here. Al Unser's uncle died here. You'd think they'd rather go in a haunted house than to the Indianapolis Motor Speedway. You'd think the sight of a turbocharged race car would make them turn white and cross themselves. Guess again.

Al Unser Jr. is a deceptively mild-appearing young man, freckled, dimpled. He doesn't really look like an Unser. But he drives like one.

He didn't get in a race car till he was well up in age – 9. For an Unser, that's practically in his dotage. Unsers usually go directly from the cradle to a cockpit.

Little Al's father, Big Al, put him in a go-cart when he was big enough to see over a dashboard. After that, he was pretty much on his own. The Unsers are not big on sharing secrets. "My father taught me everything I know," Little Al concedes. "But he didn't teach me everything he knows ."

Why do the sons and grandsons of drivers follow in the family business while chain-store magnates can't bribe their spoiled brats to show up for work?

"It's addictive," Al Unser the Younger explains. "It's hard to explain the excitement." It is, he adds, a feeling that you are more alive, more alert, more challenged in a race car than you will ever be again. The rest of life is vanilla ice cream.

Wouldn't his family rather he be a lawyer, an accountant? "I went to work in a machine shop when I was 16," young Al reveals. "I worked eight hours a day, five days a week. On the weekends, I was very glad to go racing."

Of course, an Unser out of a race car is like a camel out of sand, a cowboy off a horse. John Wayne in a three-piece suit. Legend has it Unsers don't come equipped with heart, lungs and bloodstreams like the rest of us. They have cylinders and fuel pumps, and they bleed petroleum. If you check an Unser, you find a tachometer. In a few more generations, they'll be born with tires.

Is it likely they'll have to be numbered like popes or English kings or Super Bowls?

As the scion of a family that has won seven Indy 500s and on a track on which his uncle, Jerry, died in practice, does he feel any pressure to excel?

"The public may feel I don't have my own identity," young Al concedes. "But when you're in a race car, your name won't help you."

Are his loyalties split? Will he be rooting for his father to win his unprecedented fifth Indy? "I will be rooting for me to win my first before I want him to win his fifth," Al Two insists.

Is he gaining on his father? Can he break the family tradition and impart secrets? "A 27-year-old cannot teach a 50-year-old anything," young Al claims, endearing himself to a whole generation of father-knows-bests.

"Me and Dad talk a lot. But you have to understand the Unser family is very competitive within themselves." In other words, if you're an Unser, you learn, crash-by-crash.

He's had five trips around this racetrack in the 500 now. Will he not feel like an Unser till he wins the race? "I wouldn't feel like an Unser if I weren't in the race."

Except that Unsers get in Victory Lane as well as the starting grid. Victory Lane is like Buckingham Palace, the ruling family's ancestral home. Being a racer is getting to be like being a Hohenzollern. You reign by divine right. The Indy 500 museum is going to become like Westminster Abbey, the resting place for a few monarchical families. And the father whose son won't take over the garment industry can only look on in envy. He's facing a losing battle. You can't get killed selling dresses. So who wants to spend his life doing that?

Tennis

• • • • • • • • • • • • • • • • •

JULY 30, 1998

He Needs to Stay Focused

"Image is everything," Andre Agassi used to tell us in those TV photo commercials. Never mind substance.

Well, on reflection, image isn't everything. It isn't anything if it doesn't come with performance attached.

You think anyone would give a rat's rap for Dennis Rodman's purple hair, dangling earrings, cross-dressing and toe-to-ear tattoos if they didn't come with a rebounding title attached?

You have to be good to dare to be different. Otherwise people just look at you and snap, "Act your age!"

Nothing succeeds like excess in this country, but stardom is getting in as short supply as anything these days. It is a chimera, as fragile as eggs, as insubstantial as a shadow on a wall. One day Ian Baker-Finch is winning a British Open; a few fortnights later he can't break 90. Ditto Bill Rogers. Virtuosity leaves them like a thief in the night. A pitcher wins a Cy Young Award one year and he's pitching in Norwich the next.

But nobody had a longer free-fall in the history of sports than Andre Agassi. One day, he's winning Wimbledon, the U.S. Open, about five of every eight tournaments he enters. The French Open is the only Grand Slam event he hasn't won.

He's got the world at match point. Everywhere he looks is money. He gets a hundred thousand or so just to show up at your tournament. He's married to one of the most beautiful women in the world.

He can't go anywhere without a camera following, say anything without a microphone picking it up. He makes People magazine every other issue.

He's ranked No. 2 in the world in his sport two years in a row. Some months, he's No. 1. It can't get any better than that.

Then, all of a sudden, he's ranked No. 122. He can't even see Pete Sampras from there. He's got all the recognition factor of a ball boy. He's losing to guys named D. Flach in opening rounds. He's rapping out in the first round at Wimbledon and the fourth round at the U.S. Open. He's losing to guys who are 176th in world ranking.

It's embarrassing. Tennis entrepreneurs are moaning.

Tennis always has been the most formful of sports. Don Budge, Jack Kramer, Rod Laver or Pete Sampras reaches the top, and he stays there. Bjorn Borg wins five Wimbledons in a row, four French Opens.

You're not supposed to go from No. 8 seeding to No. 122 in this man's game. You don't go from the No. 1 serve returner in the game to a guy who can't get a racket on a lob. You don't go from center court at Wimbledon to the outer courts at New York, to a spot in a tournament at Burbank.

Agassi always has fascinated the game anyway. He looks less like a Wimbledon champion than anyone since Bobby Riggs. He's got short legs, short arms, he himself is short by today's standards. He doesn't look overpowering.

He doesn't run, he scurries. He hurries everywhere, always managing to look as if he were 10 minutes late for an appointment or trying to catch a bus. His eyes dart all over the place like a gambler with a low pair. He's ubiquitous on court.

He plays that way. He never misses a trick. He seems to have a sixth sense as to where the ball is going to land. Like a great outfielder, a Joe DiMaggio or Willie Mays, when the ball comes down, he's there waiting for it.

You can't get a serve past him. He could return a bullet.

His own serve is nothing to get drunk over – a modest 120 mph or so. But he can play on any surface. His tenacity is legendary. He has an arsenal of shots and, if he plays a game that sees him move into position to better field the shot, he is a master at calculating where his opponent might not be and to whistle the ball precisely there. "Sometimes it seems like there are two of him out there," a disgusted Aussie, Mark Woodforde, once observed.

But you can see, with this arsenal, there is no margin for error, for nonchalance. Agassi has to play you 60 minutes of every hour.

Last year, he didn't. "Last year, I was just fooling around," he has acknowledged. He cannot play off the interest of his talent the way Sampras might be able to; he has to dip into the capital on every shot. "I have to hurt people," he told a magazine interviewer.

He breezed through a Washington, D.C., tournament like a wrecking ball earlier this year and, then, in the Mercedes-Benz Cup at the UCLA Tennis Center on Tuesday night, he took out the A-game to subdue young Bob Bryan of Camarillo, a young wild-card entry who is such a fan of Andre's he has his bedroom at home wallpapered with Agassi posters.

His idol lived up to his expectations, 6-4, 6-3, but the young man showed such promise, someone might someday want to paper a room with his likeness.

He paid his respects to his idol, Agassi. "He's classy, he's flashy, he put me on my heels and kept me there."

His idol, for his part, assented, "I have to find my way back. I have to channel all my energies into my game – 100%, not 99% or 6%." The ball is looking "nice and fat" again, he said.

If it's a question of image, it's coming back into focus better and better day by day and may soon overshadow the man once again.

● ● ● ● ● ● ● ● ● ● ● ● ● ● ● ● ●

JULY 4, 1993

Ashe's Days of Grace
Erasing Barriers of Race

Of all the athletes I have known, there was none whose intellect I had more respect for than Arthur Ashe's. You could get right down to the

nitty-gritty of any subject with Arthur, and that included racial har-
mony – of which he was a passionate advocate.

I remember once we were having lunch, and the discussion turned
on what he termed indissoluble differences between blacks and whites
in America, and it was suggested that one group could never understand the other because the differences went all the way to the glandular in nature.

I remember sucking up my breath and plunging in, taken aback by
my own audacity and fearing I might have overstepped our friendship.

"Arthur," I chanced it, "you know as well as I do that the so-called
'black' race in America is hardly homogeneous. For one thing, take
Sherman's army. There are an awful lot – hundreds of thousands – of
'blacks' who are descended from his March to the Sea, which was often
sidetracked to slave quarters, to say nothing of the 10 or so other
Union armies."

I held my breath. But to my intense relief, Arthur not only cheer-
fully agreed, he added anecdotal lore of his own to the mix. Arthur was
a well-read man.

When he died this year, we lost a voice of reason and reconciliation
we can ill afford.

Arthur wrote a book, "Days of Grace," and left a legacy to his people – us Americans. In a way, it was his deathbed advice. So we know it
was heartfelt, devoid of artifice or self-service. But with Arthur, we
would have known that anyway.

Arthur went through life the way he played tennis – coolly, warily.
With great style and dignity. He played the most mistake-free tennis of
any great player. Not for Arthur Ashe was the "unforced error."

He was as meticulous in his private life. No scandal ever touched
Arthur Ashe. Arthur had no problem being a "role model." He considered it a privilege. He was militant without being strident, crusading
without being contumacious. Not for him the street-corner rhetoric of
the rabble-rouser. He got things done quietly but effectively, simply
another forehand down the line. His motto was the same as that

French philosopher's: "There is no use getting angry at facts, it is a matter of indifference to them."

Arthur faced facts. Without blinking. His interest, the last weeks of his life, was in the NCAA Propositions, 42 and 48, concerning the academic qualifications of athletes. College basketball coaches such as John Thompson (interested in smuggling 7-foot centers through the eye of this needle) saw them as "culturally biased."

Wrote Ashe in his last testament: "My own position is different from Thompson's. Can one attribute a low test score to socioeconomic bias? Perhaps. Can one invoke cultural bias to explain a combined 700 (bare minimum) SAT test score? Ridiculous!"

Arthur felt that, by not forcing their athletes to meet the academic challenge, they were underestimating them.

Said Arthur: "To Thompson's objection that black athletes would be barred by the new standards, I asserted my belief that any loss in numbers would be short term. In response to the new standards, black youngsters would simply rise to the challenge and meet them."

Arthur meets what he calls the "ethos of entitlement" head on. He recalls a "distressing" visit to a Connecticut high school to meet and debate varsity athletes on Props. 42 and 48.

"I asked the kids – mostly black and male – if they thought it fair that persons who performed weakly in academics should be given athletic scholarships. The response of every black male was that he was entitled to a scholarship even if someone more qualified academically would be deprived of one.

"Not one suggested that athletes should be held to the same standard as non-athletes. They argued they had spent endless time in training, that blacks had been discriminated against (historically) and so on.

"On display was the increasingly dominant African-American adolescent ethos of entitlement, of 'You owe me,' which I consider monstrous. One can be sure that an adolescent with such an attitude will make no particular effort at scholastics. Why should he? His teacher owes him a passing grade.

"I can understand the argument that blacks should have been paid reparations for slavery and segregation. By an Act of Congress, Japanese-Americans interned in World War II received $20,000 per family. Germany is paying reparations to Jews ... but our sense of entitlement is taken too far. Should we now give up because of an oppressive sense that we have not been compensated for historic wrongs done to us? Absolutely not."

Continues Arthur: "What I and others want is an equal chance, under one set of rules, as on the tennis court. While rules are different for different people, devices like affirmative action are needed to prevent explosions of anger. But I would not want to know I received a job simply because I am black .... Such is human nature, why struggle to succeed when you can have something for nothing?"

What Arthur wants is a level playing field, academically as well as athletically. No one ever had to make a black basket count three while a white basket counted only two. No one ever had to give a black runner a head start in a 100-meter dash. No one had to make a black single count as a double or give a black batter four strikes.

Arthur suggests blacks don't need an artificial advantage off the field, either.

He was not emboldened to speak out by his intimations of foreshortened mortality. He had written scathing essays – "Coddling Black Athletes" – on that point for the New York Times years before he found out he was ill.

Arthur might have been heartened by a statistical report issued only this week by the NCAA on the progress of Prop. 48. It showed improved graduation rates for athletes who had begun college after the policy was put in effect. Black football players at Division I-A schools and black male basketball players showed the largest increases in graduation rates.

There is still work. At 100 of the nation's institutes of higher learning, only 26% of black male basketball players graduated, and 39% of black football players did. But this was an improvement, up from 23% and 33% in a previous survey.

The graduation rate for all black male athletes was 41%, higher than the rate for the black non-athlete population, 30%. The figure for white male athletes was 57%, with a 56% rate for all white males.

Arthur would be pleased, but not satisfied.

"The critics of Prop. 42 seriously underestimate the psychic value that black athletes place on their athletic success and how that could be used to motivate them academically," he wrote. "Prop. 42 – or something like it – would motivate high school coaches and their players to take education seriously. More important, that dedication ... would set a tone in the schools that would inspire non-athletes to study harder, too."

Arthur, as usual, has left us after winning, love-love. And, as usual, the count is advantage, Ashe.

• • • • • • • • • • • • • • • •

JULY 24, 1985

He Fights His Battles On the Playing Field

INDIANAPOLIS – Sportswriters couldn't believe their good luck when that young West German from Leimen won Wimbledon.

First of all, there was that name. If you sat up nights you couldn't come up with anything more felicitous: Boris Becker.

It had everything. Alliteration. Bombast. Almost rhyme. Charles Dickens would have invented it. Hemingway never had a greater inspiration. Edgar Allan Poe could have written a poem around it.

It had a fictional quality about it, almost as if it were from the Hardy Boys series, or a character in Tom Swift:

- ♦ "Boris Becker and His Atomic Racket."
- ♦ "Boris Becker at the Seashore."
- ♦ "Boris Becker Goes Hawaiian."
- ♦ "Boris Becker, Set Point."

The possibilities were endless.

Then there was that background. The boy from the small town in Germany that time forgot. The pro from the Brothers Grimm. The player from the tree house. The Wagnerian hero. Maybe he'd turn into a swan in the last act.

But, best of all, he was German. That gave the journalists free range. Visions of typical Teutonic allusions danced in their heads like a parade of wooden soldiers. The military motif was off and rampant. Blitzkrieg Becker came swiftly to mind. The field marshal of tennis.

The spiked helmet came out of mothballs. Ideas rolled. Shouldn't he be playing in jackboots and a steel helmet? Shouldn't he make the cover of Sports Illustrated with an Iron Cross pinned to his throat? Shouldn't he exchange his racket for a baton when going out in public? Shouldn't he be addressed as "Your excellency" by everyone under the rank of corporal?

You kept waiting for the headlines and leads: "Boris Becker went through Wimbledon's seeds like von Moltke through the Low Countries here today." Writers could speculate that he would goose-step onto court. Other players arrived by limo. Becker would probably come by Panzer unit.

And so on.

Alas! Herr Becker would have none of it. He put his No. 11 foot squarely down on the literary license. The war was over. Even the comparatively mildly military allegory of Boom Boom Becker left him disturbed.

"I am a sportsman, not a soldier," he complained. "When my mother calls me, she doesn't say 'Come here, Boom Boom,' she says 'Boris.'"

He made it plain that he wants it known he comes from a Germany that wins Wimbledon and a Masters, not Paris or the oil of the Caucasus. "I came to play games, not conquer territory," he said.

So the poets of the press box had to sigh and make do with what they had – which was a kind of heavy-legged German kid who, if he hit a ball with the authority of a Reichswehr 88-millimeter field piece, didn't care to have it written that way.

What he had done hardly needed the military equivalencies, anyway. This gangling reddish-blond teenage giant, barely out of high socks and lederhosen, had done something no one his age and rank had ever done before. He had routed the flower of world tennis at Wimbledon to become the first and youngest and only unseeded player ever to win that storied event.

In so doing, he had captured the hearts and minds of the world by being the first non-brat to win that tournament in years.

He did it in the most un-Germanic of ways. Given his background, tennists might have expected Boris to play the kind of classic, set-piece, mathematically perfect game of a kid who learned the game by the book, who had been programmed into position by staff manual. Clausewitz tennis.

Instead, he played tennis the way Ty Cobb or Pete Rose played baseball, or Dempsey fought. He played a scrambling, dirty-uniform, get-there-at-all-costs and hang-the-form-charts game of a member of a street gang.

"He plays tennis like you might steal hubcaps," one tennis announcer pointed out.

He was a brawler, a swarmer, an infighter. He attacked the ball as if it were a swarm of bees. He didn't hit it, he swatted it. He skidded, slipped, tumbled and lunged. It wasn't a game, it was a rumble. You didn't get aced, you got mugged. Love had nothing to do with it.

He did lots of things wrong, but the scoreboard never knew it.

Germany used to have a great player, Baron Gottfried von Cramm, who played the game as if it were high tea. He always had the correct finger on the racket, and he looked great losing. Becker doesn't even look great winning. He plays as if he's trying to plug holes in a roof during a thunderstorm.

They used to say of Arnold Palmer that the only thing he did right with a golf club was win. Boris became the tennis equivalent. He hit off the wrong foot, his backhand was unclassic, his forehand collapsible – but the ball came rocketing back like one of Nolan Ryan's fastballs. He has the nerves of a 17-year-old – i.e., none.

He is here in Indianapolis this week to play in the U.S. Clay Courts, and he has turned this non-event into the tennis soiree of the season so far.

No one minds that John McEnroe, Jimmy Connors, Martina Navratilova and Chris Evert Lloyd are, as usual, not here. Boris (Don't Call Me Boom Boom) is, and the hotels and the stands are full, TV is standing by and even the pro football Colts are taking an inside page in the local papers this week.

Clay courts are a refinement of the game in which the surface favors the player whose game is modeled after a barn door. Which is to say that he can return every shot at the same angle and velocity in which he received it. It is a form of play requiring enormous patience, somewhat like a dog fetching a stick or a bird hour after hour.

It can wear out the tempestuous player. It is a tournament that has been won by the likes of Tut Bartzen, Chuck McKinley and Manuel Orantes. It has been lost by some of the big hitters, although Bill Tilden, Pancho Gonzalez and even Connors made a point of toughing it out to win several times.

Boris believes that he can play this game, too. He grew up on clay, he said.

Besides, the German-American Davis Cup competition is scheduled for clay courts next month. Germany has never won the Davis Cup.

If Becker wins both of these feats of clay for Germany, he may have to relent – to the extent of at least answering to a single Boom if someone hails him by it.

• • • • • • • • • • • • • • • • • •

DECEMBER 3, 1992

A Band Plays the Oldies For Borg

Picture, if you can, Babe Ruth retiring from baseball while he was still a pitcher.

How about imagining Jack Nicklaus quitting after winning his second Masters or fourth major?

What if Jack Dempsey hung them up after the Jess Willard fight? What if Knute Rockne went into business after his first national championship?

Well, the exact equivalent happened in 1982 when Bjorn Borg, who was to tennis what any of the above were to their sports, suddenly and shockingly put away his rackets and headbands and announced he was through with the game. He was 26.

At age 26, Ruth had just turned outfielder and had only 103 of the 714 home runs he was to hit in his career. At 26, Pete Rose had only 723 of his 4,256 hits. At 26, Rocky Marciano had not yet had a main event. When he turned 26, Nicklaus had not yet won a British Open.

Supposing the word burnout had crept into the language a generation or two earlier? That was a day and time when you signed on for the duration. You used to have to cut the uniform off a player. Joe Louis was fighting young bulls from Brockton when he had nothing left but his powerful punch. It was like having a railroad gun – and no railroad. Mickey Mantle played till he couldn't get around on the fastball. Dempsey and Benny Leonard made comebacks when they needed glasses. People worked in factories 55 years. Burnout wasn't a word anyone was familiar with. Burnout was a copout.

Don Budge and Bill Tilden played into their dotage. Even in the amateur era, when the payoff was a silver cup and a free meal, tennists persevered.

Which is why the sports world was stunned when Borg announced he was defaulting from tennis.

How inconceivable was it? Well, consider Borg is four years younger than Jimmy Connors. He is only two years older than John McEnroe, who still dreams of winning Wimbledon or the U.S. Open.

Borg had just completed the most remarkable run in modern Wimbledon history – five consecutive victories in that tournament. You had to go back to the turn of the century, when tennis was the province only of the aristocracy, to find a comparable performance. None of the moderns could do it, not Tilden, Fred Perry, Budge – not even Rod Laver.

Nor was there any physical explanation for Borg's defection. He had been a finalist in that year's Wimbledon and U.S. Open, losing, but barely.

He had won the French championship six times, the Italian twice. He never won the U.S. Open, but he was a finalist in it four times.

He was far and away the best of his generation, maybe of any generation. He had an all-court game. He could slug, he could lob, play at the net, serve-and-volley or kill you from the baseline. He had perfected a deadly two-handed backhand, hitting a ball against a barn door through the snows of his native Sweden as a boy.

He played with the kind of poker-faced intensity and confidence of a guy who knows he has aces-full and the best you could have is a small pair. His stamina was incontestable, although he didn't always need it. He beat Connors and Ilie Nastase in straight sets in two Wimbledon finals. He played in the days before the tiebreaker. So he was ready to play all night, if necessary.

He never threw his racket, cussed out a linesman, kicked a camera or charged the umpire's chair. He didn't need anybody's help to win.

He was at the absolute height of his powers. So why did he quit? The game was just coming into the big money.

It was anti-history. It was also counterproductive.

When the flags are flying, and the band is playing and everyone is telling you how great you are, it's easy for the star athlete to believe the music will go on like this forever, to think that – like a great sculptor – you have carved an image of yourself that will endure forever.

But the scenario began to go bad for Borg almost instantly. There were business failures. There were rumors of drug use. There was, finally, a rumor of a suicide attempt.

At the very least, he had left all that money lying on a table. Given his talents, Borg was, doubtless, walking away from millions.

Why did he do it?

Borg sat in a West Hollywood hotel lobby the other afternoon, toying with a beer and reflecting on the question.

"It stopped being fun. It stopped being enjoyable. To be great at anything, to get to be the best, you have to enjoy what you're doing. Don't you think Arnold Palmer enjoyed playing golf – enjoys playing golf? I got to the point where I didn't care whether I won or lost. I remember the '81 final against McEnroe at Wimbledon. I felt as if we were just playing backyard tennis."

Tennis is a grueling game, a grueling way to make a living. But so is putting windshields on Chryslers.

Borg believed he never would play again, but now, after 10 years, he showed up with a tennis racket. It was an outdated wooden one. But so was the player.

What of the rumors, the tabloid version of the Borg saga? Bjorn shrugs. "That's the media," he says. "I sell papers for them. I tried cocaine once. That's no habit. I have no habit. They make it a habit."

And the suicide story? Borg sighs. "I go to the hospital for food poisoning. I am in the hospital (in Italy) for two hours total. I get my stomach – how you say it – pumped out? There are reporters and flashbulbs when I come out."

Borg takes the position he would have to be the first guy in history who tried to kill himself with spaghetti marinara.

But if burnout is a new word in the lexicon of sports, so is seniors. Bjorn Borg is getting a second career. Just as in golf, the entrepreneurs are finding a huge market for players on the other side of 35.

Sponsored by the financial service conglomerate Advanta, tennis is getting a senior tour, too, titled the Great Return. And it saw Bjorn Borg winning his first tournament since 1981 in Chicago, beating the American rocket Roscoe Tanner, whom he beat in a Wimbledon final 13 years ago.

The Advanta tour hits Los Angeles this weekend with a tournament beginning today at the venerable L.A. Tennis Club, a citadel of nostalgia in itself.

If Borg wins, it'll be bittersweet. In the movie "On the Waterfront," one of the most poignant scenes in film history finds Marlon Brando as the betrayed pug saying to his betrayer brother, "I coulda been a contender!" Bjorn Borg can relate. He can say reproachfully to his betrayer Bjorn Borg, "I coulda been champion!" All those years.

• • • • • • • • • • • • • • • • • •

SEPTEMBER 25, 1974

Nobody's Favorite

He wears a Prince Valiant haircut and has a baby-soap complexion – Little Boy Blue on center court.

But underneath is a street kid's face, alert, eyes darting, ever on the lookout for the cops, a crap game or a hubcap.

And he's the best tennis player in the whole-cotton picking universe.

There are those who would equate this with the news that Paris was burning or the dam at Johnstown was beginning to crack. James Scott Connors is about as popular in the world of tennis as a double fault. As one promoter said, "Nobody is neutral about Jimmy Connors. You either dislike him – or you hate him."

He dispatches opponents with a kind of impersonal contempt that is kind of obscene in a 22-year-old who looks as if he should still be collecting autographs. What's worse, he seems to win on sheer cussedness. His serve isn't big. He has a girlish two-handed backhand. He's not overpowering, just relentless. He's great for the same reasons Ty Cobb and Jackie Robinson were great. He's getting even with the world.

For what is not clear. He was born with a silver racket in his mouth. Mother was a champion of sorts. He's going to marry another champion. He never had to play with an old beat-up set of balls or an unstrung racket. He had the best teachers, the best equipment.

He has never let anything interfere with tennis. College didn't take. His hobbies include beating 39-year-old Aussies and betting on the horses. He treats newspapermen as if they were 10th-seeded human beings. You might describe him – euphemistically – as "cocky."

He seems to flourish in an aura of antipathy. The more hostile a crowd gets, the better he plays. The redder he makes the umpire's neck, the steadier his own game becomes.

No one jumps the net to congratulate him. There are some people who can beat you and make you smile. Connors, somehow, seems to rub it in.

You take the other night at the Pacific Southwest, where he was winning his third major tournament and 20th straight match. His opponent was a ballboy-sized player named Harold Solomon. Solomon is like a Labrador. He retrieves shots, he doesn't make them. His game is supposed to be 40-volley points. He just keeps hitting the ball back at your feet till you get bored.

Connors probably could have – and should have – mercifully and quickly killed him off by rushing the net. He preferred to do it like pulling the wings out of a canary. He played Solomon's game. Only when he tired of the sport did he move in for the kill. He teased the crowd into hoping for a miracle, then dashed its hopes.

At Wimbledon, the British treated him as if he had asked the queen to hold his coat.

With Connors, it is not even necessary to have proximity. He can raise the hackles on your neck at 100 paces. You half-expect people walking by on the street to start shaking their fists at him. I was perched on the rim of the Los Angeles Tennis Club the other night, determinedly neutral, in fact, secretly admiring someone who was good and was damned if he was going to be modest about it.

By the third game, my teeth were as on edge as everyone else's, and my face was flushed. I began to mutter, "Damned left-handers! How can any normal man be expected to play them? They should have tournaments of their own."

A moment later, he put one of his two-handed backhanders down the line for a point. I took it personally. I was insulted. "Two-handers!?" I screamed. "Don't they have wrists anymore? Bill Tilden would cover his eyes! That's like skating on double runners!"

On the court, Connors scowled at the umpire. I was livid. "Call that a scowl?" I raged. "As a scowl, I don't make that one-two with Pancho Gonzales. Now, THERE was a scowl! This kid is just learning!"

It didn't do any good. As usual. Connors won sweetly, and almost without touching the income of his talent. He beat Solomon after giving Solomon his best shot. Almost like sticking his chin out and saying, "Hit it, I dare you!"

In the locker room afterward, I was surprised to see the horns didn't show. Connors was not affable, but just a 22-year-old who plays his sport better than anyone else.

Did he consciously cultivate this aura of hostility? he was asked. Connors shrugged. "They're gonna have to cheer for me sooner or later." Is it an act then? Another shrug. "Everyone who plays tennis is an actor."

The thing is, not everyone picks a part for Lon Chaney.

● ● ● ● ● ● ● ● ● ● ● ● ● ● ● ● ● ●

FEBRUARY 8, 1990

No Doubt, She Graced This Game

They called her "the Ice Maiden." Penguins could live on her, they said. She had the mean average annual temperature of an iceberg.

She was so shining white, it hurt to look at her. She was like a ski slope in the sun.

She played tennis as if she were pouring tea. No one ever saw her perspire.

She was a throwback to the days when women played in hobble skirts and flowered bonnets.

She never left the baseline. She knocked everybody out at long range like the USS Missouri. She played tennis the way an orchestra played Beethoven, deftly, lovingly but with intense concentration on the notes. Other players might be rock 'n' roll or bombast. Chris Evert was a Moonlight Sonata.

It irritated some people. They wanted more dash and fire. They wanted Chris to come to the net, to slash more, serve and volley, lose her temper, come apart. Be human.

She wouldn't. She was as cold as a marble statue. She never dived for a ball, skidded into a net. She looked as easy to beat as a pair of treys.

You couldn't get a ball by her in a tank. She had the patience of a schoolmarm. She made Job seem impetuous. She would hit balls back at your feet till you wanted to scream.

The crowd wanted Dempsey and they got Willie Pep. Sugar Ray. Chris jabbed you to death.

She was at pains not to look like it, but she was a tremendous athlete. She made the two-handed backhand popular, which made the Establishment need smelling salts. Chris just smiled sweetly. She didn't run on court, she'd glide. She'd remind you of a great center fielder. DiMaggio in his prime. When the ball came down, she was there. And when she hit it back, it had hair on it.

But she elevated defense to a high art. No linebacker ever had a surer instinct for the ball than Chris Evert. She once won 125 consecutive matches on clay. She won seven French Opens. She was unbeatable where the ball bounced true.

She walked with the graceful little mincing steps of a belle at a cotillion. You half expected her to have a parasol. She didn't appear to have a nerve in her body. I once wrote that she played with the bored detachment of a pro giving a lesson to an old dowager. It was true to the end.

She played a heady game. She had to. "My serve was not a weapon," she laughs. "I put it in there to start a point, not to ace anybody off the court."

She resisted temptations to turn into a serve-and-volleyer. She stuck to what brought her. Not even when Martina Navratilova came along with a game modeled after Marines storming the beaches did Chris leave the baseline.

She won nine of every 10 matches she played. She won 157 singles titles, 1,309 matches in all, more than any female player. She won 18 Grand Slam titles, which, as it happens, is one more than Martina.

Whatever she was doing must have been right.

But I always thought Chris Evert's enduring contribution to the game was not tenacity, it was femininity. Not since Helen Wills Moody Roark had the game seen anyone with the aloof, dedicated perfection of Evert. They used to call Wills "Little Miss Poker Face." Chris Evert presented the same unruffled, confident exterior. You could never tell from looking at her whether she was down four-love or up two sets to none.

Chris Evert never managed to look as if she just got off a tugboat or just put out a cigar. She wore ponytails and earrings and hair ribbons. Even necklaces. She played in bracelets till they got in the way. Louisa May Alcott would have loved her.

Chris Evert has left the baseline. She put away the rackets and 19 years of cross-court volleys, drop shots and two-handed backhands last fall at the U.S. Open when she lost in the quarterfinals to Zina Garrison, a player who stood in line for an hour to get Chris' autograph only nine years before.

It was only the second time in her career that Evert failed to make at least the semifinals there. She played in 113 U.S. Open matches. She won five Opens and was a finalist three times and a semifinalist eight.

There is no senior tour as such for tennis. Will Chris Evert now retire with her clippings, her trophies, her ski-slope husband, Andy Mill, to a condo in Aspen?

Hardly. As a matter of fact, she's going to the net. "Don't make me out to be a dynamo," she pleads. But she will do tennis commentary for NBC Sports, her Evert Enterprises is active in the sports fashion business, and on March 3-4 at the Hyatt Grand Champions Resort in Indian Wells, she will head the pro-celebrity phase of the Virginia Slims of Indian Wells tournament to benefit the Women Sports Foundation.

She spanned the era from Billie Jean King to Steffi Graf with grace and taste. She kept Martina from swallowing the game whole.

King and Graf were/are great players. But could they have won wearing an evening gown and a diamond tiara?

Chris Evert could. All but did.

●　●　●　●　●　●　●　●　●　●　●　●　●　●　●　●　●

DECEMBER 14, 1989

Booming or Not, She's Easily The Best Around

It is not characteristic of me to offer advice to (quasi)rival publications, not even my alma mater, Sports Illustrated.

But it has come to my attention that the magazine is casting about for its annual sportsman of the year cover and candidates are coming from all over.

I have one for them, the individual I would like to see on the cover of the last issue of the year.

It's a West German tennis player who may be the best ever to play the game. Fair-haired, cat-like, No. 1 in the world. Hits the ball with the booming authority of the born slugger, has this long sweeping stride and is the most-feared competitor in the game today. Never throws a racket, curses an umpire, describes the host country as "the pits" or acts the spoiled brat. Never talks much at all. Just smiles. And wins.

Boris Becker? Who said anything about Boom Boom?

No, my candidate for sportsman of the year is a fraulein, the other half of the umlaut entry in the world of pro tennis.

Becker is good. But he's not one set better than anybody playing his game.

Steffi Graf is. There are those who think she's a set better than anyone who ever played her game – Helen Wills Moody, Mo Connolly, Martina Navratilova, Chris Evert, Billie Jean King, Margaret Court. She is better than any of them in the view of longtime tennis coach and scholar Vic Braden. "She hasn't even begun to scratch the surface of her talent," Braden insists. "She just stands at the baseline and beats your brains out. The only time she comes to the net is to get the check. As soon as she needs some other strokes and other parts of the game, she'll get them."

She is only 20 years old. She has earned $5,251,345 on a tennis court. She won 83 of 85 matches she played this year. Of the 16 tournaments she entered, she won 14 of them and was a finalist in the other two. She has won seven of the last eight Grand Slam events (French, U.S. and Australian opens plus Wimbledon) and was a finalist in the other.

She looks more like a Rhine maiden than an athlete. You imagine the Lorelei looked like this. Or it's a face right out of Grimm's Fairy Tales. She was born in a gingerbread house. You want to ask her whatever happened to Hansel.

She is as German as a glockenspiel. And fittingly, she plays this kind of Wagnerian game, full of crashing crescendoes, heroic passages, lyric transitions. She attacks. She doesn't have quite the tenacity of a Billie Jean or the stately elegance of a Helen Wills. She's a pouncer. She leaps on a mistake like a leopard on a waterbuck.

If Orel Hershiser won 83 of every 85 games he pitched, there'd be no question who'd be Sportsman of the Year every year. If a golfer won 14 of every 16 tournaments he entered, including all the majors or even three out of four, he'd be a statue in every clubhouse in the country.

Age 20 is a little young to be a figurehead for an entire industry. At 20, you're supposed to be barely out of teeth braces and Michael Jackson records. Steffi Graf is a world figure and she doesn't even wear lipstick yet.

Is it a drag?

"It's all right if you like what you're doing – and I like what I'm doing," insists Graf, in Los Angeles to play a Michelin challenge match with her No. 4 pursuer, Zina Garrison. "I have good surroundings. I feel good about what I do."

Does she find the responsibility a bit sticky – the lack of privacy, the demands on her time? "Well, I've had 2½ years to get used to it," she says. "I've been No. 1 for that time. And I just grew into (the role). I know what my responsibilities are, what's expected of me, what my obligations to tennis and the public are.

"In Europe, I'm more instantly recognized, but I'm more left alone. They say, 'Oh, it's Steffi!' But they don't bother you for autographs while you're eating. Here, they are not so considerate."

How does West Germany react to having not one but two international sports heroes in Becker and Graf? Who's seeded No. 1 in their little tournament there?

"We are equal in attention," Graf shrugs. "I don't think about it really. I am not in competition with Boris Becker. My focus is Martina or Gabriela (Sabatini)."

Graf has been the best player in the world since the day at Wimbledon in the final in 1988 when she stopped Martina's win streak of 47 matches there – three short of Helen Wills Moody's Wimbledon record.

But she admits there is a double standard in tennis. Could she, she is asked, indulge in the luxury of orbiting a racket into the stands, scorching the ears of a chair umpire with a collection of epithets more suited to the cab of a truck than a center court? Graf smiles. "I don't think it would be so good," she admits. "For me or the game."

Does she not feel like exploding at times? Graf nods. "I have a temper," she agrees. "I get angry when a call is wrong. But I control it, just as I control the rest of my game. Tennis requires concentration." So does anger.

For Steffi Graf, life has a net in it. She is either on a baseline or an airplane. It is the notion here, given gratis to the editors of Sports Illustrated, that she should be on their cover as sportsperson of the year. One thing is sure: Her record of success will outmeasure anyone else who may make it.

● ● ● ● ● ● ● ● ● ● ● ● ● ● ● ● ● ●

SEPTEMBER 23, 1986

He's the Man That the Fan Loves to Hate

"I hate funerals and would not attend my own if it could be avoided. But it is well for every man to stop and reflect every now and then on the kind of mourners he is preparing for his final event."
– Gouverneur Morris, Revolutionary patriot

John Patrick McEnroe Jr., the tennis player, may be a long way from his funeral, but a lot of people thought his tennis game was terminal. It had atrophied shockingly in a 6½-month layoff. If it wasn't dead, there was a rattle in its throat.

It was a day many people had been looking forward to like a kid to Christmas. Umpires, journalists, linesmen, opponents, the whole fabric of tennis yearned for the day when his serve no longer blistered, his forehand wobbled and his backhand netted.

Tennis could go back to being a gentleman's game again and not a Bowery Boys sitcom. After all, it is a game that starts out at love, and now it could go back to its tea-and-crumpets origins, where the royal box could be spared the kind of gutter language the lower classes use to express themselves.

McEnroe had lowered the elegant game to the level of mud wrestling. No self-respecting equerry would dare subject the Queen Mother to a McEnroe match. She would hear some perversions of the mother tongue Chaucer never dreamed of. Might as well take her to a porn house in Times Square.

It would be nice to have a Wimbledon final of "Lovely shot, Gene!" again, of silent, efficient Swedes or fun-loving but polite Aussies. No more guttersnipes to curdle the cream on the strawberries.

So when McEnroe married a movie star and retired to Malibu to reflect on his options, tennis began, hopefully, to dig out like a family that has survived a tornado, to see what was left they could rebuild upon.

They had this pointy-headed Czechoslovakian, a heavy-legged German kid and not much else. But matches could be played in library silence again. Tennis is not really a spectator sport, it is a kind of complicated tea dance. McEnroe made it seem like the semi-main at St. Nick's or a dock fight in Marseilles.

When McEnroe didn't even make Wimbledon and then got knocked out in the first round of the U.S. Open this year, tennis heaved a collective sigh of relief. The day it had been dreaming of seemed at hand.

The kind of mourners McEnroe had been training for his final event were about to throw their hats in the air. Throw a party. Uncork the champagne. Dance in the streets. Congratulate each other. The nightmare was over. Tennis was saved.

Or was it?

When McEnroe was eliminated, the U.S. Open degenerated into the Czechoslovakian Open. Four Czechs played in the two finals, which gave newspapers a field day with their "Hey, Czech This!" headlines and a chance to break out all their Czechpoints, Czechmates, bouncing Czechs and similar puns.

Other publications were not so enchanted. When Ivan Lendl won, Sports Illustrated put his picture on the cover, labeling him "The Champion That Nobody Cares About."

Inside, the magazine published a series of headless pictures of him, showing his shirts and suggesting that his wardrobe was the most interesting thing about him, that he played tennis with all the elan of a store window mannequin. The story pointed out he could empty a room faster than a loose anaconda or a smell of smoke, and said that when he took the court the aisles were so clogged with fleeing spectators it looked like the evacuation of Paris.

Lendl played the kind of robotized tennis that made you wonder where the dials were. He played such bloodless tennis that in the final against another Czech, so little known he was dubbed the blank Czech, it was reliably reported that only three people in America cared who won and only 11 would know.

Jimmy Durante used to sing, "You Know Darn Well I Can Do Without Broadway, but Can Broadway Do Without Me?"

Tennis won't have to do without John McEnroe just yet. He showed up at the Volvo Tennis/Los Angeles tournament last week and, although it was not to be confused with the U.S. Open, it had some people who have been beating McEnroe lately. The crowds came out in numbers, probably in the hopes of seeing the shadow of John McEnroe humiliated by guys who couldn't warm him up in the old days, the kind of people who slow down at freeway accidents or like chain-saw movies.

The McEnroe that showed up was no burnout. He was not the shell of a player the rumors had led the crowds to expect. He chewed out photographers, umpires, linesmen, referees, fans and opponents with equal skill and enthusiasm. He fought for every point, verbally and athletically.

If his tennis was a little ragged, his larynx was in Wimbledon form. He stood on the baseline with those cat's eyes of his, like a lion who sees a leaf moving in the bush across a clearing, and he whacked out opponents like Brad Gilbert while jawing with female fans, whom he called "low lifes."

He kept up a running commentary to himself on the behavior of the ship of fools in the stands and violently contested all calls that went against him. Meanwhile, he was playing impeccable tennis.

It was vintage McEnroe. It called to mind Muhammad Ali systematically destroying some foe in his prime while keeping up a lively banter with the ringside seats. "Call this guy a contender" – bam! – "get me somebody" – whap! whap! – "who can fight."

These verbal assaults are obviously as necessary to McEnroe's game as a forehand volley. He seems to perform best with waves of hostility washing across him from the audience.

He basks in hate. He doesn't play tennis, he provokes it. He stirs his own adrenaline, chokes his opponent's choler – and then serenely plays his best tennis while affecting a scowl as black as a polar night.

He is not fooled by the crowd's bared fangs. "People want to see me beaten in a match, until they remember that, if they do, they won't see me the next day," he explained in a postmatch press conference. "I think they want to see me the next day."

At one point Saturday night, McEnroe walked over to a catcalling fan cheering for his opponent, Gilbert, and demanded: "What do you want to see tomorrow, an Edberg-Gilbert final or an Edberg-McEnroe?"

John McEnroe knew the answer. So does all tennis. They used to call Erich Von Stroheim, the movie villain, the man you love to hate. John McEnroe makes him look like Rebecca of Sunnybrook Farm.

McEnroe is training exactly the kind of mourners he wants – and tennis needs. Paying ones.

• • • • • • • • • • • • • • • • • •

In Tennis,
She Has Set Standard

If I were to tell you one of the greatest athletes of the 20th century – and maybe the greatest of our times – would be appearing in Manhattan Beach this week, would you go there expecting to see: (a) Jose Canseco, (b) the ghost of Jim Thorpe, (c) Nick Faldo, (d) Pete Rose, (e) Joe Montana or (f) any Detroit Piston?

What you would find there is none of the above. What you would find is an athlete who is pound for pound, inch for inch the greatest of the era, an athlete who weeps in victory, smiles in defeat, wears designer clothes and actually looks good in earrings.

No one is sure whether God is a woman, but it just may be that the greatest tennis player in history is.

Listen, when you talk of all-time sports feats, hitting in 56 consecutive baseball games, pitching six no-hitters, scoring 100 points in an NBA game or winning three Super Bowls stand out.

But winning nine Wimbledons?! That makes the list with any of them at any time.

It is the tennis feat of all time. It makes Martina Navratilova the best ever to play that game. Big Bill Tilden? He won three Wimbledons, thank you. Don Budge? Two Wimbledons. Rod Laver? Four Wimbledons. Bjorn Borg? Five Wimbledons. Ivan Lendl? None.

You have to dip into antiquity to find a matchup for Navratilova. Only the elegant Helen Wills Moody, who won eight Wimbledons, is in her class.

That's what you have to do with the truly marvelous – measure them not against their contemporaries, but against their ancestors, against history. Helen Wills was to tennis what Babe Ruth was to baseball. Henry Aaron breaking Babe's all-time record was no greater an accomplishment than breaking the great Queen Helen's. People thought neither of them would ever be matched.

Martina won more than a tournament. She won her way into legend. She now plays for the ages. She escapes the fine print. To be in the same paragraph with Helen Wills is an achievement. To reduce her to a footnote is to take over tennis.

Helen Wills used to play with the fixed expression of someone trying to win a pot with two treys. Martina plays with the intensity of a deer fleeing a forest fire, but she turns as coldly efficient as a serial killer when the Queen's cup is on the line.

She is in a business where the average age seems to be somewhere between 14 and 19 but, at 33 nearing 34, she manages to dispatch these younger, fiery schoolgirls with the steady competence of someone plucking chickens.

Martina never seems to come to a game in emotional disarray. She is as tough and focused as Mike Tyson with his man on the ropes or Nolan Ryan with a guy looking for the curve.

She dispatched a schoolgirl (Debbie Graham, Stanford) in a little over 45 minutes Tuesday with almost bored nonchalance. It was like watching someone pull wings off a butterfly – except that Martina treats every match as if it is a Wimbledon final. She confided afterward that she was fearful after a five-week layoff that she might have forgotten how to play.

How could Martina forget how to play tennis? What does it take to win nine Wimbledons in the first place? What does it take to be and remain Martina Navratilova?

Plenty. It calls for the tenacity of purpose of a bulldog on a rope. In Helen Wills' time, tennis was not exactly a profession. It was more of a pastime for the not-so-idle rich. Tournaments were spaced, outdoors and relentlessly amateur. Silver cups were at stake, not silver Rolls-Royces.

The competition was genteel. Tennis was largely something to do before the cotillion started.

Today, it's Wall Street with rackets. Big bucks, high pressure. It's a jungle out there.

You need your own masseuse. You need your own osteopath. You travel in an entourage. You're on an airplane, in a limo – or on the court.

You have to watch what you eat. "Your body is like a vintage Rolls-Royce," Martina says. "You have to be careful what fuel you put in."

You have oatmeal and carrot juice for breakfast. Doughnuts are out. Even orange juice. "Sugar is a drug," Martina insists. "A mind-altering drug. It is the most abused drug in America. It gives you a high and then it does what all drugs do – brings you down and in despair. Robs you of precious energy."

Red meat is OK. Once a month. "I love hamburgers," Martina admits. "But if I ate them every time I wanted them, I wouldn't make the quarterfinals."

The body is treated as deferentially as a sovereign. Some women check the mirror for their beauty. Martina checks it for her health. It is her belief that only her mind is 33 years old. The rest of her is still in her teens.

"It's a narcissistic life," she says. "But it's necessary."

Most people wear glasses so they can see 20/20. Or even 20/30. Martina can already see 20/20 with the naked eye. She wears glasses because they correct her vision to 20/10. Martina takes every edge into the match she can muster.

She lifts weights not to build up her muscles, but to build up her endurance. Martina's body is not a set of muscular knots. It's chorus-line round.

She ices her knees after every match. She's a late sleeper. The body is pampered, but Martina shows little patience with the athlete in it. She is an expert skier, defiant of the possibility of a fracture.

If tennis were a morality play, Martina would be the villain. She has a nice smile, but in the early years of her career, she used it sparingly.

She had come into the game out of the gloom of Kafka's Czechoslovakia, where smiles were rationed like sausages. She learned to play tennis hitting a ball against a barn door. "It's hard to learn the game when your competition is a wall." When she began to beat the golden Chris Evert and everybody's darling of the center court, Evonne Goolagong, Martina was treated like a truck driver at a royal lawn party.

Not anymore. Martina is the royalty on the court now. The crowds come to see her in the Virginia Slims tournament at Manhattan Country Club this week. She is an American heirloom.

She is, typically, hardening her body and toughening her mind for the U.S. Open. After all, she has only won four of those. (Borg never won any.)

But her ambition is not a 10th Wimbledon or a fifth U.S. Open, it's to win a gold medal for the United States in the Barcelona Olympics in '92.

It's an interesting ambition. Even curious. Until you remember that Helen Wills won one in 1924.

● ● ● ● ● ● ● ● ● ● ● ● ● ● ● ● ●

August 5, 1993

Sampras' Ability Is What Sets Him Apart

The trouble with Pete Sampras is, you can't tell by looking at him whether he's winning, 6-0, 6-0, or struggling with his backhand and losing two sets to love.

He has the same bemused, stoical expression on his face. He looks as if he really doesn't care much one way or the other. In the U.S. Open last year, he was beset by stomach cramps, but no one knew because he didn't look appreciably different from when he felt fine.

You have no idea how much this annoys the British tabloids. They have come to rely on American Wimbledon champions to be tantrum-throwing, racket-throwing, self-indulgent semi-sociopaths who misbehave on court and have the most juicy off-court relationships a keyhole reporter could wish for. The Brits love Andre Agassi, John McEnroe, Jimmy Connors. They wish Sampras would either go out in the round of 16 – or get tangled up with some reigning TV or movie queen or insult the British Queen. They want a soap opera, not a sport.

All Sampras is, is the best tennis player in the world. He just doesn't act like it. On court, waiting for a serve, he frequently hangs his head like a guy who is a suspect in a child murder or has just spilled soup on his hostess.

He has the dark good looks of a matinee idol. He's as polite as a butler. He doesn't have the Huckleberry Finn-ish appeal of a Jim Courier, but he's as American as the hot rod and probably could have been a cleanup hitter if someone hadn't put a racket in his hands at age 7. He plays tennis like a guy dealing blackjack. All he does is beat you.

That's dramatic enough for most people, but the world expects tennis to be a sitcom.

Even Willie Mays' cap would fly off when he went out to rob someone of a three-base-hit – Willie used to wear them purposely one size off, so they would. Muhammad Ali used to narrate his fights for the ringside audiences. Babe Ruth used to step out of the box and point to the bleachers.

Pete Sampras just slams an ace by you. And looks apologetic.

It's a heady feeling being No. 1 in anything. To be to your sport what Michael Jordan is to his, what John L. Sullivan was ... Louis, Hogan, Nicklaus. Sampras has a chance to be to his sport what Tilden, Budge, Kramer, Perry and Laver were.

It's a responsibility as well as an honor. Sampras wears it well.

He's what the public likes – the home run hitter, fastball pitcher, KO puncher, long-drive artist. He's got the equalizer – the 140-m.p.h. serve. He's got the dunk shot. Sampras is not boring. Unless you consider a guy with a machine gun boring. Sampras plays tennis the way Dempsey fought – or Ted Williams hit. He blasts you out of there. No opponent ever considered him boring. Stefan Edberg maybe; he kind of surrounds you. But not Sampras; he terminates you.

It isn't as if he's just a poker-faced bomber. Sampras has all phases of the game – drop shots at the net, blistering backhands and, very occasionally, the lob, although that's not much needed with his firepower.

It's kind of unfair. It's like giving a lion another tooth, a bear another claw. On the nights when the serve isn't working – and it's like a fastball in pitching, he says, because there are times when he can't keep it in the strike zone – he can fall back on a variety of shots even Edberg might envy.

Now that he's about to take his place on a pedestal of the game, shouldn't he want to spice up the act – show up at Wimbledon with a bimbo on each arm, a bottle of champagne in his Lamborghini and his picture in the supermarket gossip sheets? How abut getting "colorful," i.e., smashing rackets, kicking cameras, cursing umpires, calling the All-England Championship "the pits"?

Pete Sampras laughs. "That's not what I'm all about," he tells you. "I'm not the flamboyant type. I'm not out there to overshadow the tennis. I go out to win tennis matches. And I hope people enjoy watching that."

If not, presumably, they can watch "Falcon Crest."

Sampras learned that racket-throwing was bad form from an irreproachable source, his father. "He told me if I was going to get into that, I better get out of tennis," he recalls. "Also, he told me he didn't want me to embarrass my mother."

Sampras hits every ball as if it owed him money. His serve-and-volley game is merciless when it's on. He dispatched a mystery opponent, Andrew Sznajder, who is only 155 slots below him in the world rankings, Tuesday night at the Volvo/Los Angeles tennis tournament at UCLA in just over one hour, 6-1, 6-2.

Sznajder, a likable sort, groaned, held his head in his hands and rolled his eyes skyward as eight aces and countless forehands down the line roared past him like express mail. Sampras just looked like a guy waiting for a bus. On some of his aces and winners, Sampras didn't even bother following them in to the net, just started walking to the ad court as soon as he'd hit them. They should at least have given Sznajder a blindfold and a cigarette before they lined him up.

The British tabloids may not find this exciting. But any sports fan who wouldn't find Pete Sampras exciting wouldn't find Stan Musial at the plate with a full count or Joe Louis with his man on the ropes or John Daly off a tee exciting either. Sampras finds 40-love at set point plenty exciting. So does the guy he's playing against. Pete Sampras at the net is as exciting as Michael Jordan at the top of the key any old day. Because the next sound you hear is going to be "Slam dunk!"

You're seeing No. 1 doing what he does best. That's as exciting as it gets. In any sport.

Track and Field

• • • • • • • • • • • • • • • •

MAY 10, 1988

He Landed Somewhere
In the Future

In the summer of 1920, Babe Ruth hit 54 home runs, or 30 more in a season than anyone else ever hit before and 25 more than he hit the season before, when he was only a part-time hitter and full-time pitcher. This was widely perceived at the time as, maybe, the outstanding single sports feats of all time.

In 1918, Jack Dempsey knocked out two men, Fred Fulton and Carl Morris, in a total elapsed time of 32 seconds, including the counts – Morris went 14 seconds, Fulton was tougher, he went 18 – and these were considered the standards for pugs to shoot at the rest of time.

On Oct. 18, 1924, Red Grange of Illinois scored four touchdowns in 12 minutes the only times he touched the ball, running 95, 67, 56 and 44 yards for scores against Michigan. He later scored twice more, on a run and a pass reception, and that was the day he became the Galloping Ghost, the spectral runner against whom all subsequent ballcarriers were to be measured.

On March 2, 1962, at Hershey, Pennsylvania, Wilt Chamberlain threw in 100 points in a pro basketball game, 22 more than his previous high and 29 more than anyone else ever had.

On June 10, in 1977, in the second round of the Memphis Open golf tournament, Al Geiberger shot 11 birdies and an eagle and took only 23 putts to shoot an unheard-of 59, the lowest round in pro tournament golf history.

Extraordinary achievements all. But, almost without question, the most incredible single athletic feat of all time took place on Oct. 18, 1968, at 3:46 p.m. in the gathering gloom of the Olympic long jump pit at the stadium in Mexico City. Bob Beamon jumped 29 feet 2½ inches.

It was one of the glowing moments of sports history when everything comes together almost in a flash of insight, almost as if the athlete were standing outside of himself watching, too.

Bob Beamon was in the air just shorter than the Wright Brothers. No one had ever been aloft that high or that long over a long jump pit before – or since. It wasn't a jump, it was an orbital flight.

Beamon didn't break the record, he disintegrated it. It was not only how far he had jumped, it was how high. Some thought he might have broken the high jump and long jump records at the same time.

"I thought he never would come down," I remember runner-up Ralph Boston marveling.

Rumor had it Beamon came up on the traffic controllers' screens at the airport. They thought he was the noon flight from Guadalajara. Lindbergh didn't get that high off the deck.

No one had ever jumped 28 feet before. The world record was 27 feet 4¾ inches, and the machine designed to measure the long jump at the Mexico City Olympics that year had a nervous breakdown. The optical device could not digest the information being fed back to it.

It could not, in effect, believe its eyes. It had been constructed to measure jumps of 28 feet. Everyone thought that would be enough to measure any jump on the planet Earth by any creature that didn't have horns or spots.

Bob Beamon broke the long jump record by nearly 2 feet – by 19¾ inches to be exact. He broke the Olympic long jump record by almost 3 feet – 31 inches to be exact.

"He has broken the Olympic record by a half century," the British long jumper, Lynn Davies, said later. "He has destroyed the event."

It was an enormous mark. It was like a man hitting 80 home runs, batting .502, shooting 50, winning Wimbledon love-love-love. It is an Olympic record not likely to be broken in our lifetimes.

It has had the extraordinary effect of making Bob Beamon a bigger celebrity as his achievement fades into antiquity. It is usual, 20 years after the event, for a public to have difficulty remembering either one.

But in the 20 years since the Jump, Beamon has seen the Olympic best, even with the great Carl Lewis on the runways, barely creep to 28 feet – 28-0. To be sure, word coming out of Russia is that the Soviets' Robert Emmiyan has posted a 29-foot jump, but the details are sketchy.

Few of us are ever privileged to experience the perfect moment in life. It may come to athletes, it may come to actors or actresses, opera tenors. Maybe even a poet can find words that he has no idea where they're coming from.

But Bob Beamon has worn his laurel gracefully. He's not sitting around bars, inviting strangers to buy drinks for "the world's greatest jumper ever" or showing his gold medal at cocktail parties. Beamon is still trying for that perfect jump; he's attacking the boards.

He is in town to promote the 1988 Pepsi Invitational meet at UCLA June 5, where the pharmaceutical company he works for, Glaxo, Inc., is sponsoring both the men's and women's 100-meter dash.

His long jump may never come down in our time, but the jumper came down a long time ago. Beamon became a national spokesman for the treatment of high blood pressure when he found that he, the super athlete of all time in his event, had, of all things, high blood pressure.

It is, Beamon points out, a disease without symptoms. Usually the first indication you get of it is death. Almost 50% of the people who have high blood pressure do not know it – until they die from it. It makes its presence known mainly at autopsies.

It is estimated that 6,315,000 blacks in the United States suffer from it, and that its rate of occurrence in blacks is more than three times that in whites.

This is one record Beamon would rather lower than increase. Lobbying for something as worthwhile as this and bringing the message of his company's medication is a proper application of athletic fame, and if the Jump helps him spread it, Beamon is grateful.

What of the record? Can it be broken at Seoul? Beamon smiles. "Records are made to be broken."

Maybe so. But it won't be broken by any 2½ feet.

• • • • • • • • • • • • • • • • •

JANUARY 6, 1987

Could It Be That She Really Is the Finest Athlete in the World?

The world's greatest athlete?

Don't bet that the world's greatest athlete will be in the Super Bowl, the World Series, Centre Court at Wimbledon or the prize ring at Caesars Palace.

Don't bet the world's greatest athlete is a great hulk with a beard that positively needs shaving every day. The world's greatest athlete may very well look good in high heels and mesh stockings, lipstick and bracelets.

The world's greatest athlete may be just like the girl that married dear old dad.

Which is to say, a very good case could be made for Jackie Joyner Kersee. The world's greatest athlete may very well be just a slip of a girl and not a hunk at all – just 5-10 and 155 – who can cook, has brown eyes and a nice smile and a figure that could make a chorus line.

What do you want of a great athlete? Speed? Strength? Capacity for hard work? Versatility? Determination?

This Jackie might be the greatest in all those departments since another Jackie – Robinson – also a great athlete.

You want speed in the world's greatest athlete? How about 12.8 seconds over the 100-meter hurdles? You want the ability to jump? How about 23 feet 9 inches?

You want strength? How about a 50-foot shotput, give or take an inch or so? How about a 22.8 time in the 200? How many people do you know who can throw a javelin 164 feet?

Jackie Joyner Kersee is not the best in the world in any one of the heptathlon's seven events, but she's the best in the world at all seven.

Not since the storied Babe Didrikson has America had a woman who holds the world record in a multi-event competition.

Babe Didrikson might have been the greatest athlete of her sex who ever lived – maybe of any sex.

So might Jackie J.

Unlike Didrikson, Jacqueline Joyner did not begin life as the village tomboy. The Babe, who grew up in Beaumont, Texas, could always do anything the boys could do – better. Jackie Joyner probably went to the track because her brother Al, who later won a gold medal in the triple jump at the Los Angeles Olympics, went there.

She concentrated on the long jump. She became good enough to make the Olympic final, where she finished fifth, out-jumping Carl Lewis' sister, Carol, who was favored in the event, but finishing behind the Romanian jumpers for the medals.

The heptathlon is less a sporting event than a modern Inquisition. Torquemada would have loved it. The girls who enter it are subject to every form of torture short of the rack and fingernail-pulling.

It is a seven-stage ordeal in which you are expected to hurdle, jump, run, throw. In between, you gasp for air with lungs that feel as if they have been sandpapered. People come out of it about in the condition they crawl out of a plane wreck. Your heart is on fire, your feet hurt, your back aches and your teeth don't feel too good, either.

In Babe Didrikson's day, it was popularly supposed that women couldn't take more than three events of this grueling nature. That was before they realized women had more endurance than men. By 1964, the multi-sport competition had been expanded to five events, and Soviet women, who were built more or less along the lines of locomotives, excelled at it.

By 1980, the competition was stretched to seven events, still short of the men's 10 in a decathlon but still almost as big an assignment as climbing a snow mountain in bare feet and dental floss. You run the high hurdles and the 200 meters, high jump and put the shot one day. You long-jump, throw the javelin and then wind up with a cardiac nightmare, the 800 meters, on the second.

That would be hard enough on a grown man bursting with good health, but Mrs. Kersee – husband, Bob, is also her coach and the coach of a dozen other medal-winning Olympians at UCLA – does it all despite a chronic case of asthma.

According to Coach Kersee, Jackie's is a form of the disease that is brought on by, of all things, exercise. Which is like – what? – a great chef being allergic to flour? A jockey who sneezes when exposed to horsehair?

With the defection of the Soviet Bloc at the 1984 Olympics, Jackie Joyner Kersee was a mild favorite to win the heptathlon at the Coliseum.

A heptathlete, like a male decathlete, usually stands out in one event. Jackie's event is the long jump. When she barely clipped 20 feet in her long jump at the Los Angeles Games, she became downcast. She thought she had blown her chance at the gold. She hadn't, really.

"She was so inexperienced in international meets that she got emotional, lost her concentration," explains husband Kersee.

Even then, she finished only five points behind the winner, Australian Glynis Nunn. She beat the ultimate winner in the shotput, the 200 and the javelin throw and tied her in the high jump. The long jump was the crusher. If she could have jumped within a foot of her all-time best, she would have had a lock on the gold. Jackie had to settle for the silver medal.

At the Goodwill Games in Moscow last summer, Jackie arrived with a crash. She not only set the world record, she became the first woman – and, so far, the only – in history to post 7,000 points in a heptathlon.

She has now broken that record, too. At Houston, last fall, she exceeded her 7,148 Moscow points by a "dime," totaling 7,158. Competing in temperatures up to 126 degrees, she routed her competition by 1,024 points.

It has been calculated that if she could put together a heptathlon of her lifetime personal bests, she could top 7,500 points.

If that doesn't put her in the hunt for the putative world's greatest athlete with any cornerback, welterweight, backcourt man, pitcher or hitter who ever lived, you'll have to tell her admirers what does.

On her way to Seoul in '88, Jackie will be starring in a few meets this indoor season. One of them will be the Sunkist Invitational at the Sports Arena Friday night, Jan. 16. Jackie will be long-jumping that night, an event in which she again proposes to double in the 1988 Olympics.

A 7,000 score in the heptathlon is equivalent to a 10,000 score in the decathlon. In 1912, when Jim Thorpe posted his record decathlon, the King of Sweden, no less, saluted him with, "Sir, you are the world's greatest athlete."

Of course, Thorpe could also punt the football 70 yards, catch or throw one 55 yards and play baseball for the New York Giants, things Jackie J. Kersee hasn't yet proven she can do. On the other hand, don't bet she can't.

● ● ● ● ● ● ● ● ● ● ● ● ● ● ● ● ●

APRIL 21, 1996

The Best? His Track Record Says It All

Who would you have to say is the greatest athlete of the century?

Babe Ruth? Well, a case could be made. Starred in two disciplines in ones sport – pitching and slugging.

Henry Aaron? Attention must be paid.

Muhammad Ali? Joe Louis? Would get votes. So would Bill Tilden, J. Donald Budge. Pele gets in the hunt. Joe Montana? Well, if you're only going to count throwing, make mine Sandy Koufax.

Michael Jordan? Well, couldn't hit the curveball. But maybe that shouldn't matter.

Jim Thorpe? Well, you're getting warm.

I think the vote here might go to Carl Franklin Lewis, Esq., of the New Jersey and Houston Lewises.

Look! How do you measure athletic prowess? The guy who can hit harder, run faster or jump higher than anybody, right?

Carl Lewis makes it on two out of three. And he never measured himself against the curve, the return of serve or the right cross. But when it came to running and jumping, well, nothing this side of Man o' War could challenge Carl Lewis in his heyday.

There is very little doubt Carl Lewis is the greatest athlete in track and field history. Eight gold medals and a silver in the Olympics close the argument. Mark Spitz rolled up seven golds in one Olympics. But he needed water. Also, you can't butterfly stroke your way to a track gold.

Lewis' staying power in a sport in which only youth has historically been served is awesome. For 18 years, he has been dominating track meets. His Olympic medal count was rolled up even though the 1980 Olympics were boycotted by the U.S. and he wasn't able to compete. The 100-meter dash was won in Moscow that year in 10.25 seconds. Lewis could run that carrying groceries. Jesse Owens ran nearly that fast winning the Berlin Olympics 44 years earlier.

Carl Lewis duplicated Jesse Owens' feat in the 1984 Los Angeles Olympics when he won the 100, the 200, the long jump and ran a leg on the winning 400-meter relay. That is the Quadruple Crown of track and field, a .400 average, a Grand Slam, a 2,000-yard season.

By any yardstick, Carl Lewis is to his sport what Man o' War was to horse racing, Jack Dempsey to boxing or, for that matter, Nijinsky to dancing. One of a kind. Above-the-title billing. Academy Award stuff.

That his sport is non-generic, unlike baseball or football, and is universally understood and played figures in the equation. It's a melancholy fact that Lewis will stop traffic quicker on the Champs Elysees or the autobahn or the Via Veneto than he will on Broadway or Sunset

Boulevard in his own country. At the Barcelona Olympics four years ago, his arrival had all the hype of a papal visit to East Lansing, Michigan. Rumor had it that the king wanted his autograph.

He will be 35 at the start of the Games in Atlanta this year, but nobody is ruling him out. In any of his specialties. In fact, he requested that the international track federation reschedule the events and space them out so it will be possible for him to have a chance to duplicate his 1984 feat.

Carl even thinks he may be wanting the federation to do the same at Sydney in 2000. He shocked the track world at Barcelona four years ago, winning the long jump from a man who had just set the world record, Michael Powell.

Track stars had career spans of meteorites in the days of mock amateurism. Getting Leica cameras didn't pay the rent, and today's gold-medal winner was tomorrow's playground director.

But even in the face of economic liberation, Lewis' longevity defies the odds. He ascribes it to stability, explaining, "I have had the same coach [Tom Tellez], the same manager [Joe Douglas] and the same practice facility [the University of Houston] all my career.

"There are a number of other factors: I have been a vegetarian. I keep control of what I eat, how I rest and I keep mentally fit."

Winning is often cerebral, he points out:

"You want to make your best jump first. It demoralizes the competition. That's what [Bob] Beamon did when he jumped 29 feet 2½ inches on his first jump at Mexico City. After he saw that, Ralph Boston didn't even jump 27."

Lewis was as good at the mind games as he was at the rest of the Olympic Games. In the '84 Olympics, he won the gold medal with one long jump, passing on his other jumps to save energy for the 200. He wanted to use all his reserves for a four-gold-medal Olympics and a duplicate of Owens' Olympics rather than waste them on a forlorn chase of Beamon's 29-foot record.

You wonder why a farewell tour isn't on the agenda for a legend of his magnitude. Sarah Bernhardt had one. So did Mickey Mantle, Charles Dickens, Kareem Abdul-Jabbar. Sometimes the farewell tours were premature. Bernhardt had four.

No one is willing to bet Carl won't be around for the Sydney Olympics. Have-jump-will-travel.

But today may be your last chance to see the last of the great Olympians in California. He will compete in the Mt. SAC relays at Mount San Antonio College in Walnut. This is the venerable meet Lewis has been competing in since 1981 and in which he will be taking part without his customary appearance fee and at his own travel expense. A sentimental journey.

It won't be a farewell appearance, but it may be close to it. In any event, it will be a last chance to see a legend before you have to fork over thousands for the privilege of doing so at Atlanta this summer.

He will be running in the 200 at Mt. SAC. Maybe you didn't see Ruth bat, Dempsey hit, Koufax throw, Tilden serve, Bird shoot or Mays catch, but you can say you've seen Lewis run – which is the same thing.

● ● ● ● ● ● ● ● ● ● ● ● ● ● ● ● ● ●

FEBRUARY 11, 1988

Tulare's Best Became Best in the World

There were better athletes. But not many. There were guys who could run faster, jump higher, throw farther. But not all three at the same time.

You want to talk running with the football? Bob Mathias once ran 96 yards for a touchdown against USC to put Stanford in the Rose Bowl. The last guy between him and the goal line was Frank Gifford, to give you an idea. He missed.

If basketball was your game, he was the original power forward. He threw in 18 points a night in high school in Tulare, California, and out-rebounded whole teams.

He could hit the curve ball, return the serve, he could putt a little.

But what Bob Mathias really was, was a one-man track team. He didn't have to do much about it. God and nature anticipated him. Whatever a mountain lion could do, Bob Mathias could do. He was brought up in the sunshine and breezes of the San Joaquin Valley, where vegetables and men grow in size to twice the national average.

He won the first decathlon he ever saw. Two weeks before, he had never even had a javelin or a pole vault in his hands.

His form was atrocious. He gripped the spear like a guy killing a chicken. He went over the vault like a guy falling out of a moving car, and his high jump looked like a guy leaving a banana peel. All he did was win.

He was like a guy dropping a handful of aces in the middle of a card game and saying innocently, "Are these any good?"

People who had to work at it wanted to kill him. It was almost the old cliche: Someone strained and grunted and sweated – and put the shot. And, Mathias, passing by, picked it up and threw it back at his feet – underhanded.

Four months after he took up the sport, he was beating the world at it – at the '48 Olympics in London. He was 17 years old. "We sent a boy to do a man's job," wrote the columnist Vincent X. Flaherty, "and he did it."

As if the process weren't daunting enough, the London decathlon was played out in a driving rain better suited to kayak pairs than pole vaulters. You almost needed a coxswain instead of a coach. "You couldn't even see the crossbar half the time," Mathias recalls. The shot-put not only sank into six inches of mud, so did the shotputter.

The contestants sat under blankets between turns in the pit. "The only lights they had were for the dog track, and most of our events were by flashlight. The British had just come through a war, and they didn't believe in spoiling you."

A decathlon has to be competed for in a 48-hour period, but Mathias remembers both days going on to the witching hour.

"I think there were two minutes left to midnight the day when we finished the pole vault in the rain." The 1,500-meter run, last event of the sport, was held in a blackout as dense as any in the blitz, with Big Ben just about to boom 12.

Four years later, when he had time to perfect form and technique, Bob Mathias not only broke his own record, he won the decathlon by a whopping 900 points, more than anyone ever had or would.

He retired to try his hand at movies, where he was no threat at all to Laurence Olivier, and at politics, where he went to Congress but stopped well short of the Oval Office.

"I was working for John Wayne's company when someone asked him to do a TV series and, when he turned it down, to recommend someone in his company. Unfortunately, he recommended Jim Arness. That program was 'Gunsmoke,'" Mathias says wryly.

No one had ever won two Olympic decathlons before. Now the brave Brit, Daley Thompson, has. He will go for his third at Seoul.

It is a matter of history that Thompson won one Olympic decathlon boycotted by the West and the other boycotted by the East. It is also a matter of history that he beat one bloc in one Olympics and the other in the other.

He will be 30 years old, 9 more than Mathias was when he won his last decathlon. The man whose record he will break if he wins his third says, "My hat's off to him if he can do it."

Said Mathias: "Ours is the only country in the world that doesn't provide government funds for its athletes. We have to depend on donations by companies like Hilton. Imagine what it would mean to history if Jesse Owens never got to Berlin. What if Mark Spitz never got to Munich, or (then) Cassius Clay never got to Rome, or Billy Mills to Tokyo or Bob Beamon to Mexico?"

Or if Bob Mathias never got out of Tulare?

• • • • • • • • • • • • • • • • •

The Baryshnikov
Of the Barriers

I like to see Edwin Moses run the hurdles for the same reason I liked to see Rod Carew bat, Bing Crosby sing, Joe DiMaggio drift under a high fly, Joe Louis throw a left, Sammy Snead hit a drive, Swaps in the stretch. Palmer putt, Koufax with the hitter in a hole, Marcus Allen hit a line – or, for that matter, a Swiss make a watch, an Arab sell a rug, a Manolete fight a bull or a Hemingway write about it, an Englishman do Shakespeare, or Roosevelt make a speech.

I love those guys who make it look easy. Who have that special combination of grace and talent that puts no strain at all on the viewer. They make it not a contest but a recital, a fugue for 10 hurdles by the artist. It's like watching Paderewski do the Moonlight Sonata or Heifetz do Bruch.

I'm getting so I don't like those guys whose hats fly off, whose faces look as if someone is holding lighted cigarettes to their feet, or who look as if they're going to die at the tape. I don't like those high-wire acts who pretend to slip, singers whose voices crack on the way to the high notes, and I hate it when they say, "And now, a stunt never before performed before a live audience anywhere!" I like to be able to say "Watch this!" when Nolan Ryan breaks off a high hard one or Dempsey is measuring his man for the hook.

It's a principle called "empathy," and it has to do with identification. It's what makes "fans." That's not Sandy Koufax and Steve Garvey out there, that's you. The easier a performer makes it for you, the more you enjoy it. When he makes it hard, you go home exhausted, wrung out, emotionally drained. You are the one who struggled through all those 3-and-2 counts, who had to foul seven off before you got the home run.

317

The great ones send you home relaxed and confident and with a new faith in yourself and a new outlook on life. The strainers put your teeth on edge, your nerves in a ball, and you want to go home and kick the cat and ask the world how anybody can drink this slop they call coffee nowadays?

Edwin Moses is one of the great virtuosos. You imagine Man o'War was like this. This modern Moses, this patriarch of the games Olympians play, comes on a track like Caesar inspecting the battlefield, a king trooping the guard. It's as if the other seven runners hadn't shown up. In a sense, they haven't.

Moses affably inspects the 10 hurdles, satisfies himself they are properly placed and heighted, like Padereswki checking the concert grand, Caruso testing the acoustics. He runs nonchalantly in place, strides out a few steps and then takes off over a hurdle or two.

The concert is ready. A little traveling music, maestro, the artist is on stage.

He could run the 400-meter hurdles in top hat and tails. It's like Muhammad Ali and George Chuvalo, a contest only if you consider the Johnstown Flood one. It's really just a complicated solo. When you see Baryshnikov dance, you're glad Tchaikowsky wrote. When you see Moses hurdle, you're glad the Greeks invented. And De Coubertin revived.

A 400-meter hurdle race is as technical as grand opera. It requires a calculating skill as well as enormous raw talent. There are lots of Olympic races where you just get out there and do the same things lions do on the track of a zebra. There's nothing cerebral about a 100-yard dash. If God didn't take care of everything first, there's nothing you can do about it.

The hurdles appealed more to Edwin Moses. In the first place, he's a scientist. Physics is as uncomplicated to him as the infield fly rule to Tommy Lasorda. When other kids were making snowmen on the block, he was making rockets in the cellar.

He fell in love with the hurdles. He could run the 200 and the 400 on the flat. But there wasn't enough geometry in that. The 200 is for truck drivers. Cheetahs. The 400 intermediates is the thinking-man's race.

They say that Edwin Moses' edge in the 400 hurdles is that he doesn't jump them, he just sort of ignores them. That is to say, he jumps the first hurdle – and then doesn't come down till the last. The joke is that Edwin doesn't really run the hurdles, he just breaks the long jump record three or more times during a round. They say it's just a rumor that he takes steps between the sticks (13 of them, by the way, or two fewer than anybody else usually takes). His stride is just shorter than Man o'War's, but he could probably win the event in leg chains.

He's now won 90 straight races or 105, depending on whether you count heats or not. Only three other runners have ever broken 48 seconds in the event. Moses has done it 28 times. Of course, he holds the world record. He keeps setting it.

The thing is, Edwin Moses' 90th and probably most important race was not exactly vintage Moses – and yet he won it by daylight and was, as usual, the only one in the field to break 48. But he jump-started once, and his time – 47.75 – was hardly Mosaic. He appeared to go fractionally higher over the hurdles instead of shaving them on the way over as usual.

But what was Mosaic was that, typically, it was no strain on the viewer. For the biblical seven years, this Moses has been undefeated. The pharaoh of time cannot catch up with him either. He was his usual affable, congenial self before and after the event. It's not only no strain on the spectator, it's no strain on Edwin, either. ("The race went about as I expected," he said calmly after it. In other records, the piano was in tune and the scenery stayed up.) It was like Crosby singing, or Kelly dancing in the rain. Moses in the hurdles is one of the great soothing sights of all time. A great way to end your day. Beats even sunsets into the Pacific or springtime in the Rockies.

• • • • • • • • • • • • • • • • • •

APRIL 21, 1987

She Won't Take It Lying Down

Mary Decker Slaney is one of the greatest runners America has ever produced. She holds the world record for the mile and every American record at every distance from half a mile to 10,000 meters.

So it's a ticker-tape parade, flowers on opening night, an adoring public, America's sweetheart, right?

Wrong. Mary comes into focus in the public mind lying on her stomach on an Olympic infield, teeth gnashed, tears coursing down her cheeks while she pounds the ground and wails "Get away from me!"

She has the negative image of the spoiled child holding her breath till she turns blue or gets her way. She comes into range with the public infamy most people would have to rob banks or burn flags to obtain.

It would seem unfair. No one remembers Babe Ruth striking out with the bases loaded or Dempsey on one knee at the end of the Tunney fight. We remember them in their triumphs, pointing to the bleachers, standing over a fallen Firpo.

Mary gets remembered for a series of mistakes at the 1984 Olympics not the least of which was not running her normal race, which was way out in front of everybody, like Secretariat at the Belmont of '73.

Mary fell from more than a gold medal. She fell from grace.

When she ran into Zola Budd that fateful day, it was like a motorcycle gang running over a statue of the Virgin.

Zola Budd was everybody's orphan that year, a mere slip of a girl who ran like a blithe animal but who got caught up in the insane politics of the time. She had to run for a country not her own and in front of "countrymen" who jeered and spat at her as if she were responsible for the sins of a lot of old generals and bankers.

In addition to everything else, Decker had actually run up on the heels of Budd, and the mood of the press was pretty much summed up by the Sporting News journalist, Dave Nightingale, who observed dryly: "When I got my first driving license, years ago, my father said to me, 'Son, if you ever rear-end anyone with this car, just reach for your wallet 'cause it's going to be your fault.'"

But fault is one thing. Historical injustice is another. And Mary Decker Slaney rear-ended more than Zola Budd that Aug. 10, 1984.

For Decker Slaney not to have won a gold medal is as depressing a footnote to history as Rod Carew never playing in the World Series or a Barrymore never getting an Oscar.

Never mind that Mary was all-world before the Olympics – Sports Illustrated's Sportsman of the Year in 1983, undefeated in 20 finals at all distances and on all surfaces. Never mind that she, along with hundreds of others, lost all chance to win anything in the '80 Olympics.

The injustice was underscored in the post-Olympic year, 1985, when Mary not only won 14 straight races but trounced the Olympic champion, Maricica Puica, and Zola Budd, both, five times, setting a world mile record against them. The last and only time Puica beat her was in the Olympics and Budd has never beaten her since.

But Mary realizes that none of that erases the awful image of the infield that August twilight. Heroic measures are called for.

She plans to make them. She plans to win a gold medal at Seoul in '88. Then she plans to win another at Barcelona in '92. Then she plans to get the women's mile record down to 4 minutes flat. Since it is currently at 4:16.7 – held by her – that would be major time shaving.

The fall might have been a blessing in disguise. It might have given Mary a new purpose, although she scoffs at the suggestion that she might have retired after the incident. "Never!" she hoots. "I was making plans to go to Europe for meets that very night!"

The new Mary Decker Slaney will, thank God, look a lot like the old one. In a sport practiced by a lot of women who look as if they should be running tugboats, Mary looks as if she just stepped off the runway at Givenchy's.

Not even a new baby – Ashley, 11 months – can mar the chorus-line perfection of Mary's 5-foot 6-inch, 105-pound silhouette, and the new season will feature probably the most beautiful set of legs ever seen outside of net stockings. Ten years ago, Doris Day would have played the Mary Decker part.

Mary will start her Seoul search May 16 in the Pepsi Invitational track meet at UCLA. She will run in the mile there and she will, subsequently, put in some 800-meter work. She plans to make it so that if anyone wants to collide with her in the 3,000 meters at Seoul, they will have to do it by parachute.

She wants an Olympics where they'll carry her on their shoulders, not on a stretcher, where she'll be laughing on a victory stand, not crying in the dirt. Mary is nobody's little lamb anymore. That one was a kid. This one *has* a kid.

Ice Hockey

• • • • • • • • • • • • • • • • •

AUGUST 11, 1988

He'll Bring L.A. Hockey Out of Ice Age

Listen! Would Caruso want to spend his career singing Gilbert and Sullivan in Leeds? Would Rembrandt want to paint barns? Is Nijinsky going to dance on street corners in Pocatello?

No. If you know anything about show business, you know you've got to bring the act to Broadway. No matter how good you are in Bridgeport, it's still Bridgeport.

What made anybody think the greatest hockey player who ever lived was going to stay up there by the North Pole forever? I mean, did Jack Nicklaus stay at Scioto, putting for quarters with school chums?

It must have killed Wayne Gretzky to walk down a street in L.A. or New York and not have 12 people in the entire city recognize him on sight or have any clear idea what he did for a living. It must have been galling to go to a cocktail party and have people looking over his shoulder to see if they can spot any celebrities while they murmur, "Oh, and are you in pictures, too, Mr. Grobsky, er, Grinsky?"

Now that he's married an actress, you can bet me she doesn't want to be sitting up there, 2,000 miles from the sound stages and the power lunches. I mean, you can be a hockey player in Edmonton but you can't be an actress. Trust me.

At times like these, I'm always reminded of the line in the play "Magdalena," where the Parisian general is transferred to the jungles of Colombia in South America and he tries to convince his mistress that she'll love it in the moonlight down there. "We'll be great lovers!" he cries. "Bah!" she says. "In Paris, great lovers. In the jungle, two monkeys."

Is it the greatest, most cynical sale in sports history? Well, it's close.

In 1919 a show biz entrepreneur named Harry Frazee owned the Boston Red Sox, but his heart was on Broadway. Among other things, he wanted to bankroll a musical called "No, No, Nanette." To get cash, he sold the greatest player in all the annals of baseball, Babe Ruth, himself. He got $100,000 cash and a $350,000 loan on his ballpark.

The sports world was stunned. The park-bench lawyers were out in force with their dark warnings of antitrust. But it was the greatest single move baseball ever made, unless you count Walter O'Malley's move to California.

Could Ruth have become Babe Ruth, a universal symbol for domination of a profession, if he had stayed in Boston? Highly unlikely. In that day and age, if you didn't do it in New York, you might as well not have done it.

Press box denizens recall one night in a World Series when an Oakland outfielder, Joe Rudi, made a catch that was right out of Lourdes. "If he does that in New York, they write songs about it," pronounced writer Jack Lang. "Here, it's just 'F-7.' "

In 1969, in concert with the complicated – and extralegal – draft laws of the sport, Kareem Abdul-Jabbar, undoubtedly the greatest single player in the annals of basketball, found himself playing the game in Milwaukee. Now, Milwaukee isn't Edmonton. They have summers there. It may be a fine place to raise a family. But it ain't 42nd Street. Sunset and Vine.

Abdul-Jabbar played the Good Soldier Schweik for six years. Then he told the team and the league that was enough. He would play either in New York or Los Angeles. The tryout was over. The show was ready for the big top.

Even ricocheting between Philadelphia and San Francisco wasn't enough for Wilt Chamberlain, although neither of those metropolises is exactly bucolic. Wilt wanted out and maneuvered his way to Los Angeles.

Jack Kent Cooke was an owner who very well understood the nature of the sports business, which was, after all, show business. It needed stars. Cooke went out and got Abdul-Jabbar and Chamberlain – and later Magic Johnson – for his basketball team. There is no hard evidence that he twisted the league's arm but it is evident the league was more than glad to see a contender in the L.A. market annually. Any game needs L.A. and New York.

George M. Cohan once said that once you get west of the Hudson River, everything is Bridgeport. Well, that's no longer so true. But superstars need super-cities.

I have always felt Henry Aaron would have been a megastar if he'd done what he did in New York. Ty Cobb's and Roger Hornsby's feats didn't go unnoticed – all those years over .400 – but they would have been ticker-tape parade starters in the Big Apple. Ted Williams might have had leagues named after him if he'd starred in Yankee Stadium. Musial earned the nickname "Stan the Man" playing against New York teams.

I think Gretzky had all the "Nice game, eh's?" that he wanted. He wants to play the Palace.

I think Bruce McNall is in the Jack Kent Cooke mold. Hollywood was built on the star system. So were professional sports.

Anyway, the league should be happy. I don't know whether Edmonton owner Peter Pocklington was another Harry Frazee who needed the quick money or whether he knew he couldn't keep Gretzky in the closet. Either way, you hang the "Mona Lisa" in the Louvre, not some curio shop in downtown Lyon.

Gretzky will fill the seats. If he can fill the nets, too, he'll be the biggest bargain since Babe Ruth. The game needs glamour more than goals. He's already pulled the hat trick. He's put hockey on Page 1. In Los Angeles. In August.

● ● ● ● ● ● ● ● ● ● ● ● ● ● ● ● ● ● ●

MARCH 12, 1974

A Legend in Disguise

You listen to old-time hockey people and you get the idea Robert Gordon Orr was born with skates for feet and a hockey stick for a right arm.

He was drafted by the National Hockey League at the age of 3. He became the Boston Bruins at the age of 16, won the Stanley Cup all by himself two years later. He could stick handle the puck through the Florida Everglades, score on the German Army, win the Olympics speedskating championship skating BACKWARD. He was so good, he could skate on water.

Compared to him, Babe Ruth had a long, uphill fight. He made Bobby Hull look like a gorilla trying to learn to skate. He was so fast he would disappear on his way to the goal. His reflexes were so good, he was the only guy in the league who still had all his teeth. And he won the junior championships while he still had his baby teeth.

Even rival players discuss Bobby Orr as if he died a long time ago. People don't get to be a legend like that until they're in a position not to disgrace it. Bobby Orr is the only player in the game who can get booed for merely doing the hat trick. Bobby Orr doesn't need a number, you can spot him by the halo. He's the one with the puck. He's personally responsible for 28 nervous breakdowns on the part of goal-tenders. He can score from downtown. On his days off, he changes water into wine.

His height has been variously estimated at 8 to 10 feet. He can see 360 degrees. At night, he turns into a swan. No one's ever seen him bleed or sweat. And so on.

I went out to see this living apparition, this paragon who stepped right down from a stained-glass window, the other night at the Forum.

I was not sure he could be seen by the naked eye, but I bought a program just in case. The Kings were to furnish the token opposition – something they've been good at over the years.

I kept waiting and waiting for Bobby Orr to show up. I finally guessed my worst fears were realized: You couldn't see Bobby Orr unless you BELIEVED. For instance, I could see a "No. 4," all right, but he was just a little guy with blond curly hair and big baby blue eyes and skin like a baby on a soap ad. I figured he was the ballboy or whatever is the hockey equivalent. I figured he would spend the night bringing towels to Phil Esposito.

I figured when Orr came on the ice, the house lights would dim and the arena would begin to tremble and this whistling sound would come out of the rafters and maybe the heavens would open.

"When's Orr coming out?" I asked somebody. The guy looked at me. "That's him over there," he said, pointing to this, this – boy!

"That's ORR?!" I said in disbelief. "THAT'S the scourge of the NHL?! Why, he looks as if he should be on double runners!"

"Wait'll he gets the puck," said the other fellow grimly.

I had figured the real Bobby Orr would score from the dressing room. I was surprised the Bruins bothered to suit up 18 other guys. But the game went clear into the second period before this Bobby Orr scored. I did notice the Kings treated him as though he were ticking, though. I have seen guys go after a buried bomb more recklessly than they went after Bobby Orr.

In the National Hockey League, they figure it's a power-play goal every time the Bruins score with Orr on the ice, no matter how many players the other team has, but this night the Bruins were resting on their ORR. The hat trick (three goals scored in the game by one player) was turned by a Kings player named Gene Carr, whose three scores gave him a lifetime total of 24, or only 185 behind Bobby Orr.

The Bruins, down 4-2, tied the game in the last six minutes, largely, it seems, on reputation. The Bruins are the "good hit, no field" team of hockey. But they intimidate the other guys. They beat you 9-8 – or 12-

0. They try to score from the seats. Some nights, the guy in the goal looks as if his job is to dodge the pucks, not stop them.

I went down to the locker room to interview Orr before he became a statue on the Boston Commons. He was easy to find. You just picked your way through the biggest crowd of movie and TV stars and autograph seekers. I noticed water ran off him like everybody else.

I wanted to say, "Why aren't you 9 feet tall, and how come you have those pink cheeks with down on them instead of barbed-wire whiskers, and why aren't your calves 22 inches around, and how come you're wearing shoes and have fingers?"

Instead, I just said lamely (as if he were just a hockey player), "How come you score so much for a defenseman? Defensemen are supposed to be around their OWN net, aren't they?"

The statue who looks like a choirboy grinned. "I get caught out of position when I shouldn't, because I carry the puck and cross the blue line a lot. They scored a couple of goals tonight when I got caught where I shouldn't be."

I closed the book. This legend doesn't look, act or talk like a legend. I haven't been so disappointed since I found out Napoleon was only 5-2 or Lincoln had warts.

● ● ● ● ● ● ● ● ● ● ● ● ● ● ● ● ●

MARCH 14, 1968

Here's How to Gordie!

You ask a Canadian about Gordie Howe and the first thing he does is take his hat off and place it carefully over his heart. His eyes film up, this lump comes to his throat, and you get the eerie feeling that Citizen Howe is at least one of the 12 Apostles. He wasn't born, he was found in the bulrushes.

There may be some things Gordie Howe can't do better than anyone else who ever lived, but you have to check through the late pages of the Spalding Guide to find out what it is. I mean to say, no one ever checked him out on skittles, horseshoe pitching, the luge or the kayak pairs competition.

If you do it on ice, he's a mortal cinch. He is, by common consent, the greatest hockey player who ever lived – Willie Mays, Babe Ruth, Red Grange, Sandy Koufax, Ty Cobb and Jack Dempsey all rolled into one.

Boxing? He's undefeated, and about 40 lifetime KOs ahead of Cassius Clay. No one ever hollered "Fake!" after one of his fights. How do you fake a broken jaw?

Golf? Well, his game has suffered a little because of an off-season job. Arnold Palmer might have to give him a stroke. He's clear up to a three handicap because of the layoff.

Baseball? Well, he worked out with the Detroit Tigers once and the legend has it, drove two starting pitchers into retirement and had three American League managers standing in a puddle of drool.

Fishing? He hooked into the first five sailfish he ever saw and boated all of them. If you're watching "The American Sportsman" on TV one of these weeks, he'll be the one netting all the trout.

He tried skiing last winter. He's not quite as good as Jean-Claude Killy. It took him one whole day before he was skiing the cornices.

He's been on more ice than a polar bear. He's the most durable hockey player who ever lived. He was on an operating table once at 2 o'clock in the afternoon and on the ice at 8 that night. Around the league, they say if Gordie Howe died, he might miss three days. He plays 40 of the 60 minutes of every game and holds the all-time record for games (1,467) and years (22) and goals (682).

He wasn't born on skates but, unlike most babies, he didn't learn to walk, he learned to skate. The first time he put shoes on, he fell down.

He leads the game in everything but penalties. It's not that he's that extraordinarily clean. He's just like an old rubber-hose cop. He knows how to hurt a guy without it showing or getting caught at it.

Now, on the verge of 40 (March 31 he makes it), he's like the old opera singer who doesn't try to break the chandeliers with every note any more. But the younger players still approach him as if he were wired and ticking. He's also like an old slugger who waits for his pitch. He doesn't shoot on a goal until he's close enough to hear the goalkeeper begin to sob. Much of the time he tries to pretend he's just a guy out for a few figure-eights in the park on a Sunday afternoon. Then, all of a sudden, he becomes a red blur and lights the red light.

He did it for the Detroit Red Wings against the Kings at the Forum the other night. The Kings had a one-goal lead. There were only 32 seconds left in the period. Everyone relaxed when Gordie Howe went flat on his face. Raising himself thoughtfully to one elbow, he carefully flicked the tying goal past a goalkeeper who acted as if he had just been scored on by a guy in the third-row seats. As the goalie skated disconsolately off, a fan comforted him. "Son," he said, "never take your eyes off Gordie Howe on ice till the coroner tells you." In Canada, they feel even that may be too soon.

Other books from the Los Angeles Times

Drawing the Line
by Paul Conrad

Two hundred drawings, spanning the period from the late 1960s to President Clinton's impeachment trial, from America's premier political cartoonist. $25.45

Eternally Yours
by Jack Smith

Who can forget Jack Smith, the Los Angeles Times' columnist for nearly 40 years? When he died in 1996, we all lost a treasure. But at least his words survived. In this volume, Jack's widow Denise, and sons, Curt and Doug, have collected some of their favorite columns as well as those that explain Jack's life as well as his death. $16.95

Curbside L.A.
An offbeat guide to the city of angels
by Cecilia Rasmussen

Enjoy a truly eclectic tour of Los Angeles. Explore the L.A. you've not seen with enticing excursions into the city's peerless history and diversity. $19.45

DAY HIKERS' GUIDE TO SOUTHERN CALIFORNIA
by John McKinney

Walks in Southern California, from the simply scenic to the challenging, as described by Los Angeles Times hiking columnist and author John McKinney. $16.45

52 WEEKS IN THE CALIFORNIA GARDEN
by Robert Smaus

How to make the most of your garden by the foremost authority on gardening in Southern California. $17.45

GOD AND MR. GOMEZ
by Jack Smith

This is the hilarious account of how Jack and Denise Smith learned that it would take both God and Mr. Gomez to build their vacation dream home in Baja California. $16.95

HIGH EXPOSURE/HOLLYWOOD LIVES
FOUND PHOTOS FROM THE ARCHIVES OF THE LOS ANGELES TIMES
by Amanda Parsons

In this beautiful hardcover book you'll see photographs of Marilyn Monroe, Liz Taylor, Mae West, Jane Russell, Frank Sinatra, Rita Hayworth, Errol Flynn and scores more stars at the height, and sometimes the depth, of their Hollywood lives. $29.95

L.A. UNCONVENTIONAL
by Cecilia Rasmussen

Where some people see roadblocks, others, such as the men and women in L.A. Unconventional, see possibility, opportunity, and excitement. $30.95

Lakers Encyclopedia
by Steve Springer

Any sports fan would want this: an A to Z compendium of the first 50 years of Los Angeles' favorite basketball team. Foreword by Magic Johnson. $30.95

Last of the Best
90 COLUMNS FROM THE 1990S BY THE LATE JIM MURRAY

The best of Jim's columns from the last decade of his life are included in this paperback volume compiled by Times Sports Editor Bill Dwyre and featuring a foreword by Dodger legend Tommy Lasorda. $19.45

Low-Fat Kitchen
by Donna Deane

From the pages of the Los Angeles Times Food Section now come more than 110 recipes that use fresh food flavor, not fat, to satisfy your taste buds. $20.45

SOS Recipes
30 YEARS OF REQUESTS
by Rose Dosti

This best selling hard-back book offers hundreds of tried and true recipes for all-time favorite dishes that literally range from soup to nuts. $19.45

••

To order, call (800) 246-4042 or visit our web site at
http://www.latimes.com/bookstore

Colophon

The text is set in 10 point Minion, a face designed by Robert Slimbach, and issued in digital form by Adobe Systems, Mountain View, California. The column headlines are set in HTF Saracen, designed by Jonathan Hoefler and issued by the Hoefler Type Foundry, New York, New York. The chapter titles are set in Adobe Latino Elongated.